RAPAN LIFEWAYS

*Society and History
on a Polynesian Island*

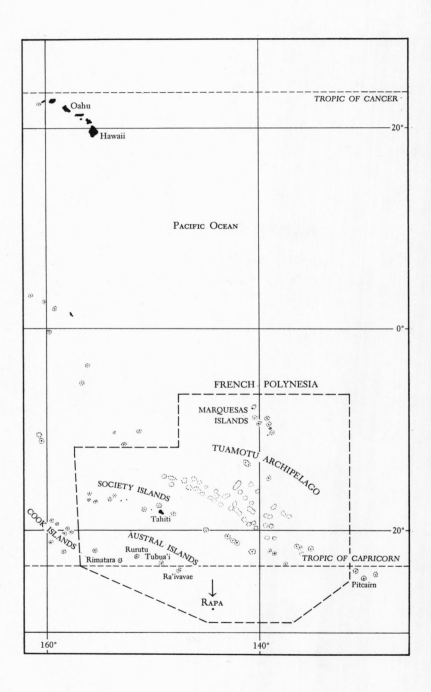

TROPIC OF CANCER

20°

Oahu

Hawaii

PACIFIC OCEAN

0°

FRENCH POLYNESIA

MARQUESAS
ISLANDS

TUAMOTU ARCHIPELAGO

SOCIETY ISLANDS

Tahiti

COOK ISLANDS

20°

AUSTRAL ISLANDS

Rurutu   Tubua'i

Rimatara   TROPIC OF CAPRICORN

Ra'ivavae   Pitcairn

RAPA

160°   140°

RAPAN LIFEWAYS

*Society and History
on a Polynesian Island*

F. ALLAN HANSON *The University of Kansas*

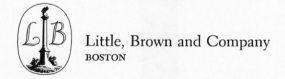 Little, Brown and Company
BOSTON

This is for
Louise

Acknowledgments

This book owes its existence to the generous support of several institutions and the encouraging assistance of many individuals. Fieldwork in Rapa, extending from December, 1963 to November, 1964, was supported by a National Science Foundation Graduate Fellowship. A grant from the National Institute of Mental Health (MH14562-01) made it possible to undertake archival and library research on Rapan history in Paris and Chicago in 1967. This, plus grants from the General Research Fund and the Graduate Research Fund of the University of Kansas, allowed me to obtain photocopies of most manuscripts and documents dealing with the island. Free time to write the manuscript was afforded by a Summer Faculty Fellowship from the University of Kansas, while other expenses connected with historical research and manuscript preparation were met by a grant from the Kansas City Association of Trusts and Foundations. For the financial support of all these institutions, I am profoundly grateful.

Governor Grimald, Administrator Allain, Admiral Thabaud, Captain Bastard, the officers and crew of *La Bayonnaise*, and many other civilian and military officials of French Polynesia extended every courtesy and assistance. Fellow anthropologists Paul Ottino and Henri Lavondès of the *Office de la Recherche*

Scientifique et Technique Outre-Mer generously contributed much practical assistance and intellectual stimulation. I owe special debts of gratitude to Father Patrick O'Reilly of the *Société des Océanistes* and René Bonneau of the *Tribunal Supérieur d'Appel* in Tahiti. The success of my archival research in Paris is due directly to the advice of Father O'Reilly, while M. Bonneau has been quick to lend his support to every facet of my Polynesian research ever since my first visit to Tahiti ten years ago.

I am grateful to Fred Eggan and Lloyd Fallers of the University of Chicago for their guidance when I first wrote up my material on Rapa as a doctoral dissertation. Much has been derived from the penetrating comments of Jon Cook, Marc Rucker, Martin Silverman, Carlyle Smith, and Murray Wax, who kindly read all or parts of this book in various stages of its preparation. Thanks are due also to Bill Hart, who extracted much valuable information from the microfilmed archives of the London Missionary Society.

My wife Louise has been part of this book from the day we set foot on Rapa's shore to the moment we wrote the manuscript's final sentence. No list of services rendered could begin to express my gratitude to her. Suffice it to say that the immensely rewarding experience of coming to know another culture by living in it, pondering over it, and writing about it deepened in meaning because it was shared with her.

Final thanks belong to the people of Rapa.[1] Although few of them understood why we had come so far to learn their lifeways, they welcomed us with warm hospitality and spared no effort to assist our research. No year has been more rewarding and memorable than that spent with them. We are especially grateful to our Rapan hosts, the households of Te'ura and Fa'atu. If we have gained any appreciation for life in Rapa, it is due most directly to these good and generous friends who, without thought of payment, shared with us their homes, their food, and their thoughts.

[1] To protect their privacy, many Rapans mentioned in this book have been given fictitious names.

Contents

List of Figures and Tables

Figures

Tables

RAPAN LIFEWAYS

Society and History
on a Polynesian Island

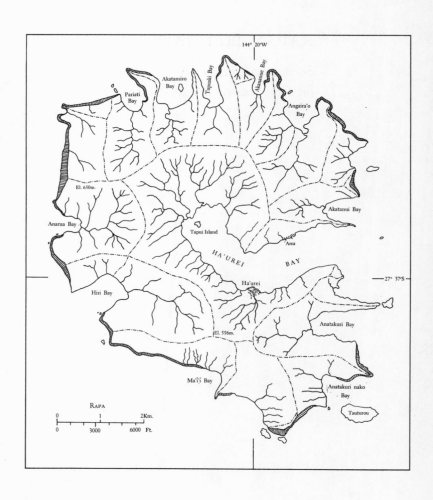

144° 20′W

Akatamiro
Bay

Tupuaki Bay

Akatanue Bay

Pariati
Bay

Angaira'o
Bay

El. 650m.

Akatanui Bay

Anarua Bay

Tapui Island

Area

HA'UREI   BAY

27° 37′S

Ha'urei

Hiri Bay

Anatakuri Bay

El. 556m.

Ma'ïï Bay

Anatakuri nako
Bay

Tauturou

RAPA

0   1   2Km.

0   3000   6000 Ft.

CHAPTER ONE

Introduction

BODY AND SPIRIT

"In Rapa we divide life in two sides: the food side and the belief side." The violent hurricane had prevented Fa'atu from fishing or farming for several days, and I took advantage of his forced leisure to engage him in long conversations about life on this Polynesian island. Fa'atu's statement about the two "sides" reminded me of an incident that occurred several months before, when we were living in another household. One evening I attended the caucus of a Rapan political party. Talk turned to that meeting at lunch the next day as we sat on the straw floor of the cookhouse. I happened to mention that the caucus began with a prayer. Te'ura Vahine rapidly spoke up in criticism. "Those idiots should not pray at political gatherings," she said. "Meetings like that are work of the body, not of the spirit."

Work of the body is opposed to work of the spirit, the food side to the belief side. These are different ways of expressing a fundamental division in life and the world as these are perceived by the Rapans. Essentially this is the distinction between the secular and the sacred. Approximating it another way, on the "food side" or "body side" (*pae ma'a, pae tino*)[1] Rapans class those elements of life which we would term economic, social and political. On the "spirit side" or "belief side" (*pae varua, pae fa'aro'o*) they place the religious and the moral.

This book is about the "body side" of life in Rapa. One of its aims is to describe Rapan economic, social and political life as I found it during a year's residence in 1964. While casting the description in a form coherent to Western readers, whenever possible I will attempt to show how the various customs, beliefs and organizations which compose the "body side" are significant to the Rapans themselves. Here we adopt the goal of the ethnographer as enunciated by Bronislaw Malinowski. "This goal is, briefly, to grasp the native's point of view, his relation to life, to realize *his* vision of *his* world" (Malinowski 1922:25, Malinowski's italics).

The anthropologist is seldom content with simple description. He aims to analyze his data: to explain why people behave as they do, and to relate his findings to general problems and theory. Shreds and patches of explanation will be found scattered throughout this book, although it is of course impossible to pursue the theoretical implications of everything described. However, Rapa is particularly relevant to two problems in social scientific theory, and for these more detailed analyses will be offered. One of these problems is in our understanding of kinship and social organization. Until the last fifteen years or so, anthropologists were most familiar with societies based on unilineal descent: where special importance is attached to relationships traced exclusively through

[1] The correct pronunciation of Tahitian words in this book may be approximated if consonants are given their English values and if vowels are read as follows:

> a = ä as in "father"
> e = ā as in "ate"
> i = ē as in "meet"
> o = ō as in "wrote"
> u = ōō as in "troop"

Unmarked vowels are short. Those with a bar (as in *tāne*) are long: they are pronounced with greater duration than short vowels. An apostrophe in Tahitian words represents a glottal stop.

males (patrilineal) or through females (matrilineal). Unilineal models had become so deeply intrenched in social anthropology that in 1935 one of the leaders of the field could write "unilineal institutions in some form, are almost, if not entirely, a necessity in any ordered social system" (Radcliffe-Brown 1952:48). More recently, reports from Southeast Asia, the Pacific islands and elsewhere have shed light on social systems where descent for validating membership in social groups, rights to property, and other purposes is reckoned cognatically (along any line of ancestry) rather than unilineally. Thus the theories of descent clearly needed revision, and this subject has been a dominant one in anthropological literature in recent years. Rapa represents one of the most thoroughly cognatic systems yet described. I hope that this account of how the Rapan systems of descent and kinship actually work, and the discussion of some of the theoretical issues involved, will contribute to our understanding of cognatic systems in general.

The other problem for special analysis is social change in Rapan society since European discovery in 1791. As with most islands of Polynesia, European contact drastically altered Rapa. During the nineteenth century, indigenous religion gave way to Christianity, political autonomy succumbed to French rule, and Rapa was linked in a network of inter-island trade. Without doubt the most devastating blow was a series of epidemics which swept away fully 90 percent of the population. So destructive was the impact of European disease and culture that, according to one authority, the Rapans were doomed to extinction (Caillot 1932:24). But history has belied this opinion, and today Rapa's population is increasing vigorously. After a period of rapid change following European contact, the modern social system was forged by the latter part of the nineteenth century and since then has changed relatively slowly. From this perspective, Rapan history contributes to at least one gap in our general understanding of social change. The massive depopulation occasioned by epidemics qualifies Rapa as a case of change in time of disaster. The immediate effects of disaster on society have been studied in some detail, but "we do not know much about the long-term changes that may be wrought by disaster, because almost no research has undertaken to follow a stricken community over any great number of years" (Chapman 1962a:22). Since the reorganized Rapan society emerged from a period of disaster and rapid change about a century ago, the history of change on this island should illuminate this problem.

Summarizing the plan of the book, the next chapter tries to reconstruct the pre-European society and outlines Rapan history throughout the nineteenth century. Following chapters delineate the network of relations that define modern Rapan society. The first focus is on the relations between men and things. The native concept of property and means of ownership are examined in Chapter 3, while property exploitation — the technology and sociology of Rapan economy — is the subject of Chapter 4. In succeeding chapters the network of social relations is described in an ever-widening context, beginning with relations between spouses and moving outward through the household, the kinship system, and, finally, the village and the island community. The concluding chapter presents an analysis of Rapan history and social change.

THE ISLAND AND ITS PEOPLE

Rapa is the southern outpost of French Polynesia, a territory of far-flung South Sea islands covering as much of the globe as Europe but with a total land area only slightly larger than Rhode Island. Stretching south from Tahiti, capital of the territory, are the five Austral islands: Rimatara, Rurutu, Tubua'i, Ra'ivavae and Rapa.[2] Mostly high volcanic islands, the Australs form one of French Polynesia's five administrative districts, or *circonscriptions*. No French official resides in Rapa. Intermittent visits are paid by the administrator of the Australs and a military doctor (both based at Tubua'i, administrative seat of the archipelago) and by the gendarme stationed at Ra'ivavae. A measure of self-government is provided by the locally-elected District Council, and a native policeman represents the law on the rare occasions it needs representing. Rapa has a weather station, run by a Tahitian (who doubles as radio man and postman), and an infirmary, staffed by a Tahitian nurse.

[2] For books on other Austral islands, see Aitken (1930) and Marshall (1961).

4

With the coordinates 27°37′ south, 144°20′ west, Rapa lies some 700 miles south-southeast of Tahiti and 300 miles south of Ra'ivavae, its nearest inhabited neighbor. Given its location over 300 miles below the Tropic of Capricorn, Rapa experiences a marked seasonal variation in climate and can get noticeably cold in the Austral winter. In the period 1951–64, the average monthly temperature varied from 63° F. in August to 75° in February. The absolute minimum for 1951–63 was 48°, the absolute maximum 88°. Rainfall is heavy, averaging 106.5 inches annually during 1955–63. The skies are often overcast, especially in the cold season. Violent thunderstorms occur periodically, causing the streams to rise several feet. Then all of Rapa becomes a marsh, and the cataracts tumbling down every cliff and hillside create the impression that the island has sprung a myriad of leaks. I was told that especially cold winters have experienced sleet. The island is visited by high winds several times annually. Occasionally these attain hurricane velocities and wreak considerable damage.

The English ship *Discovery*, commanded by George Vancouver, discovered Rapa on December 22, 1791. Vancouver described the island as

. . . a cluster of high craggy mountains, forming, in several places, most romantic pinnacles, with perpendicular cliffs nearly from their summits to the sea; the vacancies between the mountains would more probably be termed chasms than vallies, in which there was no great appearance of plenty, fertility or cultivation; they were chiefly clothed with shrubs and dwarf trees (Vancouver 1801 I:214–215).

Rapa is the cone of a long-extinct volcano. The island is irregular in shape and indented on all sides by numerous bays. On the east the mountain wall has been breached and the volcano crater has become the large, elbowed Ha'urei Bay.[3] The mouth of the bay is about half a mile wide but very shallow. Entering ships must follow a sinuous channel between dangerous formations of coral. Within, however, the bay is deep in many places and makes an ideal harbor, sheltered on nearly all sides by the crater wall.

The population, 362 in 1964, lives in two villages, Ha'urei and

[3] In other publications this bay and the village of the same name are usually termed "Ahurei." I use "Ha'urei" because this corresponds to the native pronunciation.

'Area, situated about a mile apart on either side of Ha'urei Bay. The villages are dingy at first sight: polyglot collections of off-white or unpainted masonry houses with corrugated iron roofs, house shells (some abandoned, others in the slow process of construction) with no roofs at all, and low, dilapidated pandanus huts. A touch of color is added by flowers and, on laundry days, by clothes draped to dry over every available bush and shrub. The coastal pattern of residence on other islands, where the open sea fills half or more of the horizon, is for me a constant reminder of being on an island, remote from the rest of the world. But Rapan villages, surrounded on all sides by mountains, create the impression of a self-contained universe. The world beyond seldom comes to mind. Only upon crossing the mountains, when the ocean can be seen rolling off to infinity on every side, did I feel remoteness on Rapa.

If Rapa is a world unto itself, it is a small one. At its greatest dimensions the island measures only four by five and one-half miles, and covers a total area of approximately fifteen square miles. There is no barrier reef, and in the night one can hear heavy waves dashing against the rocky and uninviting shoreline. Scattered just off shore are a number of small islets, many no more than huge chunks of rock 100 or more feet high which have broken off from the mainland and tumbled into the ocean. In several places sheer cliffs rise from the sea for as much as 1,500 feet. Some of these are infamous as places where men have plunged to their deaths while hunting barehanded the birds that nest there.

Rapa lacks the lush vegetation, placid lagoon, and broad beaches of the tropical islands to the north. Its magnificence lies in the spectacular cliffs and bold mountains of black basalt which pierce the sky in fantastic panoramas of needle spires and razor-back ridges. The highest of these peaks exceeds 2,000 feet. The central ridge, rim of the volcanic cone, traces a rough semicircle around Ha'urei Bay. At many points the central ridge is met by peripheral ridges, rising from the outer shore or from the bay. The highlands present a barren aspect: hillsides clothed in coarse light-green grasses sprinkled with wild raspberries and culminating in the naked rock of the peaks. Valleys fan out between the ridges,

The village of Ha'urei: top, *the village as seen from Ha'urei Bay;* bottom, *some Rapan homes. The photographs used in the text were taken by the author.*

sloping gradually down to the bays at their feet. Each valley is well watered by one or more permanent streams. Along these, as they twist through the narrow valley head, are found stands of lumber trees, groves of coffee, bananas and oranges, and a few lemon and lime trees.

The lower temperature ranges preclude the presence of a number of plants of great importance in the islands to the north. Breadfruit, mangoes, and papaya will not grow at all. A few coconut palms may be seen and although they attain maturity, they bear no fruit. Some pineapples are cultivated but are of an inferior, woody quality. By far the most important crop is taro. The starchy root-stock or corm of this plant is Rapa's staple food. Taro is grown predominantly in the broad lower reaches of the valleys. Here the face of the land has been much altered by the handiwork of man. The valley floors have been cut and leveled into large systems of irrigated taro terraces which fan out in shallow steps from the rivers as they reach their estuaries.

The highlands are largely given over to animals, predominately goats and cattle. Some 400 to 500 goats roam wild in all parts of the mountains. The northern side of the island, from Akatamiro to Angaira'o Bays, is the domain of the cattle. In 1964 the herd numbered about 200 head. Like the goats, the cattle are left to forage for themselves. Goats and cattle are occasionally killed for local consumption at feasts, or when stormy weather prohibits fishing. Every few years a portion of the cattle herd is exported for sale in Tahiti. The mountains also afford pasturage for a few small flocks of sheep, totalling about 20 head, and 5 to 10 horses. No use is made of the horses, nor of an increasing population of rabbits confined to the islet of Tauturou.

Hordes of rats (the small Polynesian variety) forage in the mountains and at night descend on the villages to nibble at unprotected food in the houses. One would think the rats would be controlled by the cats, which also roam wild in the highlands. The cats, however, seem to prefer the role of accomplices in crime, stealing into the villages at night to prey upon chicks. Some Rapans keep dogs as pets — unsavory-looking mastiffs who spend their days battling the pigs for slops since their owners seldom feed them. The dogs might be expected to curtail the nocturnal depredations of the cats, but instead they head for the hills after dark to devour a lamb or a kid. So much for the balance of nature.

Like most Polynesians, Rapans tend to be large people with brown eyes, black hair, broad noses and skin hues varying from tan to brown. Men dress in tattered European-made shirts and shorts, women in equally ragged blouses and sarongs. For church the men don ill-fitting trousers and ancient suit jackets and the women wear white or brightly printed dresses and 1940-style hats. Sundays and weekdays, both sexes omit shoes.

Men spend their days cultivating taro and other crops, fishing, and building houses, boats and canoes. Women are responsible for household tasks and child care, and they share in agricultural labor. Since 1950, when the first school was built, Rapan children have been required to attend school to the age of fourteen. All instruction is in French, although besides the teachers, very few persons (including the school children) ever use or appear to understand that language. They speak Tahitian, with a few words of the nearly-extinct Rapan dialect thrown in. Thanks to the efforts of the church school, nearly all Rapans are literate in Tahitian.

Except for three or four Roman Catholics, the entire population is made up of Protestant Christians and has been for well over a century. Each village has its whitewashed church. The one pastor, a Rapan with seminary training in Tahiti, divides his Sundays between them.

RAPANS FROM THEIR OWN POINT OF VIEW

Measured by his outlook, temperament, and image of the good life, at different points in his lifetime a Rapan is four quite distinct persons. These correspond to the native division of life into four stages: infancy, childhood, youth, and adulthood. In general, an individual becomes a child (*tamari'i*) when he learns to walk, a youth (*taure'are'a*) around the age of sixteen to eighteen, and an adult (*ta'ata pa'ari*) in the late twenties or early thirties. Chronological age, however, is a sadly inadequate measure of these stages. For example, one young woman of eighteen is an

9

adult, another of twenty-one is a child, while a third of forty-two is a youth. Beyond infancy, Rapans define each stage of life by a particular mode of acting, and most important, a certain way of thinking. Thus they told me that one shifts from youth to adulthood when one changes from the *feruri taure'are'a* to the *feruri pa'ari:* from the youthful to the mature state of mind.

The Innocence of Childhood. Childhood is a time for learning. To the age of fourteen the children attend school, learning multiplication tables, French verb conjugations, and so on, through unison repetition. Twice a week they go to church school, where they become literate in Tahitian by learning to read the Bible. Their free time is spent chasing each other through the village, jumping rope, and playing marbles or games imitating the work of their elders. Girls often have the responsibility of looking after their infant siblings, whom they carry even at play, strapped to their backs in cloth pouches. Beyond this and occasional help with the coffee harvest, little work is expected of children.

Children are considered to be incomplete beings. Partly this refers to their incomplete knowledge, to the fact that they are in the process of learning those things necessary to operate as full members of society. (Rapans often refer to a child as *tamari'i ha'api'i,* or "learning child.") They are also incomplete economically, since they do not participate fully in work required for subsistence. Perhaps most important, they are incomplete sexually. This whole dimension of life is lacking in children; one might almost say they are sexless. Graphic evidence of this view of children may be seen in church seating arrangements. Youths and adults are segregated by sex, the women sitting in front and the men behind. The children occupy the first few pews, boys and girls mixed indiscriminately. In Rapa the hallmarks of childhood are innocence and purity, especially with reference to sex.

No social recognition is taken of a girl's first menstruation. Boys are superincised[4] around the age of puberty, but this is done privately and is not marked by any special ceremony. After

---

[4] The Polynesian form of circumcision, whereby the foreskin is cut longitudinally along the top. This exposes the glans, the foreskin falling to the sides and below.

puberty sexual desires awake in the children. Usually these are unfulfilled for a few years, although the girls become flirtatious and groups of boys roam the village at night in a vain quest for adventure. Eventually, however, virginity is lost and this is a prime sign that a child has lapsed into youth.

The Abandon of Youth. To my question of when children become youths (taure'are'a), one man laughed and said, "When they begin to lie to you." His point was that they become secretive about their activities and anxious to evade parental control. Several others summarized the transition as "they want to have a good time." Rapan youths are oriented toward pleasure, particularly the sensual variety, and spend their free time vigorously pursuing it in athletics, singing, dancing, drinking, and sexual adventures.

Two or three evenings a week the youths gather outside the store in Ha'urei. They produce guitars and sing the songs and practice the dances which are currently the rage in Tahiti. Girls do not drink, but the boys become especially exuberant on the rare occasions when wine purchased from a visiting ship is available, or when a coffeepot filled with locally brewed orange beer surreptitiously makes the rounds. (Alcoholic drinks are scarce because the island's only store is not licensed to sell them. Orange beer is made infrequently and is illegal, although the law is not enforced as long as the drinkers maintain a facade of secrecy and cause no serious disturbance.) These sessions shatter the night air until 10 o'clock, when they terminate in accordance with a local ordinance. Afterwards young lovers meet secretly and boys with no steady girlfriends scour the village in search of a partner for the night.

By day the youths are the workhorses of the economy: they do most of the heavy tasks such as rowing boats, carrying heavy loads of taro and firewood over the ridges, running down cattle and goats, and making *popoi* (the favorite preparation of taro, a paste made by smashing boiled corms with a heavy rock). But the youths leave the authority and responsibility for running the households and society at large to their elders. They have no taste for long-range planning or for the burdens of community responsibility. They relish a carefree present, and when their work is done they enthusiastically devote themselves to the quest for pleasure.

In many ways youth is the precise opposite of childhood. Children participate only incidentally in the economy, while youths are the most important segment of the labor force. In the native view, the sexual contrast seems to be the most significant: children are pure and sexless, youths are impure and eminently sexual. Again, the church provides the clearest delineation of this view. Youths sit with adults in pews behind the children, where the sexes are separated. The church frowns on premarital sexual relations, and since these are by definition a part of youth, the young people hold low ritual status. They may not take Communion or attend church business meetings. It would be defiling for a youth to sit in the pew reserved for the pastor's wife, which is almost sacred. The interior of the church is periodically cleaned by the married churchwomen, and youthful girls are not allowed to help.

Although a time of ritual impurity and, insofar as the church is concerned, second-class citizenship, the taure'are'a years are highly appreciated by most Rapans. Children look forward to them in eager anticipation, youths live them enthusiastically and are often reluctant to leave them, and adults look back on them with nostalgia. It is human nature to kick up one's heels before settling down, they say, and those experiencing this carefree period are regarded by the rest of the community with benevolence occasionally tinged with envy.

The Fullness of Maturity. Eventually, Rapans say, youths tire of the taure'are'a way of life. As they mature they turn to more substantial things and gradually their frame of mind changes from carefree gaiety to sober responsibility. This change in outlook defines the transition from youth to adulthood.

One of the most diagnostic traits of of adulthood is formal marriage. By marrying, a Rapan publicly commits himself to a lifetime of devoted responsibility and fidelity to his spouse and provision for his children. In fulfilling these commitments, married adults accept the duties of planning for the present and future well-being of their families and households. By their forties most

12

Rapans find the heaviest tasks in the economy increasingly difficult and leave these to the youths. Adults head most households, however, and in this capacity they have the responsibility of planning and directing the work of all household members to insure a steady supply of food and other necessities. Adults also make plans to raise the level of living for themselves and their dependents. They save money to buy cement for more substantial houses, outboard motors, and modern toilets to replace the outhouses. Some families even hope to do away with their smoky cookhouses in favor of kitchens complete with sinks, gas stoves and refrigerators. Children are sometimes sent to Tahiti for advanced education in the hope that lucrative and prestigious occupations, such as school teachers or civil servants, will be opened to them. All these aspirations betray the sources of familial satisfaction in the adult mind: seeing one's planning and work bear fruit in the form of a harmonious, well-fed and well-sheltered household, a rising level of living, and healthy children who are given the opportunity to have a better life than their parents.

Shortly after marriage, Rapans normally become communicant members of the church, and this is the other diagnostic trait of adulthood. The church is by far the institution most concerned with the well-being of the Rapan community as a whole — not only the spiritual and moral state of the society, but all facets of social harmony and solidarity. Church festivals are the only occasions which bring all Rapans together in a unified community. Through baptism a new member is inducted into society, through the church wedding his conjugal relationship is legitimized, through the church funeral he is ushered into the next world and his stricken family is comforted and gently reintegrated into society. All church activities are planned and controlled by the communicant members. Other positions of community importance, as in local government, tend also to be held by adults. Thus, in addition to their familial and household commitments, adults shoulder the responsibility for the well-being and stability of society at large.

Symbolically, adulthood is distinguished from childhood and youth by position in the church, and again the criterion is sex.

Unlike children, adults are sexual beings and therefore they occupy pews with the youths, males separated from females. Unlike the illicit sexuality of youths, adult sexuality is sanctified: a condition established by marriage and maintained by strict conjugal fidelity. Therefore a mark of adulthood is admission to communion, for in Rapa this sacrament is limited to those who are old enough to make a reasoned commitment to Christ and who come to the table free of sin.

CHAPTER TWO

Rapa
in
History

RELICS OF THE PAST

Rapa's ancient inhabitants carved the ridges and hilltops of their island into large forts, the remnants of which have fired the imagination of visitors. Vancouver, discoverer of Rapa, wrote:

The tops of six of the highest hills bore the appearance of fortified places, resembling redoubts; having a form of block house, in the shape of an English glass house, in the center of each, with rows of pallisadoes a considerable way down the sides of the hills, nearly at equal distances. These, overhanging, seemed intended for advanced works, and apparently capable of defending the citadel by a few against a numerous host of assailants. On all of them, we noticed people, as if on duty, constantly moving about. What we considered as block houses, from their great similarity in appearance to that sort of building, were sufficiently large to lodge a considerable number of persons, and were the only habitations we saw (Vancouver 1801 I:215).

Vancouver saw only a few of the forts; in all, at least fifteen dominate Rapa's mountainscape (Stokes 1930:367[1]).

Typically the forts are located at high points along the central ridge, where subsidiary ridges branch off. The forts were constructed by excavating the ridge so as to leave a central tower surrounded by two or three terraces; often further terracing branched out from the central section along the ridges. The tower and many of the terraces were faced with dry masonry walls. One fort, Morongo 'Uta, was completely cleared and excavated by William Mulloy of the Norwegian Archaeological Expedition in 1956. He found the total terraced surface of the site to cover approximately 5,406 square meters (Mulloy 1965:23). There can be little doubt that the forts were designed for defense. Their strategic position, the vertical masonry-faced walls, the concealed pitfalls and deep trenches cut nearly or completely through the approaching ridges — all bear testimony to the military design of these structures. Moreover, the Rapans of the early twentieth century told both Caillot and Stokes — the two major authorities on the island's history — of many ancient wars and the central role of the forts in them. The conclusion seems inescapable that warfare was chronic in pre-contact Rapa.

To discover the fundamental reason for the existence of the forts and the conditions of war that they imply, we probably need search no further than in the facts of demography. Vancouver estimated that not less than 300 adult men, none exceeding middle age, came out to his ship in canoes. From this he calculated the island's population to be at least 1,500 (Vancouver 1801 I:216–217). The English missionary Davies spent about a week in Rapa in January, 1826. Although "there had recently been a great mortality among the people," he estimated the population at the time of his visit to be more than 2,000 (Davies 1827:331, 1961:280). Of Rapa's total area of about fifteen square miles, I would estimate that no more than two or three square miles are level enough to support taro agriculture. Thus, population pressure on available land must have been very great indeed. This assumption

[1] Each page of the Stokes manuscript bears several numbers. References here are to the circled numbers.

16

The fortified village of Morongo 'Uta: top, conjectural restoration of the central section from the northwest, taken from Mulloy (1965), with the kind permission of Thor Heyerdahl; bottom, Morongo 'Uta as seen in 1964.

is supported by Ferdon's conclusion from a land-use survey that suitable land had been extensively terraced for irrigated taro (Ferdon 1965:12). Stokes interprets the major cause of warfare as the need for land (1930:703); Caillot writes vividly of raids to steal taro and the bloody battles which resulted, and of wars in which one group would nearly or totally exterminate another in order to appropriate its land (1932:38–42, 64–68). Ferdon (1965: 12) and Mulloy (1965:58) agree that the major cause of warfare was probably competition for territory and, given the ratio of population size to arable land, this seems entirely reasonable.

In addition to serving as points of refuge and defense in time of war, it is probable that the forts were sites of permanent habitation — at least in the period when population pressure had become acute and warfare was endemic. Caillot's view is that the people moved to the highlands in order to free more land for cultivation (1932:67–68), while Stokes is of the opinion that mountain residence provided security against surprise attack (1930:366–367, 705). Archeological evidence makes it clear that a large population certainly could have lived in the highlands. Morongo 'Uta, apparently one of the larger fortified villages, was capable of housing at least 400 persons according to estimates by Stokes (1930:437) and Mulloy (1965:58). Stokes surveyed most of the fortified and unfortified terraced mountain sites in Rapa (there are at least thirty-five such places, each capable of holding from 25 to 400 residents) and calculated that they could house a total of 3,027 inhabitants (Stokes 1930:438–440). While we do not know how many sites were occupied at any given time, it is clear that Rapa's highlands contain more than enough terraced residential space for a population in the neighborhood of 1,500 to 2,000.

From the foregoing we can derive a reasonably certain understanding of the conditions of life in Rapa prior to European discovery. A dense population placed a high premium on arable land. The increasing requirements for land led to a state of endemic warfare between different groups. The people lived in the highlands, where they hewed impregnable fortresses out of the ridges. These fortifications show considerable planning and certainly required a unified effort to build and defend, suggesting a fairly centralized social and political organization (Mulloy 1965:58).

ANCIENT RAPAN SOCIETY

Caillot reports that Rapa contained a number of "tribes," or even "States." By the latter term he means that each of these groups had its chief, controlled a portion of the island, contracted alliances and waged wars within the miniature world of Rapa. The number of states varied at different times in the island's history; around the beginning of the eighteenth century there were eighteen. Normally a state controlled a single valley and owned a fort situated on the ridge commanding its domain. The state also held exclusive fishing rights over the waters extending for a short distance off its shores (Caillot 1932:32, 63–66). Caillot's "states" become "clans" in the terminology of Stokes, who depicts Rapa's ancient social organization in greater detail.

What sort of organizations were those "clans" or "states"? The clan (to use Stokes's term temporarily) was agamous, meaning that a person could marry either inside or outside his clan.[2] Rights of membership in a clan passed from parents to children by descent. Children inherited these rights from both parents (Stokes 1930:723–724). A system like this, in which descent may be traced along any chain of ancestry be it patrilineal, matrilineal, or of any combination of male and female links, is termed a cognatic descent system. That descent was reckoned cognatically means that children and descendants of inter-clan marriages held membership rights in more than one clan. Although Stokes is not perfectly clear in these matters, it appears likely that people who traced descent in more than one clan did not enjoy equal status in all of them. To develop this point and to extend our understanding of clan structure, we must examine the system of land tenure.

[2] Stokes recorded forty-one marriages of people born between 1700 and 1800, all of whom would have been of marriageable age before the arrival of the missionaries in 1826. Of these marriages, six were between members of the same clan and twenty were between members of different clans. The remaining fifteen cannot be identified, as Stokes could ascertain the clan affiliation of one spouse only (Stokes 1930:Table 13).

While all land belonged ultimately to the clan as a unit, individuals held two sorts of rights over it. These were termed *arakaa* and *moekopu* (Stokes 1930:723). The arakaa referred to the rights of members to cultivate specific portions of the clan's territory. Arakaa were assigned originally by the chief of the clan, and then descended cognatically from parents to their children. Adoption was frequent, and adopted children inherited the arakaa equally with biological children. During his lifetime an individual could administer his arakaa land as he wished, including the right to allow any other clan member to cultivate portions of it. Upon the holder's death the arakaa passed to his heirs. Normally a parent, approaching death, divided his arakaa lands among his own and adopted children. Should heirs be lacking, the arakaa reverted to the direct control of the clan. Presumably the chief could then reassign that land to another arakaa holder (Stokes 1930:659–660, 723).

Of the rights termed moekopu, Stokes writes (1930:724):

Children of parents from different clans . . . inherited from both parents. This was a right known as the *moekopu*. . . . The *moekopu* in the *arakaa* was recognized and sustained until an heir opposed the clan in war, when it automatically lapsed. Apparently, the blood relationship was stronger than the attainder, for it was stated that any clan descendant had the right to demand an *arakaa* from the head of any clan in which he could prove ancestry.

We may conclude that the arakaa was a device whereby lands belonging to the clan were distributed among its members for cultivation. That is, the arakaa may be understood as rights of land-use actively exercised. Given cognatic descent and interclan marriages, numerous persons traced ancestry in more than one clan. Very likely they did not actually use land — hold an arakaa — in all of these clans. Yet they did retain the right to demand land to use — to demand an arakaa — in all clans in which they traced cognatic descent. These rights, which we might term "latent rights of use," constituted the moekopu.[3]

[3] Linguistic evidence may provide further support for this interpretation of arakaa and moekopu as referring to active and latent right of land-use. There is no direct linguistic evidence from Rapa, but in the closely-related Tahitian dialect *'ara* means "awake," while in both Rapan and Tahitian one meaning of *moe* is "asleep" (Jaussen 1949:116, 152; Stokes 1955:335).

The clan could not command the loyalty of, and exercise authority over, everyone who had rights of one kind or another in its land. These considerations held only for those persons who lived in the area associated with the clan. Thus a woman who married a man of another clan and took up residence with him was subject to the authority of her husband's clan. Similarly, an inmarrying husband was "adopted" by his wife's clan, and "would war against his original clan if necessary" (Stokes 1930:714–715). On this basis I assume that persons exercised active land-use rights (arakaa) only in the clan in whose territory they resided. Given the high premium placed on land due to population pressure, it is unlikely that a clan would award an arakaa to someone residing elsewhere. The clan would have little authority over him, could not count on his loyalty in defending or expanding the clan's territory, and might even find him among the ranks of its enemies.

My conclusion is that the clan was a localized cognatic descent group. Active membership in the group — being under the authority of its leaders, supporting it in battle, and cultivating its land — depended upon residence in its territory. Each group had also a periphery of latent members: persons who traced descent in it but who exercised active membership in some other group in which they also counted ancestry. Such individuals could activate their membership in the descent group by applying for and receiving rights to cultivate its land (an arakaa). As this entailed taking up residence in the group's territory, doubtless their active membership in the group of former residence lapsed. Persons who did not trace descent in the group, and thus could not be considered its full members, might also have resided there and used its land. Among these were inmarrying spouses from other groups. In addition, probably fugitives from descent groups which had been defeated in war and had lost their lands could petition for and receive land to use from the chiefs of groups in which they traced no descent (Stokes 1930:682, 707–708).

From the foregoing it seems evident that ancient social organization in Rapa was based on descent groups of the type described by Goodenough (1955) as residentially restricted, nonunilinear descent groups, and labeled "ramages" by Firth (1957). Our confidence in this interpretation may be increased by the fact that other societies in the same general area were organized on the basis of ramages.[4] Henceforth we shall refer to the Rapan descent groups as ramages in preference to Stokes's term "clan." Each ramage was headed by a chief, or *ariki*. According to Caillot (1932:29), "this king made war and peace, dispensed justice, directed public works, and collected contributions of food from his subjects. Occasionally he exacted dues and even forced labor from them."[5] Stokes agrees that the chief led in war, attributes to him general authority over the ramage, and adds that he alloted land-use rights (arakaa) to ramage members (Stokes 1930:659–660). But "the real authority lay with the elders, who in conclave with the chief decided matters affecting extra-clan relations, such as war, and who had authority to displace the chief" (Stokes 1930:660). The office of chief passed from father to son, although if a male heir were lacking, a daughter might succeed, or the ramage elders might elect a close relative of the previous chief (Stokes 1930:659). Most probably the ideal order of succession was from father to eldest son. While chiefs might have had several wives, most other persons contracted monogamous marriages (Caillot 1932:35–36).

The entire ramage was stratified. Highest in rank were the chief and his near relatives. The middle class according to Caillot was composed of the *hui ragatira* or landowners (1932:29); Stokes terms them the *'uri rangatira* and describes them as warriors (1930:658). Caillot's lowest class is labeled *kio* or servants (1932: 29); Stokes learned nothing definite about a commoner class or slaves (1930:658). In all likelihood these classes were further differentiated by minor gradations of rank according to degree of relationship to the chiefly line and seniority (Stokes 1930:658). That seniority was important to rank is suggested by indications that in the administration of land inherited from a parent "the eldest child's ideas were predominant" (Stokes 1930:723). The

---

[4] A few examples are the New Zealand Maori (Firth 1957, 1963), Mangaia (Buck 1934) and Rangiroa in the Tuamotus (Ottino 1965).
[5] This and all subsequent translations from French works have been made by the author.

practice of assigning rank by seniority of descent line was wide-spread in Polynesia (Sahlins 1958).

Many of the ramages segmented from common sources. The informants of both Caillot and Stokes maintained that all of the ramages were descended from the first man, Tiki (Caillot 1932: 61–62, Stokes 1930:665). While Caillot assumes that the pre-European population was derived from a single migration (1932: 61), on the basis of their names, territorial distribution and legendary history Stokes concludes that the various ramages must have stemmed from five or six groups which arrived on Rapa at different times, with first settlement around 950 A.D. (1930:20–21, 700). In his analysis, twenty-two different ramages emerged from these basic stocks. Figure 1 summarizes his tentative reconstruction of ramage segmentation. Stokes had to work with accounts of unwritten historical events, many of which apparently occurred two centuries and more before his time, gathered from informants who were usually biased one way or another. In these circum-stances one can be sure of nothing, but his research was thorough and his reconstruction of relationships between ramages does bring some coherency to the many pages of legendary history he re-corded. In my opinion, however, the data are far from adequate for determining either the date of first settlement[6] or whether all ramages sprang from a single source or from several arrivals. Nevertheless, the chart reflects Stokes's ideas concerning a se-quence of migrations, with the Mana'une arriving first and the Aureka last.

ANCIENT HISTORY RECONSTRUCTED

Earliest Rapan history must have been a relatively peaceful period as one or a few small groups of immigrants increased their num-bers in conditions of abundant resources, and the ramages were formed and consolidated themselves in their various territories. As the population increased, expanding ramages began to covet the same land. Legends indicate that the first such confrontation was between Ngate Mato (originally centered around Tupuaki Bay)

---

[6] The earliest radiocarbon date from Rapa is 1337 A.D., plus or minus 200 years (Smith 1965:83).

FIGURE 1   SEGMENTATION OF PRE-EUROPEAN RAMAGES *

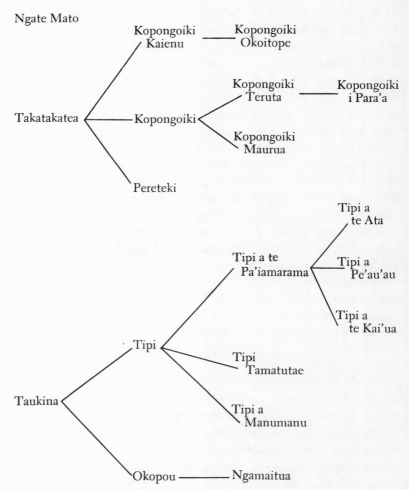

Mana'une

A

Ngate Mato

Aureka (Ngaitapana)

*The information in this chart is taken from Stokes (1930: 678–679, 681–698).

and one or more of the Takatakatea groups (first located around Anarua Bay). Both were expanding into the large fertile plain of Tukou at the head of Ha'urei Bay. War may have ensued; if so, Ngate Mato was probably defeated. Takatakatea, however, was soon threatened from the rear by the Taukina ramages. Probably beginning around Hiri Bay, Okopou held the fertile lowlands at the head of that bay and expanded across the central ridge into the flat land around modern Ha'urei village. Their impregnable fortress Napiri guarded these two areas and the narrow mountain corridor which Okopou controlled to connect them.

The more important part of the Taukina group was composed of the various Tipi ramages. These first came into prominence by defeating Takatakatea at Anarua, on the west coast. The Tipi retained the valuable lowlands and drove the Takatakatea ramages into the highlands of the southern and western portions of the island. Under the leadership of their senior segment, Tipi a te Pa'iamarama, the Tipi ramages followed the same course of eastward expansion as the Takatakatea before them — toward Tukou. Here outposts of Ngate Mato were again met. Ngate Mato was defeated, so disastrously that only one man is said to have survived.

The expansions by Okopou and Tipi probably mark an era of turmoil during which the people left the lowlands and built their fortified mountain villages. By virtue of their military successes, the chiefs of Tipi a te Pa'iamarama were acknowledged as the kingly dynasty of Rapa. Apparently while they directly controlled only those areas they had conquered, other ramages recognized the hegemony of the Tipi and probably paid some tribute.

Eventually a coalition challenging Tipi sovereignty was formed under the leadership of the Aureka ramage, centered at the time of its first ambitions in the highlands between Akatanui and Angaira'o bays. After severe initial reverses, Aureka forged a network of alliances which ultimately toppled Tipi power. Aureka's most spectacular military success was the reduction of Okopou's supposedly invincible fort Napiri. Aureka is said to have built Tevaitahu, a rival fortress very close to Napiri, expressly for the siege. In a further campaign the Tipi ramages were defeated at Anarua, and Aureka's military primacy was established. Stokes believes that these events occurred around the beginning of the eighteenth century. The Aureka ramage changed its name to Ngaitapana, and its chiefs became Rapa's "kings" — again having a loose control stemming from acknowledged power of arms, and consisting largely of collecting tribute from the other semi-independent ramages. The Ngaitapana dynasty held hegemony over Rapa for eleven generations until the French abolished the monarchy in 1887.[7]

1791–1865: CONVERSION, COMMERCE, AND DEATH

After Vancouver's discovery in 1791, Europeans next appeared off Rapa's shores in 1814 or 1815 when a Captain Powel was becalmed near the island, and again in 1817 when the English missionary Ellis passed en route from New Zealand to Tahiti. While not exactly hostile, the Rapans displayed a disconcerting exuberance on both of these occasions. Finding a hawser trailing from Powel's ship, about fifty swimming natives attempted to tow the vessel to shore. They were induced to relinquish the design only in the face of brandished cutlasses. A group of natives invited aboard Ellis' ship stole every article of iron they could lay hands on, and manifested keen disappointment upon meeting determined resistance to their efforts to jump overboard with the ship's cabin boy (Ellis 1829 I:42–45, Caillot 1932:72–73).

The early visitors who went ashore found the Rapans living in the most primitive conditions. According to Paulding, who visited in 1826:

They had a sickly look, almost without an exception. Their dress differed altogether from any we had before seen. It consisted of a heavy mat of grass, weighing from ten to fifteen pounds, which was thrown over their shoulders, and another light mat of the same material, for the loins. . . . A few of their houses were scattered about

[7] The preceding information concerning pre-European history is taken from Stokes (1930:681–713, 727, 736). He advances it only tentatively, and we have no assurance that this rendition is accurate. Caillot's information is that endemic warfare between autonomous "tribes" continued until just after Vancouver's visit in 1791, when one ruler finally exerted his sway over the entire island (1910:447, 1932:71–72). Stokes's version is given here since he spent more time in Rapa and seems to have researched the matter more closely.

26

upon the hills. They were extremely miserable, and might, without disparagement, be compared to dog kennels. They were long, and very narrow, and about three or four feet high, so that when one entered them, it was necessary to get down upon the hands and knees (1831:253–254).

Davies who also called in 1826, wrote "their complexion is darker than that of the Tahitians, but their features are much the same; and were it not for their savage appearance, going without clothes, with long hair, and long beards, several of them might be considered as good-looking people" (Davies 1827:331).

Among the first to be seriously interested in Rapa were the Tahiti-based Protestant preachers of the London Missionary Society (an inter-denominational organization of basically Calvinistic theology). In 1825 the Tahitian cutter *Snapper* called at Rapa and, apparently fearing attack from the fleet of canoes which set off to meet her, sailed away with two natives who had already boarded the ship. The Rapans were placed under the care of the missionary Davies in Tahiti. Initially terrified, they soon became fond of their English and Tahitian hosts, and manifested great interest in the cattle and crops they saw and in the Christian religion. In late 1825 the *Snapper* returned them to Rapa, in the company of two Tahitian missionaries who were to determine the potential for spreading the Gospel in that island. As the ship's boat approached the land, the Rapans, delighted at seeing their two compatriots whom they had presumed dead, literally picked up the boat with all its occupants in it and carried it ashore. Frightened by this reception, the Tahitian missionaries were calmed by a most hospitable welcome from the king. He invited them "to go and fetch their families, and come and reside at Rapa, and teach them some of the good things known at Tahiti (Davies 1827:325). Early in 1826 Davies sailed to Rapa to establish these same two native missionaries, their wives, and two more Tahitians on the island. They brought seeds, tools, Tahitian spelling books and Bibles, and timber for a chapel. They were received less enthusiastically than their first visit, probably because an epidemic had recently struck, counting the king among its victims. "The ignorant superstitious islanders attribute the mortality to the visit of the ships," especially to the contagious effects of the muskets some previous visitors had used in duck hunting (Davies 1827: 328). However, the missionaries received a reasonably cordial welcome. Having seen his missionaries well installed, Davies left after a week's stay (Davies 1827, 1961:279–280).

Rapa has never had a resident European missionary. English preachers visited at intervals of from one to five years until about 1865 and less frequently thereafter, but the mission was left in the hands of native teachers. These were Tahitian until 1862, when the first native Rapan returned from training in the Society Islands to take up the work of the church (Morris 1862). The first Tahitian teachers, arriving in 1826, must have been fairly effective, for conversion proceeded rapidly. "The profession of Christianity had become general thro' the island since the beginning of 1828, . . . a considerable number had learned to read, and know the Tahitian Catechism, and made some progress on Civilization" (Davies 1961:280–281).

During the early years of Rapa's Christian era the natives seem to have espoused the new religion enthusiastically. In 1831 or 1832, for example, a self-appointed missionary from Rapa turned up in the Gambier Islands (located northeast of Rapa) and began to preach Christianity. His evangelical attempt aborted, however, when sickness broke out among the natives, the missionary and his God were blamed, and he was forced to leave (Jore 1959 II: 109). Again, when the English missionary Orsmond visited Rapa in 1834, he brought Tahitian translations of the Scriptures for distribution among the natives. The people gathered around shouting:

"For me one! for me one!" The best readers were supplied first. A greyheaded woman sat down, and as her children gathered around her, she said, "I have a Salmo; mine is a Salmo!" (copy of the Psalms). She read a little, then pressed it to her bosom: she read again, and laughed loudly, wondering, as I supposed, at herself at being able to read a new book as easily as her old one. After reading a few verses, she pressed it to her head, and exultingly said, "Oh! these good foreigners who bring us the word of the true God! My desire is fully appeased. Come let us read, etc." . . . As I gazed from an unobserved quarter, I could not restrain my tears. Satisfaction dwelt on every brow; gratitude flowed from every heart (Orsmond 1835:519).

Orsmond's more austere colleague Pritchard, however, called at Rapa a year later and was less enthused about the progress of Christianity on the island.

It is to be regretted that there is not more evidence of real conversion to God among the people generally. Many are satisfied with a mere profession of Christianity, while they are destitute of the power of vital godliness in their hearts. . . . As most of those who are united in the church fellowship, have during the last year, acted in a manner unbecoming the gospel of Christ, it was thought most prudent not to administer the ordinance of the Lord's Supper. . . . The members were admonished and exhorted to look to God by fervent prayer for grace and strength to manifest more of a Christian spirit in the future (Pritchard 1835).

The severity of the blow which struck Rapa during the years following the arrival of the missionaries is difficult to imagine. Epidemics, probably introduced by visiting ships and foreign residents, reaped a devastating harvest. The first wave of death had already struck when Davies, on the basis of a week's stay to install the missionaries in 1826, estimated the population to be "upwards of 2,000" (Davies 1827:331). If this estimate is accurate, Rapa lost nearly three-quarters of her population within five years. In 1831 the missionary Darling conducted the first exact census of Rapa, writing down the names of all the inhabitants. He found there to be 357 adults and 243 children, for a total of 600 (Davies 1961:281). To aggravate the disaster, three renegade whites took up residence in Rapa and began to distill liquor from a local root. Probably this further decayed the health of the islanders, and rendered them even easier prey to the ravages of disease. When Darling again wrote down the names of all inhabitants in 1836, he found the population had dropped to 453 (Darling 1836).

During the 1830s and 1840s Rapa's demographic history is a monotonously dismal tale of continuing decline. Moerenhout (1837 I:139) found the population diminishing daily in 1834; Heath found them still ravaged by disease in 1840; in 1843 Lucett wrote, "there has been great mortality amongst them of late"

(1851 I:342); "it is amazing how the population has decreased within these few years" recorded Platt and Krause in 1845; and in 1846 John Barff found them reduced "by disease, chiefly consumption, dysentery, worms, and spasms of the stomach and bowels." Table 1 gives a few population estimates during this tragic period.

TABLE 1. POPULATION OF RAPA, 1791–1964*

Year	Population	Source
1791	c. 1500	Vancouver (1801 I:216–217)
1826	c. 2000	Davies (1827:331)
1829	c. 500	Pritchard and Simpson (1830:167)
1831	600	Darling (Davies 1961:281)
1836	453	Darling (1836)
1840	c. 200	Heath (1840)
1846	150–160	John Barff (1846)
1858	300–350	Charles Barff (1858)
1862	c. 360	Morris (1862:271)
1867	120	Méry (1867:127)
1871	200–250	Saville (McArthur 1967:308)
1881	c. 176	? (Teissier 1953:21)
1887	192	Official Census
1897	170	Official Census
1907	183	Official Census
1926	230	Official Census
1946	299	Official Census
1951	310	Official Census
1956	279	Official Census
1964	362	Hanson

* A few additional figures may be found in Caillot (1932:25) and McArthur (1967:307–309). For discussions of the reliability of early population estimates and official censuses in French Polynesia, see Schmitt (1965) and McArthur (1967:306–309, 314–318).

Caillot (1932:25) gives a figure of 70 in 1851, and identifies its source as the French government. If accurate, this marks the low point of Rapa's population. But I have been unable to verify this figure, and my research indicates that for more than a decade after 1849 the population was actually increasing (see Charter and Krause 1849, C. Barff 1858). At any rate, the conclusion seems inescapable that during the twenty years following the arrival of the missionaries in 1826, fully 90 percent of Rapa's population was swept away. Nearly every visitor during these fatal years describes the Rapans as a wretched lot, diseased and dying in bewilderment and despair. Some natives attributed the destruction to the anger of their pagan gods at the progress of Christianity (Moerenhout 1837 I:139). Lucett reports (1851 I:342): "They seem to entertain the most melancholy forebodings, hinting that in five years they believed there would not be one of them left upon the island." Certainly little comfort could be drawn from the missionary Platt, who resignedly attributed the disastrous depopulation of Rapa and other islands to an act of God, "for reasons known only to his infinite wisdom" (Platt 1848).

Traders were attracted to Rapa about the same time as the missionaries. When the *Snapper* returned the two natives to Rapa in late 1825, it profited for its pains by procuring a few tons of sandalwood (Ellis 1829 I:47). In 1826 an English merchant resided on the island collecting sandalwood and sea slugs, a culinary delicacy in China (Paulding 1831:254–255). Pearlers visited Rapa in the 1830s, and the natives earned cash and cloth from diving. Rapa's own resources of pearls and shells were soon depleted, probably before 1840, but by this time the men of the island had established a reputation as the finest divers in the eastern Pacific. Pearlers made the trip to Rapa to procure divers for work in the Tuamotus, and on the basis of their renown the Rapans commanded especially high wages (Lucett 1851 I:305, 308). During this period many men also took jobs as sailors on trading vessels and whalers, and their fame as excellent seamen persists to the present day.

The natives' moral and spiritual concerns seem to have diminished in proportion to the increase of bodily comforts afforded by these commercial enterprises. In 1836 the missionary Darling wrote:

I could not help observing a marked difference in the conduct and appearance of the people, from what it was when I was here in 1831, they appear to [have] much more foreign cloth amongst them, but there is nothing like that attention, which all seemed to pay formerly to learning, and hearing about the word of God, and Jesus Christ the true Savior (Darling 1836).

Davies, the founder of the Rapan mission, was also concerned. The opportunity to work as divers for payments of cloth and other articles "proved a great temptation to most of the men to leave their island, and so leaving the means of instruction, and being exposed to the example of the sailors they have been greatly injured" (Davies 1835). Perhaps the trader Lucett, calling in 1843, best captures the spirit of Rapan Christianity in this era.

The day was Sunday, and the natives would not enter into any conversation about business; but, strange to say, though they were rigidly strict in abstaining from labour and barter on this day, they made not the slightest scruple to enter into certain negotiations about their wives and daughters (Lucett 1851 I:307).

Intensive pearling died out in the eastern Pacific around 1850, and the Rapans looked to other means of acquiring the money to which they had become accustomed. For about twenty years they became remarkably successful entrepreneurs in their own right, selling their surplus taro in the Tuamotuan atolls where the crop does not grow (Caillot 1932:76). Possibly diminished pearling meant that fewer ships visited Rapa. If this is true, it may be related to the happy fact that after 1849 the epidemics ceased and the population began to grow. The missionaries Charter and Krause found little sickness on their visit in 1849, and in 1858 their colleague Barff could make the (for Rapa) astounding report that "only one had died during the year." Between 1846 and 1858 missionary estimates of the population rose from 150–160 to 300–350 (J. Barff 1846, C. Barff 1858).

A moment of triumph brightened Rapan history in 1863. A Peruvian blackbirder (slave ship) called at Rapa for provisions and perhaps in hopes of procuring slaves for labor in South America. The Rapans were aware of the criminal acts of blackbirders among the Pacific islands, and resolved to act. They smuggled weapons aboard and captured the ship. The Rapans sailed the blackbirder to Tahiti and turned its captain and crew over to

French justice (Caillot 1932:76–77, *Messager de Tahiti*, 21 and 28 February, 1863.)

But the nightmare was not yet over. The following events occurred later in 1863.

> The Peruvian Government took a stand against this system of slavery [blackbirding]; and as an earnest of their sincerity they chartered a vessel, and re-embarked 360 natives of various islands, extending from Easter Island, on the east, to the Tokelau group, on the west. Soon after leaving the coast, small-pox and dysentery broke out on board, and, before they reached *Rapa*, 344 of the poor creatures had been committed to the deep, after almost brutal treatment and inhuman neglect. On sighting the island of *Rapa*, the captian bore down, and as they approached shore, they lowered a boat, the natives from the shore looking on with mingled feelings. Soon, however, they were enlightened as to the nature of the visit of this ship, as the captain and crew conveyed sixteen poor emaciated human beings to their shore, with a peremptory order to the people to receive them. At first they hesitated, seeing disease was still abiding on them. The captian replied, saying, he would not take them any farther, and, if they would not receive them, he would take them back to the vessel, and then throw them overboard, and they might swim for their lives. The Rappans then received them into their houses, and the result is. . . over one-third of their population have been taken off by the disease (Green 1864a:267).

The loss was closer to two-thirds — from about 360 in 1862 to 120 in 1867 — by the time the tragedy was done (see Table 1, page 30).

1865–1887: RAPA AND THE GREAT POWERS

After 1860 the dominant thread in Rapan history was the anticipated construction of a Panama canal. This presaged brisk trade between Europe and the thriving colonies of Australia and New Zealand via Panama. Since the trans-Pacific run was extremely long for steamers of that day, it was considered essential to establish a coaling station somewhere along the route. The British considered annexing Fiji for this purpose, but in about 1858 a Colonel Smythe argued that Rapa, located much closer to the most direct route and with a fine harbor, was more suitable. In 1861 the British Admiralty agreed to investigate the island (Scholefield 1920:30–31).

33

But the Admiralty was slow to act. In 1866 or early 1867 the Panama, New Zealand and Australian Royal Mail Company began its service between New Zealand and Panama (goods and passengers were transported across the isthmus by rail). The company was strongly interested in Rapa as a coaling station, but learned that the latest report the Admiralty had on the island was Vancouver's, on his discovery in 1791. The company made its own survey of Rapa early in 1867, established a coaling station near the village of 'Area, and its steamers made monthly calls for refueling beginning later that year. Meanwhile the company tried to convince the British government to establish a protectorate over Rapa, pointing out that the large and well protected harbor would make an excellent naval base. The government was reluctant, fearing Rapa would become a drain on the British treasury. By September, 1867, however, the government seemed prepared to establish the protectorate, provided the steamship company would meet all expenses involved. But it was too late, for in April of that year the French had made Rapa a protectorate of their own (Ross 1964:67–68).

The French had tried to convince the company to use Tahiti for its coal depot, largely because this would establish regular communication between France and its Tahitian protectorate. When La Roncière, commander of the Tahitian protectorate, learned that the steamers would not stop at Tahiti, he surmised they had chosen Rapa and wrote: "As for the English, who often sacrifice their own interests in order to obstruct the development of a country belonging to France, this determination [not to stop at Tahiti] does not surprise me. We see them at work" (La Roncière 1866). La Roncière soon learned from a Rapan visiting Tahiti that his suppositions were correct: ships from the company had called at Rapa. Perhaps motivated by the idea that "if the company would not use Tahiti as the coaling station, all the more likely islands in those waters should be taken under French protection" (Ross 1964:68), La Roncière sent the warship *Latouche-Tréville* to Rapa and the natives signed a request for a French protectorate on April 27, 1867. A French resident agent arrived in Rapa early in 1868 and established his residence in

34

Ha'urei, across the bay from the coaling station (Caillet 1868, 1886).

Great Britain's tardy action in the Rapan affair and in a few other incidents concerning mid-Pacific islands provoked New Zealanders to strong criticism of the British government. In the opinion of Edward Stafford, New Zealand's Premier,

. . . the Imperial Government was not acting in a truly imperial way, but rather as the local goverment of the United Kingdom. Ignorant of the French actions at Rapa, Stafford suggested that if the French had not secured the island then New Zealand should obtain its annexation, holding that, if the British flag were once hoisted and the colony guaranteed the expenditure involved, the British Government would be too apathetic to send a man-of-war to haul down the flag (Ross 1964:69).

Rapa's prominence was short-lived. The operation of the steamship company was apparently not profitable and after about a year the Panama route was discontinued. The last steamer called at Rapa in February, 1869, the coaling station was abandoned, and the French resident agent returned to Tahiti immediately thereafter. During the next decade Rapa again receded into the backwater of history, a forgotten protectorate of France.

The prospect of a Panama canal was strongly revived when, in 1882, a French company began construction. This of course foretold the reestablishment of a trans-Pacific steamship line, and sparked new interest in Rapa as a coaling station and a strategically placed naval base. Spurred mainly by the colonial government of New Zealand, between 1883 and 1886 the British negotiated with France for the cession of Rapa. At one point in these complex negotiations Great Britain was about prepared to recognize French annexation of the large New Hebrides archipelago of the western Pacific in exchange for Rapa. However, the Presbyterian and Anglican churches in New Zealand and Australia (which had carried on missionary work in the New Hebrides for some time) stirred up public opinion in these colonies against any accommodation which would give France the New Hebrides. This ultimately forced the governments of New Zealand and most of the Australian colonies to oppose the arrangement (Ross 1964: 211–227).

Voices in France were also raised in opposition to the exchange of Rapa for the New Hebrides. Rapa was anticipated to have a strategic importance equal to Gibraltar once the Panama Canal was completed (Richard 1886/87:23–24). Some parties felt that if Tahiti and other French establishments in the Pacific were to develop commercially, France must control each and every port anywhere near the route between Panama and Australia–New Zealand (Deschanel 1888:175–176). The question of the New Hebrides came up, wrote Richard (1886/87:23–24), simply because "the Anglican missionaries of New Zealand, those same missionaries whom we meet everywhere where there are French interests to combat and French rights to annihilate, began to make loud cries." The upshot of the affair was that the New Hebrides came under the joint rule of France and Britain (Ross 1964:229) while Rapa remained French.

Shortly before these negotiations, France had moved to strengthen her hand in Rapa. After neglecting the island entirely since the departure of the resident agent in 1869, the French warship *Guichen* appeared in 1881 with the aim of changing Rapa's status from a protectorate to an outright possession of France. When M. Chessé announced he had brought the tricolor to replace the protectorate flag, the king and chiefs replied:

We have no need of either one. After the departure of M. Caillet [the resident agent who left in 1869], we thought that your country no longer wished to protect us; today we have returned the [protectorate] flag which was left with us . . . and we do not want the one which you bring. We want to retain our independence (Chessé 1881).

The Rapans maintained their position in the face of Chessé's coaxing, arguments and threats, until he said he was taking command of the island himself and that they were all relieved of their offices. He left them and prepared to go on shore with a party of twenty armed men. The chiefs huddled in consternation and conferred with the interpreter, who then brought Chessé the message: "They see that they have made a mistake; they ask that you not be too severe with them and they will be your children." The Rapan leaders were then induced to sign a brief document

36

accepting the French tricolor (implying that the island was annexed to France), but stipulating that internal government and laws were to remain in native hands (Chessé 1881). The next year a French resident agent arrived, carrying orders not to interfere in the local government except in cases which involved foreigners (Instructions 1882).

In 1887 progressing construction in Panama again focused French attention on Rapa. M. Lacascade, Governor of French Oceania, sailed from Tahiti to Rapa in the *Scorff* to check on the island's affairs. To his dismay, he found Rapa "in open revolt against the government of France" (Lacascade 1887c).

Lacascade was concerned that the Rapans had recently given a warm welcome to a British man-of-war, and he reasoned that if French possession was to have any meaning, French control over the island's internal affairs must be established (Lacascade 1887a). When he came ashore to announce his plans for the island, the Rapans replied, "We neither understand nor admit your intervention in our affairs. We accepted the flag of France, but we stipulated that we wished neither its government nor its laws." Lacascade replied that as a French possession they had no right to make such stipulations. He pointed to the recent succession of monarchs, informing them that

. . . in naming Parima's daughter queen of Rapa, at the death of her father, they had committed a very serious fault that I could punish as an act of treason against France. This speech, made in a firm voice and a resolute tone and in the presence of a detachment of marines which escorted me, produced a salutory effect. I returned on board a few instants afterwards.

The next day Lacascade was told that the Rapans remained firm in their intention to retain their queen, their laws and their administrative organization, and they rejected the right of the governor to meddle in their affairs. "However, they consented to accept the gifts that I had brought them 'because', they say, 'they had made the mistake of accepting them in the first place.'"

Lacascade immediately summoned the chiefs on board and delivered his ultimatum: "If the next morning, at precisely eight o'clock, they had not made their voluntary submission, I would consider means of wrenching their compatriots away from their exploitation and cause them to return to obedience to the orders of the Representative of France." The chiefs were surprised at being allowed to return to shore. They told the interpreter, "The English would have made us prisoners; the governor is an upright man."

The next day dawned stormy. Lacascade paced the deck, a detachment of fifteen marines drawn up behind him, ready to make a landing. Just as they were about to debark, a boat bearing the chiefs arrived with the news that "after having ascertained the opinion of the population, they agreed to execute the orders that I had given them." Thus loosened Rapa's last grip on independence. The monarchy was abolished, native laws gave way to the French civil code, and France took a direct hand in the affairs of the island. The now submissive Rapans watched Lacascade sail away, pondering the ramifications of his final warning and exhortation.

Be respectful of the law, first because everyone owes it obedience and also, because I am determined to punish very severely all who transgress it, whomever they may be.

Finally, always love France, which wishes only your happiness and that of your children; in a word, make yourselves worthy of the title which France has given you and the protection that you will always find under her flag which is, forever more, the flag of Rapa.[8]

RAPA VS. TAHITI

Rapa's potential as a " 'perfect Gibraltar' " which " 'would bar the route of all traders crossing Oceania' " (Scholefield 1920:31) has never been realized. In 1900 the oft-delayed prospect of a Panama canal again emerged and New Zealand officials tried once more (and again unsuccessfully) to stimulate negotiation for the cession of Rapa to Great Britain (Ross 1964:784). In 1903 a French engineer named Kunkler made application to construct at Rapa all the installations of a major port. For a time Kunkler had the blessings of the French government, and had his project succeeded, it is possible that Rapa instead of Tahiti would have

[8] The above information concerning Lacascade's visit is from Lacascade (1887b).

become the most important island in the eastern South Pacific. But Rapa is very small, and while it is close to major trans-Pacific shipping routes .it is decidedly remote from other islands in the area and thus not well placed as a center for local trade in copra and other products. Tahiti is far larger, infinitely richer in resources, much better placed for inter-island trade, and historically Tahiti had always been the political and commercial center of the French establishments in Oceania. There were, therefore, powerful reasons and interests opposed to abandoning Tahiti in favor of remote Rapa. By 1909, before construction had begun in Rapa, the French government withdrew its approval of Kunkler's proposal and turned its energies to the development of a port and naval base at Tahiti.[9]

Rapa has remained a lonely island, commercially and politically of little importance; an island from which one can see passing ocean liners but where as late as 1964 three months might elapse without a visit from the outside world.

[9] See the numerous letters and reports between 1903 and 1910 on the Kunkler project in the Archives de la France d'Outre-Mer, Paris, Océanie A 93.

CHAPTER THREE

Land and
the Ramage

The first focus in this study of the network of relations in modern Rapa is the economy: the relations between men and things. One major concern is how Rapans own and exploit property to secure their material livelihood. No economic system can be truly understood, however, without a knowledge of the cultural meanings and values associated with it. How can one appreciate the American economy, for example, unless something is known of the value placed on hard work as an end in itself, the exalted ideal of the "self-made man," the complete faith in technological research and innovation, and the manager's quasi-religious quest for ultimate efficiency? Rapan culture has its own set of meanings associated with things economic. These, as much as the more practical aspects of the system, form the subjects of this chapter and the next.

Rapans divide real property in two conceptual orders or categories: territory (*fenua*) and improvements. Improvements consist essentially of taro terraces and other sorts of cultivated gardens, planted trees, and houses. Improvements cannot be divorced entirely from territory; they are of course fixed in location, and the usual way of referring to them is by the name of the territory where they are situated. Still, territory and improvements are distinct orders of phenomena, so distinct that improvements may be owned separately and independently from their locale. It is no exaggeration to say that the majority of improvements existing on any tract of territory are owned by persons or groups other than the territory's owners.

The distinction between territory and improvements may be clarified by a consideration of two native concepts. The English term *land* combines two ideas which are sharply differentiated in Rapa. The first of these is conveyed in the word *fenua*, which has been translated above as "territory." *Fenua* is fundamentally a concept of location; it would be the proper translation for *land* in the sentence "America is a land of liberty." *Fenua* refers solely to some named portion of the earth's surface, be it as large as a continent or as small as a back yard. Whether that place is mountainous or flat, a site for houses or pasturage, under cultivation or left unexploited is in no way relevant to its status as fenua.

The term *repo* marks the second idea. *Repo* would be the proper translation for *land* in the sentence "Iowa has good land for growing corn." The closest English approximation of *repo* is *soil*. Strictly speaking, fenua is not productive; fertility is a quality of repo. Taro terraces are made and trees grow in repo. In the Rapan mind, then, improvements are associated with repo, not with fenua. Given the sharp semantic distinction between these concepts, we may begin to appreciate the rationale behind the Rapan idea that improvements exist separately from the land (a word henceforth used exclusively in the sense of *fenua*) on which they are located.

Malinowski wrote, "Ownership . . . is the sum of duties, privileges and mutualities which bind the joint owners to the object and to each other" (1959:20–21). It follows that to own something need not universally mean the same thing. In different cultures owners may be assigned different kinds of rights over their property and, in the case of joint ownership, different sorts of social relations may obtain between co-owners. In Rapa the concept of ownership varies with the type of property in question. Landownership implies a different set of rights over the property and relations among joint owners than does ownership of improvements, and there are further variations according to the different kinds of improvements.

LAND

To a Rapan the physical world is divided into the sea and a hierarchy of named fenua (places, tracts of land). The island of Rapa is a fenua of that name, and it is divided into a number of districts which are also fenua, bearing names such as Anatakuri, Ma'i'ī, Tupuaki, and so on. These districts are usually congruent with the valleys rising above the various bays (see the map of Rapa, facing page 1). Each district is again divided and subdivided into yet another named fenua. Here boundaries are determined with reference to permanent natural markers like outcroppings of rock, or by special stones planted firmly in the earth for this purpose. (Although on a much smaller scale, the system is not unlike our own, where the United States is divided into states, the states into counties, and so on, each division and subdivision having its name.) The boundaries separating the various fenua are thought to have been unchanged since time immemorial.

Land in Rapa is held by groups of joint owners. At times they show little concern over landownership, betrayed in statements like "The land is God's" or "The land belongs to everyone." This nonchalance over landownership is not difficult to understand because land is a remarkably unproductive form of property in Rapa. The kinds of property with economic significance are improvements, such as taro terraces and groves of trees. As explained above, these represent a conceptual order of property distinct from

42

land. Furthermore, landowners have almost no control over the uses to which it is put. Anyone may make a taro terrace, or plant fruit or lumber trees, on unused land anywhere. He is not obliged to secure the permission of the landowners, nor do they have any means of preventing his project if they disapprove. Once the improvement is established it belongs to its maker and his heirs in perpetuity. The landowners may not confiscate it; they have no rights whatsoever over it.

Rights of landowners are essentially limited to giving or refusing permission for grazing rights for goats or cattle, for planting coffee and, in certain circumstances, for building houses. Theoretically they may also order a house owner to remove the building from their land. Finally, they may prohibit cutting certain wild trees and basket wicker, and catching sea birds on their land. Gathering basket wicker is often prohibited as a conservation measure, but none of these other rights have much meaning today. Permission to build houses seems invariably to be granted, and although an eviction order may be served in the heat of an argument, it is never seriously pursued. Goat and cattle herds have been established for some time, and nearly all the locations suitable for coffee are already under cultivation. Thus, few if any requests for these rights have been lodged during the last decade or two. For other purposes, including taro cultivation (by far the most important element of the subsistence economy), land-use is free to all. Rapans are aware that in other places landownership is more important than on their island, and they are proud of the generous conception of land-use implied in their own system. To them, the fact that anyone may assure his subsistence by making and cultivating taro terraces freely on available land anywhere, regardless of its ownership, is proof of their moral superiority over those islands where landless unfortunates must pay rent.

Paradoxically, the same persons who sometimes maintain generously that the land belongs to everyone may on other occasions show such a deadly concern over landownership that it is impossible to avoid the conclusion that this is their most valued form of property. Although the free use of land described above means that landownership has almost nothing to do with the standard of living, those with little or no land are said to be *veve* — "poverty-stricken." In generous moods they are mentioned with compassion; at other times they are dismissed with contempt. Often when an informant would try to convince me of the utter worthlessness of someone, the ultimate condemnation was that he was landless.

An indication of the importance of land is how seriously Rapans regard attempts to steal it. If someone tries to confiscate a coffee grove or taro terrace, he may become embroiled in heated disputes and possibly litigation, but little more will happen. Should he attempt to steal land by moving a boundary stone, it is believed that the moment he lays hold of the stone he will fall to the ground in convulsions, lose the power of speech, and die within a few hours.

Rapan families often record births and deaths in notebooks which are jealously guarded and kept in locked chests. They regard these genealogies as proof of their inheritance rights in land. Perhaps the greatest injury one can inflict on an enemy is to steal his family books, thereby depriving him of validation of his land rights. However, this procedure can be dangerous. Several years ago a family discovered its books were missing, and shortly thereafter a man fell strangely ill. On the verge of death, he called his wife and told her where he had hidden the books. She found them in the indicated spot and returned them to their rightful owner. The man died anyway, a punishment for his deed. As often occurs in Rapa, his wife changed her name in his memory. Thenceforth she was known as "Husband Calls Me," commemorating the summons to make his confession about the books.

These books are in fact the only written records of landownership, for Rapa is one of the few islands in French Polynesia where the administration has not surveyed the land and recorded deeds. Rapans know it is only a matter of time until this is done, and they await it with fear. Many of their books have been lost or stolen and others are sadly incomplete. People are afraid they will be unable to offer adequate proof of their holdings in land, and worry that the administration might take it or might accept the false claim of some unscrupulous compatriot. Meanwhile the French, lacking official documents upon which to judge cases, leave the entire system of property ownership in native hands. Even if offered liberal compensation Rapans refuse to alienate their land. In 1963 a school was built in the village of 'Area. The administration approached the landowners with an offer to buy a lot for the school and a house for the teacher. They positively refused to sell or lease the land. In the end the administration was forced to create new land for the school by filling in a part of the bay with rocks. Motives behind behavior like this are difficult to unravel. A similar event occured in 1964, when the administration desired to buy a piece of land in Ha'urei for a new weather station. I attended the meeting where the numerous co-owners of the land deliberated this matter. Again there was absolute refusal to sell, although this time they did agree to a lease. The objection to a sale was not dissatisfaction with the offered price. This was scarcely mentioned in the meeting, and the terms of the lease entailed no exchange of money whatsoever. The Rapans said compensation would be adequate if, at the end of the lease, the administration would leave the small building it planned to erect on the site in the hands of the landowners. Nor was the issue that they wished to give up the land for a short and specified period only. As the Rapans stipulated the terms of the lease, the administration could use the land for as long as it desired. They simply wanted to continue to *own* that land, although the ownership was devoid of control and apparent meaning.

The situation is puzzling; more, it is downright aggravating to someone who wants to understand these people. Why must they place such stress on merely *having* land when having it does them no good? The answer, I think, is that having it does them a great deal of good, but the good is not defined in economic terms. We of the West endow certain possessions — wedding rings, family heirlooms, cherished gifts — with sentimental value. These objects are valued because they symbolize something personally meaningful which cannot be measured in dollars and cents. When Rapans are nonchalant about landownership they are viewing it from an economic perspective, for on their island the economic value of land is slight. When they exhibit intense concern over land it is because for them land holds something akin to sentimental value. Here we encounter one of those cultural meanings which extend the economic system beyond the purely utilitarian plane and integrate it with the Rapan world view.

TIME, SPACE, AND THE ANCESTORS

Different cultures have adopted diverse ways of bringing a sense of order to what happens in the world. In the Western tradition, for example, the concept of time probably reigns supreme. We classify the confusion of events by arranging them in chronological sequence, and we then assume that antecedent events have a causal effect on subsequent ones in a lineal progression of history.

Time is far less significant to the Rapans. When speaking of past events they seldom concern themselves with precisely when, or in what temporal sequence, they occurred. Many Rapans have only the vaguest notion of their own age, much less that of people close to them. One middle-aged woman, for example, told me she is about forty, and she figured her first child must be about twenty-five and her third around thirty! Time is not even the final measure of a person's passage through life. As we have seen, an individual is classed as a child, youth, or adult not so much on the basis of his age as his state of mind.

If Rapans appear, by Western standards, insufferably dull in matters pertaining to time, they are remarkably acute with reference to space. In fact, they seem to be preoccupied with location. Where people are, or are going, or have been is a topic of great interest. The usual greeting called out to someone walking through the village is "Where are you going?" or "Where are you coming from?" When the activities of the day are recounted at supper, household members invariably specify where they had been, where they saw other people, and the location of all noteworthy incidents. One gets the impression that by exchanging this information the Rapans are mentally classifying the jumble of events occurring around them according to *where* they occur. The categories in their scheme of classification correspond not to sequential points along the stream of time, but to named tracts of land (fenua) on the map of their island.

The principle of location serves to order past as well as current events. One striking feature of myths and legends, in both Rapa and Tahiti, is the careful specification of the location of all events in the story by means of place names (fenua names). In travels around Rapa my companions would often point out locations famous in mythology, and seeing these places would frequently stimulate a retelling of the story. Again, certain noteworthy events of recent history have been immortalized in humorous songs, such as that which vividly describes how, about fifteen years ago, a pair of three-year old twins and their ancient great-grandmother discovered a couple in the act of adultery. By means of place names the song faithfully describes exactly where the twins had been playing at gathering molluscs, the various places where the old woman went looking for them, and the location of the tall weeds in which the homeward-bound trio stumbled over the luckless lovers. Another song which holds humor for them was unfathomable to me, seeming to be nothing but a string of names of the places a man passed on his way to dive for crayfish.

The most permanent thing Rapans know is the division of their island into named tracts of land. They maintain that boundaries separating the fenua have always been as they are today. I would suggest, then, that, in addition to ordering current events, the map of the island is the Rapans' history book. In their view of history, past and current events are related in ordered series not so much because they occurred in the same chronological sequence as because they happened in the same place.

To own land is of such tremendous importance to the Rapans, I believe, because this is how they relate themselves to this spatially-oriented view of world order. This relationship has several facets. First, a tie may be established between the individual and the land at birth. When the placenta is expelled, Rapans customarily bury it under the floor or threshold of the family home. I unearthed no satisfactory explanation for this in Rapa, but

Michel Panoff investigated a similar custom in Tahiti and other islands in French Polynesia. Nearly all of his informants explained that the buried placenta establishes an "indestructible tie which will oblige the infant, become adult, to return to the family land regardless of the voyages he might undertake" (Panoff 1964:118–119).

Again, landownership is one basis for the social order. Land, like most other forms of real property, is owned by groups rather than individuals, and joint ownership of property is the whole reason why these groups exist. Therefore, land and other forms of property provide one basis for classing people together in groups. In this sense, it might be said that the map of Rapa serves as a social charter. Panoff's research again indicates a similar situation elsewhere in French Polynesia. "Land turns out to be a sociological instrument: it situates the family in society. Furthermore, through the rights of use and ownership associated with it, land is a means of identifying all of the individuals who, in diverse degrees, participate in a group or gravitate around it" (Panoff 1964:120).

Finally, landownership provides a link with the ancestors. The groups which own land are descent groups: their members belong by right of descent from a common ancestor. The man who has rights in much land is a man with many illustrious ancestors, and therefore a man who is firmly entrenched in the heritage of his society.

The map of Rapa can be characterized as a philosophical treatise, a history book, a social charter, and a family tree. Although the utilitarian value of land is small, these meanings endow it with extreme nonutilitarian or "sentimental" value. A man with no land is a nonentity; his life has no meaning and no permanence for he simply does not fit into the scheme of things. Through the ownership of land one's own existence gains meaning in the world order and history. Quite literally, and with all the connotations this holds in native thought, by owning land a Rapan finds his *place* in the world; he puts himself on the map.[1]

[1] See also Johansen's excellent discussion of the intimate relationship between the New Zealand Maori and his land (1954:93–95).

48

The modern system of landownership dates from 1889. In that year Rapa's local governing body redistributed the land, awarding the various tracts to individual owners. Improvements are also originally owned individually by the person who created the improvement: who made the taro terrace, built the house, planted the grove.[2] Few improvements are older than seventy-five years; new ones are made every year. Regardless of where an improvement is established, and regardless of whether its maker shares ownership in the land on which it is located, it is the exclusive property of its creator.

A piece of property normally outlasts its original owner. He may will it to an individual heir, such as a child or foster child. (Some taro terraces and coffee groves have passed through two or three generations in this manner.) Invariably in the case of land, however, and often in the case of improvements, the individual owner leaves his property jointly to all his children. Later it is passed on to all their children, and so on through the generations, by a rule of cognatic descent. With the passage of time, then, groups of co-owners are established around the various estates of property. Rapans call these groups 'ōpū a word which also means "abdomen." Since each 'ōpū consists of the cognatic descendants of a common ancestor, the appropriate term for these groups is "ramage." Each ramage is named for its founder: the ancestor who owned the estate individually. The modern ramage is clearly descended from the ancient ramage, although it has changed greatly in form and function since pre-European times. These changes will be analyzed in Chapter 9.

As with any ramage system, a modern Rapan may hold rights in more than one ramage. He may receive rights in one or more ramages through his mother, and rights in one or several others through his father. However, a crucial difference from the ancient system (and from most other societies with cognatic descent) is that in modern Rapa no mechanism restricts the individual to

---

[2] A few improvements are said to have been made, thus originally owned, by very small groups, such as a married couple or a set of siblings.

active membership in just one ramage, with latent rights in the others. Regardless of where he lives on the island, and whether his pedigree from the founder is patrilineal, matrilineal, or of some combination of male and female links, he simultaneously exercises full and equal rights in every ramage in which he traces cognatic descent.

The only limitation is that descent be legitimate. That is, to qualify for membership in a particular ramage an individual's chain of descent from the founder must entail legal recognition at every parent-child link. Legal recognition follows the precepts of French law as these are understood in Rapa. Any child born of a married woman is automatically recognized both by the mother and her husband, and this is recorded on the Birth Registration. Recognition of children born of unmarried women is optional for both parents. This too may be recorded on the Birth Registration or, in a more complicated procedure involving several witnesses, at any subsequent time in an Act of Recognition. Due to the common practice of lengthy premarital cohabitation, many children are born to unwed women. My information indicates that unmarried mothers nearly always recognize their children, but the fathers may not.

The stipulation that descent be legitimate limits the number of ramages to which some persons belong, but seldom reduces it to just one. Very few Rapans belong to less than two or three different ramages; most contemporary adults hold membership in four, five, or more. The fact that each individual belongs to several different ramages means that the ramages do not form discrete or mutually exclusive segments of society, but overlap in membership to a high degree.

The estate of a ramage may consist of one or more tracts of land, or taro terraces, or groves of trees, or a house or two, or any combination of these forms of property. This depends on what improvements the founder created, and whether he was awarded land in the distribution of 1889. Usually a ramage's estate is not concentrated in a single location. In 1889 it sometimes occurred that two or more tracts in widely separated areas were awarded to a single individual. Furthermore, when a Rapan decides where to establish an improvement, he is interested primarily in the fertility of the soil, convenience of access, and a place appropriate for the kind of improvement he plans. He builds his house in one of the villages, makes taro terraces in the lowlands near a river, and plants trees in the higher reaches of the valleys. All of these improvements pass into the possession of the ramage he founds. Thus it is common that different parts of a ramage's estate are located at diverse points around the island.

Its estate is the ramage's sole reason for existence. Perhaps we come closest to the native view by saying that members of a ramage do not conceive of themselves as forming a group because they are directly related to each other, nor even because they are indirectly related through the medium of a common ancestor. Rather, by descent from the founding ancestor each person is related to the estate. The basis of the members' association in a ramage is their common relationship to that estate. In line with this, a ramage undertakes no activity not directly connected with the ownership and administration of its estate. This varies with the type of property in question, but since the ramage itself does not exploit most forms of property, the activities under its jurisdiction are normally few. With reference to its land, as we have seen, the ramage is essentially limited to passing on requests to establish certain kinds of improvements on it, and to controlling the use of a few types of wild trees, basket wicker and birds found there. Ramage activities with reference to other types of property will be discussed later.

The ramage carries on its limited affairs by means of a simple internal organization. Primary responsibility for looking after the estate and coordinating ramage activities is entrusted to a *ha'apa'o*, or "manager." The manager's term is for life, although he usually steps down when he feels too old to continue his duties. Ideally a new manager is elected in a meeting of the entire ramage, but usually an outgoing manager simply designates his successor. His decision is rarely disputed by other ramage members. Unless the heir-apparent is incompetent or obnoxious, succession to the office of manager follows a stated rule: the manager should be the senior male of the ramage. That is, he should be the male

FIGURE 2   ORDER OF SUCCESSION TO
THE OFFICE OF MANAGER *

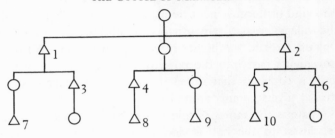

$\triangle$ = male
$\bigcirc$ = female $\triangle \quad \bigcirc$ = sibling relationship (brother and sister)

*In this and all subsequent genealogical charts, elder siblings are placed to the left, younger siblings to the right. Numbers denote the order of succession.

in the eldest living generation of the ramage, who traces the most senior line of descent from the founder.[3] A diagram (see Figure 2) should make this line of succession clear.

It will be noted that this rule of succession is cognatic — that no distinction is drawn between male, female, and mixed lines of descent. Since in the Rapan system of descent an individual may simultaneously belong to several different ramages, this cognatic rule of succession implies that conceivably a man may become the manager of more than one of them. Such is in fact the case. Several men in Rapa are currently managers of two or more ramages.

The Rapan descent system is inherently unstable. If children receive rights of membership in all ramages to which both parents belong, then with each successive generation individuals will belong to more and more ramages. Were this process allowed to proceed unchecked, its logical culmination would be a situation

[3] In a few cases at the time a manager died all other males of the ramage residing in Rapa were children or youths, and thus not yet qualified to succeed to the position. In such an event the ramage may go without a manager for a few years, or the position may be held by a female member. It has even happened that a respected man who does not belong to the ramage has been asked to act as its manager.

52

where each individual would belong to every ramage on the island or, the other side of the coin, each ramage would be composed of the entire population. In other words, the Rapan rule of descent implies a progression toward communal ownership of all property. We shall term this process "augmentation."

Two factors arrest augmentation and thus impart stability to most parts of the system. The first is the "life-span" of property. Improvements do not last forever: taro terraces revert to the status of unused territory if left uncultivated for fifteen or twenty years; groves of trees are cut down; houses are dismantled or destroyed in hurricanes. It sometimes occurs that all of the property in a ramage's estate ceases to exist. Since the estate is its whole reason for being, in such an event the ramage itself ceases to exist. Thus in some cases augmentation is stemmed by the extinction of the ramage. From what I could learn, no improvements in Rapa are older than about a century or are owned by ramages spanning more than five or six generations from founder to most remote descendant.

If the founder was prolific, a ramage may contain forty or more members within the space of three generations. In these cases Rapans often decide the ramage is too large for effective administration of its estate. Thus enters the second mechanism which controls augmentation: property division. All the improvements are divided between two or more sections of the ramage, each section consisting normally of the descendants of a child of the original ramage founder. When property is divided, it is divided absolutely. Each section of the ramage gains full and exclusive rights over the property allotted to it, and forfeits all rights over the property awarded to other sections. Having thus gained possession of an estate of its own, each section becomes a new and autonomous ramage, retaining no special relations with the other sections because of their common origin. We may term this process "ramage partition."

New improvements are created in every generation. At any point in time, then, a number of improvement-owning ramages are in the process of being founded, and others have existed only a generation or two. As time passes, such a ramage grows with the process of augmentation, but the twin factors of property extinction and ramage partition restrict augmentation within certain limits. I am aware of no improvement-owning ramages currently in existence which (1) are deeper than five or six generations, (2) have more than forty or fifty members residing in Rapa, or (3) contain adults more distantly related than second cousins. These three limits seem to mark the maximum augmentation in those ramages which own improvements. By the time a ramage reaches any one of these limits, either its estate will have ceased to exist (and the ramage with it), or the ramage will have partitioned into two or more smaller ones. Thus we may conclude that the descent system is stable as far as improvements are concerned, for under current conditions the system could persist indefinitely, but improvements would never be owned by ramages which exceed the limits listed above.

Neither of the restricting factors operates with respect to land. Improvements may be created at any time and they are finite in duration but, for sociological purposes, land is eternal. Moreover, Rapans do not divide their land. Perhaps this is because its utilitarian value is so slight that no economic advantage is to be gained from dividing land, while its nonutilitarian value is so great that no one is willing to give up his rights in any tract of land. At any rate, no ramage has divided its land since the general land distribution of 1889. Thus with respect to land, augmentation proceeds unchecked and the descent system is clearly unstable. Less than a hundred years ago, most land was in the hands of individuals. Today many landowning ramages probably contain fifty to seventy-five members, and contemporary children belong to as many as eight or ten of them. More time will be required before augmentation approaches its logical culmination wherein everyone belongs to every landowning ramage. An accident of history, however, affords a glimpse of the future. Apparently a few tracts of territory were not included in the distribution of 1889, and these were owned by groups at that time. The ramages which own these tracts today had a head start in the process of augmentation, in that their members trace descent from a *group* of "founders" who lived in 1889 rather than from an individual of that period. These historically special cases are much larger than other landowning ramages. At least one of them now contains a majority of the population.

Earlier we stated that some ramages own both land and improvements. This was more common a generation or two ago than it is today, and the trend is toward its disappearance. Every ramage which owns land is now over eighty years old, having been founded in the land distribution of 1889. If such a ramage also owns improvements, these are of about the same age, and hence are approaching the end of their life-span. When its improvements cease to exist, the ramage's estate will be composed exclusively of land. Furthermore, many ramages of this age are quite large. In recent years a number of such ramages have divided their improvements among two or more sections while the land has continued to be held in common. In this way land and improvements are segregated into the ownership of different ramages. The improvements pass into the hands of two or more new — and smaller—ramages, while the original ramage continues to hold the land. A few examples of divisions of this sort, as well as a discussion of some of the finer points of this descent system and the theoretical issues it raises, may be found in the Appendix.

COFFEE—THE CASH CROP

Coffee groves represent the only form of property exploited by the owning ramage as a unit, so here the ramage is seen in by far its most active role.

The upper reaches of valleys and moist shady hillsides are dressed in the dark green leaves of coffee trees. During the coldest season, from about May through August, the coffee harvest is the major task in the Rapan economy. The berries are allowed to fall and the flesh to rot away or be eaten by rats, and the beans are gathered from the ground. A line of people moves slowly through a grove on all fours, picking up every bean and brushing aside fallen leaves and twigs to be sure none are missed. Each worker gathers beans into a small basket or an old paint can which, when full, he empties into a gunny sack for the journey home. Both males and females gather coffee, and many of them detest it heartily. One man told me this is the hardest job in the entire economy. It is not heavy work, but it is tedious. Inching through a grove all day long, crouched low to the ground and picking up beans with both hands, is boring and it cramps the muscles. The annual school vacation occurs at coffee harvest time, so children are often drafted to help. The work does not require strength, and children do it fairly well until their attention span snaps and they run off to play with friends in the woods.

When the coffee arrives in the village, its processing is left largely to the women — especially the older ones who are no longer much good at heavier work. They husk the beans by placing them loosely in a burlap bag and beating it with a heavy stick or rock. The beans are then winnowed in a stiff breeze (men occasionally do this) and are washed by standing in a sieve-like basket under a running faucet. Finally the beans are spread out to dry in the sun on a piece of corrugated iron or a large square of cloth. Often in this season one sees old women sunning themselves by these drying "tables," idly turning over the beans with a long stick.

Most of the coffee is exported, but each family roasts and grinds enough for its own use. It is strong and excellent. Heavily sugared coffee is always served at breakfast and often at supper.

About a third of the coffee groves are owned by individuals, and the rest by ramages. Most ramages are composed of an adult sibling group and its descendants, though a few ramages are old and large enough that the adult members are as distantly related as second cousins. No one should gather coffee in a ramage's grove until a specific day, appointed by the ramage manager. On that day all ramage members, including proxies for those unable to attend personally, go as a group to harvest the crop. Ramages vary as to how the profits are distributed. Some allow each member to keep what he or she personally gathered after a day of joint work. Others pool all of the coffee and the manager measures it out in equal portions for all workers at the end of the day.

Most property disputes are over coffee groves. Probably because the ramages are most active with reference to coffee groves, here is the greatest opportunity for internal friction. In fairly large ram-

Typical Rapan labor: top, *gathering coffee;* bottom, *tying up a load of firewood.*

ages it is often difficult to select a time when everyone is free to gather coffee, and some members may not even be informed of the day. Those who are not represented in the harvest usually do not share in the profits, much to their discontent. While ideally the ramage is internally undifferentiated, descent criteria lay down fault lines which define factions when strife occurs. For instance, when the ramage is three or four generations deep, difficulties may develop between the descendants of the various children of the founder. A few coffee groves were planted by two or more individuals. These may have been siblings, more distant kinsman, or even unrelated friends. As the descent lines within the ramages are more distantly related, the chances of rancor between them are multiplied. One dispute involved a coffee grove planted jointly by two persons some two or three generations ago. One of them has had many more descendants than the other. When the harvest of beans was divided among members of this ramage, those descended from the more fertile founder maintained that each member should get an equal share of the profits. The descendants of the other founder claimed that first the total should be divided in half, and that those stemming from each founder should then divide their half equally among themselves. The dispute finally ended when the coffee grove was divided between the two factions and the ramage partitioned. As far as I could ascertain, finer points of the system, such as in this case how the profits really should have been divided, are left largely undefined. Thus, sources of friction are readily available should ramage members be disposed to use them.

Although all improvements are normally included in the division, the catalyst precipitating nearly all decisions to divide property and partition the ramage is some problem involving coffee groves. While the partition of some ramages is achieved amicably, and others are split by farsighted older persons while tension is still latent, many partitions are accompanied by ill feeling. Occasionally the friction becomes so intense that the offices of the District Council (Rapa's locally-elected governing body) are required to achieve the division of the jointly owned groves. A few ramages owning coffee groves are as deep as four or five generations, contain three or four adult sibling groups, and are quite successful. Usually their managers are thought to be very fair, and they do not contain any of the more contentious members of the population. But on the whole, given the considerable amount of activity undertaken by them and the ease of measuring discrepancies in the distribution of profits when these are as tangible as coffee beans, large coffee grove-owning ramages are not effective associations. People find it more convenient and more bearable to cooperate in coffee cultivation with small groups of close kinsmen. Here arrangements for joint harvesting are more easily made and minor inequities in labor or profits are more readily overlooked.

Inter-ramage relations usually involve coffee groves, and again these take the form of disputes. These are often over the boundaries between adjacent groves. While an alley may have been left when the groves were originally planted, new trees which have sprung up over the years have largely obscured it. Mutual accusations result that one group is gathering coffee belonging to the other. Again, if a coffee grove was divided between two disputing factions of a ramage, after partition one of the new ramages may accuse the other of gathering in its grove. Such inter-ramage disputes may linger for years, limited to an occasional shouting fest when one suspects the other of some new outrage. These confrontations take place in the village and always draw a large crowd. Threats are boisterously made that the matter will be taken to the highest tribunal, but usually they are empty and the dispute is resolved by the passage of time. When the adversaries are more serious, the matter may be taken to the District Council. This body has only the power of mediation. If its settlement is not accepted, the issue may be taken to the highest authority — the French Circuit Court. The Circuit Court, however, tries to follow the terms suggested by the local council whenever possible.

Coffee agriculture in Rapa is not efficient. Beyond the harvest, the only attention paid to coffee groves is to clean out the occasional choking invasion of raspberry vines. (Raspberries were first planted by a semi-sane French resident agent about thirty years ago, and they seem bent on taking over the island. See t'Serstevens 1950/51 II:332.) Most of the trees are forty and more years old, too old and too large for optimal bearing. In 1964 the administration's agricultural service attempted to introduce a plan of gradually replacing old trees with new ones of better quality, and a program of systematic pruning to keep the trees at the most productive size. The agricultural officer who visited Rapa was confident that this would multiply the island's coffee crop. The Rapans, however, were skeptical that such measures would substantially increase the yield, and further opposed the plan because it would mean a drop in income for a few years until the new trees reached bearing age. When I left Rapa, several months after the plan had been proposed, it did not look as if anyone would adopt it. As matters stand now Rapa exports about seven metric tons of coffee annually, although informants told me in a bad year the figure drops to two or three tons and in an exceptionally good year it may climb as high as forty or fifty tons.

CHAPTER FOUR

Food and
the Household

Rapans live essentially in a subsistence economy. Cloth and most tools and utensils are imported, but they produce the great bulk of their food, shelter and other material necessities themselves. Most of their economic activities by far are devoted to the food quest. This is no desperate endeavor, for Rapans live far from the edge of starvation. They have plenty of taro and much fallow land to grow more if needed, and their waters teem with fish. The food is there, and they go hungry only when tempestuous weather for prolonged periods prevents them from going to get it. What must be stressed to those of us accustomed to a highly specialized cash economy is the *time* Rapans devote to securing food. Many tasks in the food quest take them to remote parts of the island or well out to sea. It is not uncommon to spend two or more hours a day just walking or rowing to and from the place of work. Lacking means of preserving taro and fish at home for long periods, such trips must be made frequently. Most Rapans spend most of every day in some work connected with food.

As with fenua, *ma'a*, or "food," is a concept of pervasive significance in Rapan culture. One indication of this is that one of their terms for the entire secular side of life is pae ma'a, the "food side." Rapans seem preoccupied with food; it is a constant topic of conversation. The importance of food certainly stems in large part from the time and energy they must devote to securing it. More than this, however, Rapans endow food with a rich symbolic content. Food is their measure of happiness and security, of friendship and hospitality.

Rapans summarize the good life as plenty of food, and unhappiness as the lack of it. Families who live well in Rapa are not described in terms of fine houses, many clothes, or size of income. They are singled out for admiration because of the quality and quantity of their food, while the poor are defined as those who do not eat well. Rapans enjoy discussing the relative merits of the various islands in French Polynesia. My wife and I would talk of scenery, climate, and the friendliness of the inhabitants. The last of these was considered important by the Rapans, but their highest praise was the phrase "Fenua *ma'a* tera!" freely translated, "That's a land of abundant food!"

The emphasis on food is not unique to Rapa (see Bell 1931, Johansen 1954:212). Rapa's location below the Tropic of Capricorn means many plants important in the islands to the north do not grow there, and our Tahitian friends, hearing we planned to go to Rapa, often shook their heads and said: "You won't like it. They have no breadfruit, no coconuts, no mangoes, no papaya." Those who had visited Rapa, however, remarked that its saving grace is taro and fish, among the best in French Polynesia. As a final example from Tahiti, I am reminded of a mammoth old Tahitian who has succeeded rather well in combining indigenous values with French influence. Sinking into his chair after an excellent dinner, he beamed across at me in contentment and, indicating the prominent place his refrigerator holds in the living room, said expansively, "Le *ma'a* dans le frigidaire; voilà la vìe tahitienne!" "Food in the refrigerator; *that's* life in Tahiti!"

In ancient Polynesia sharing food marked one of the most intimate relationships between people. This social significance of food remains in Rapa, where food represents far more than physical nourishment. The epitome of hospitality is to call out to someone walking by the house, "Come in and eat!" People are visibly happier and more solidary when they eat together. Seated around a meal, they repeatedly urge each other to eat well; and then, when they are full, friendly conversation flows easily. The intimacy of eating together is captured in a subtle figure of speech. When asking someone to pass a particular dish, Rapans often use the possessive. Thus Te'ura, in whose house we ate, would say not "Pass the sugar" but "Pass *our* sugar." His voice carried a comradely warmth, and the possessive implied that the sugar or other dish belonged to the two of us. He conveyed the impression that our joint relationship to the food bound us closer to each other.

In the presence of large quantities of food Rapans may become absolutely exuberant and their urge for banter and joking is often irrepressible. Large feasts are given for weddings, the birth of a woman's first child, and on certain church holidays. These occasions are always filled with laughter and manifest good will. For some reason watermelon, which provides a welcome sweet supplement to the diet during the warm season, puts the Rapans in an especially jovial mood. When it is served at a feast the affair often ends in a gay riot, with hunks of watermelon rind flying in all directions.

The uplifting effect of food is unmistakable at a funeral. Before the burial the bereaved family and closest friends sit in the house with the corpse. Outside many are busy preparing the feast: some butcher a cow and several goats; others roast coffee; and still others make *popoi* (taro paste). The difference in mood is striking. Inside the atmosphere is heavy with grief; those outside, in the presence of abundant food, laugh and joke. Children run about excitedly playing with balloons made from goat intestines, and the festive air is dampened only momentarily by sporadic outbursts of wailing from the women holding watch with the corpse. One can see smiling faces turn somber and become gay again as people enter to view the deceased and then rejoin those preparing the feast.

All is quiet and sober during the short funeral service and the walk to the cemetery. Once the coffin has been lowered into the grave, women with disheveled hair wail loudly and may try to throw themselves into the grave, and men hold back tears only with difficulty. Underpinning it all are the depressing notes of their funeral hymn and the dull thuds of dirt as the young men hurriedly — almost frantically — fill in the grave. Then, within an hour, the feast begins. A hundred or more people seat themselves along rows of banana leaves spread out on the ground and laden with food. Here the expression of solidarity and good will is at its zenith. While the immediate family of the deceased is cheered only with difficulty, others smile broadly and engage in vigorous conversation. It is not long before many who were apparently distracted with grief at the grave are caught up in lighthearted chatter.

THE HOUSEHOLD

Rapans band together in the food quest in groups termed *utu'a fare*, or "households." Given the great amount of time they spend in tasks related to food, the household is beyond any doubt the most important social grouping in daily life. Households range in size from two to fifteen members, with an average of 6.7. These are nearly always close kinsmen. Ideally a household consists physically of a masonry house for sleeping, a pandanus hut for cooking and eating, and a privy. In actuality, a few households have two or three masonry buildings, and many are limited to a single pandanus hut used for sleeping as well as for cooking and eating. A house belongs to its builder or, if deceased, to the ramage composed of his cognatic descendants. Usually ramages which own houses are no larger than an adult sibling group, their children and (perhaps) grandchildren, for houses rarely last more than forty years. Since some of the builder's children usually move out to join spouses in other households or to form new households of their own, only a few ramage members may actually reside in the house. Yet it is considered the property of the entire ramage. The sociological nature of the household will be treated in a later chapter; here the discussion is limited to the household's role in the economy.

Members of a household act as a unit in the subsistence economy. They cooperate in all matters pertaining to food cultivation, fishing, firewood gathering, and so on, and they jointly consume the fruits of their labor. Consistent with the emphasis they place on food, Rapans define the household as those persons who habitually eat in the same cookhouse. Eating and sleeping arrangements do not always correspond. In one case the persons who eat in a single cookhouse sleep in four different houses spread throughout Ha'urei; in a few others those who eat in different cookhouses sleep in the same masonry house. In all such examples, however, the group which cooperates as a unit in subsistence economy, and therefore forms the household, is composed entirely and exclusively of those persons who eat together.

Not surprisingly, then, the focal point of the household is the *fare tutu* or "cookhouse," (although "hut" describes it more accurately). Cookhouses usually measure about fifteen by eight feet, with parallel sides and rounded ends. Most are remarkably low. The ridgepole is about six feet above the ground, and the roof slopes down to about three feet at the walls. The squat form with rounded ends saves construction materials, and also lessens the probability of destruction by high winds since there is little flat wall surface. Frame and rafters are made of logs and saplings, the roof of pandanus leaves and the walls of tough reeds or bamboo. Cookhouses are picturesque when new, but after a few years they look dilapidated.

One must bend double or even crawl through the low door, and move about inside in a crouched position or on all fours since there is no room to stand erect. Within, a cookhouse is a study in black. Windows are lacking, and especially in cold weather, the door is often closed. The walls and ceiling are coated with the years' accumulation of soot from cooking fires. There is no chimney; the plan is for smoke to filter out through the doorway.

Top, *filling in the grave after a funeral;* bottom, *mealtime in the gloom of the cookhouse.*

When the wind is wrong the cookhouse becomes unbearable: people suffer through their meal in a thick cloud of smoke, their eyes red and weeping, the sound of sniffling universal. An unmistakable mark of a Rapan, and of anyone who lives with them, is the odor of woodsmoke which permeates the clothes, the hair, and the skin itself.

It takes a few moments for the eyes to accustom to the gloom upon entering a cookhouse. Even then one is not sure of seeing everything. One day my wife and I had been eating and chatting with a family for about half an hour when suddenly a new voice startled us. Obscured by the shadows, scarcely six feet from us, sat an old woman whose presence we had not previously realized. It is always well to exercise some caution in a cookhouse, to avoid sitting on a sleeping infant hidden by the darkness.

One soon discerns, however, that the cookhouse is composed of two sections. One is the hearth, with a floor of packed dirt and ashes. Here the women crouch to cook food over a small open fire, placing their pots and pans on a grill made of an iron rod bent in a U-shape and resting on two rocks. A small pile of firewood is within easy reach. Hanging from the ridgepole directly over the fire may be a small bag of watermelon seeds drying for the next planting or the rubbery tentacles of an octopus, which are smoked for several days before being served.

The larger section of the cookhouse is for eating and relaxing in the quiet hours after lunch and supper. Here the floor is covered thickly with straw, upon which household members sit cross-legged at mealtime, eating from common platters with their fingers. At night those who have no separate sleeping houses spread their mats and blankets on this straw floor. Most cookhouses contain a light cabinet on stilt legs with screened sides and door, where various sorts of food and native medicines are stored immune from rats, the night marauders. A string of fish often dangles from the ridgepole. Strewn about the floor are baskets of taro ready to be boiled or baked, bundles of clothes and blankets and perhaps a locked wooden chest for valuables. Excepting only the outdoors, Rapans spend more time in this setting than in any other.

Gathering firewood is an odious task and is left mainly to the men. Trees are fairly scarce; most pockets of woods are located in the upper reaches of the valleys or in the outer bays remote from the villages. Trees used for firewood grow wild and may be cut by anyone, anywhere. Once cut, the wood is left to dry and brought to the village on a later trip. Carrying loads of firewood is one of the heaviest jobs in the Rapan economy.

One of the minor intrigues that spice daily life revolves around firewood. Ideally, drying wood belongs to the person who cut it. He may even stand up in a church meeting at the time set aside for such announcements and inform the people that the wood drying in such-and-such a spot belongs to him and should be left alone. But few people are foolish enough to do this, for ownership rights over firewood are respected far less than those over other forms of property. Rare is the person with enough scruples to pass up dried wood he way stumble across on his trips about the island. A public announcement identifying the location of drying is usually enough to send thieves promptly to the spot. One's best bet is to remain secretive about his woodcutting, and hope that no one else finds it. (Probably freshly cut firewood is not brought directly to the village because it is much heavier than dry wood.)

One evening Te'ura Vahine burst into our house, gleeful about a coup she had just made in the firewood game. The only wood anywhere near Ha'urei is a small copse on the shore, about 200 yards east of the village. No one cuts firewood there because the site used to be a cemetery and people are afraid of ghosts. Sometime earlier Te'ura Vahine had allowed economic convenience to outweigh superstition. She cut some wood there, careful to work only in the center of the copse, out of sight of any people walking along the path on one side or passing in boats on the other. (Women occasionally do firewood work when the distance to the village is not great and the load not too heavy.) On this day she had returned to find her wood dry and intact. She cut more for future use and brought home the load already dried. Bursting with pride at her bravery, she had high hopes for a continuing source of convenient wood. When word gets out, however, doubtless the copse will be quickly depleted.

TARO AGRICULTURE

The staple of the Rapan diet is taro. As much time is spent in cultivation and preparation of taro as for all other economic activities combined.

The taro plant (*Colocasia esculenta*) consists of a rounded tuberous rootstock, known as a corm, and slender stalks supporting large and roughly triangular leaves. (See Figure 3.) Rapans distinguish fifteen or more varieties of taro, mainly on the basis of stalk coloration, size and shape of the leaves. In Rapa the stalks generally grow about two feet high, and the leaves are eight inches to a foot in length. The portion of the plant used for food is the starchy corm, which is normally about the size and shape of a fist and, when scraped clean, chalky white. In its raw state the taro corm is actually inedible because it contains acrid calcium

FIGURE 3 THE TARO PLANT*

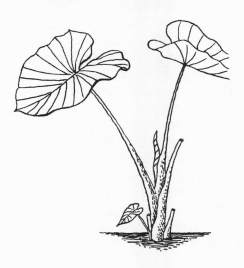

*From Neal (1965:157), with the kind permission of the Bernice P. Bishop Museum.

69

oxalate crystals; working with raw corms may even irritate the hands. Cooking removes the crystals and renders the corm edible. Taro is grown in irrigated terraces, termed *roki*. Ruins of taro terraces are etched over almost every inch of flat and gradually sloping land on the island, although now probably less than one-third of the land suitable for taro is under cultivation. Most terraces cluster along the rivers in the valley floors; seen from the surrounding ridges they look like a patchwork quilt of reflecting pools. Here the terraces are rectangular and are about forty or fifty feet long by twenty to twenty-five feet wide. Even in the sinuous upper reaches of the valleys tiny terraces, some no larger than five by ten feet, cling precariously to the river banks. Often in such places the streams have been banked with stone walls just below the terrace to protect them from erosion when heavy rains turn rivers into torrents raging several feet above their normal level. Taro terraces are irrigated by narrow ditches, at the most a foot wide. Walking near rivers demands caution, for a person could easily break a leg plunging up to his thigh in a deep irrigation ditch concealed by the underbrush. The streams are dammed at points where irrigation ditches branch off, to insure a stable water level. In large terrace systems a few arterial ditches irrigate large sections of the complex, each branching several times to serve terraces in various areas. The water runs through notches cut in the curbs surrounding the terraces, descending from terraces on one level to those on the next lower level, and so on through the system to the sea. Thus each terrace is covered with moving water about two inches deep. In addition to taro, the terraces provide a home for large black eels.[1]

There are no elaborate rules pertaining to the maintenance of irrigation systems. After a heavy rain the narrow ditches often become clogged, and the norm is that all those households which cultivate terraces served by any ditch should share in the labor of maintaining it. This is done informally by members from various households who go out to check the condition of their terraces. There is some grumbling that certain households shirk their fair share of this work, but this seldom leads to serious dis-

[1] Rapans make no use of these eels.

70

putes. In the event that some major change is made in the arterial ditches which serve a large system, a group containing one or two representatives of most or all households that cultivate terraces there undertakes the task. This occurs rarely, and I discovered no preordained rules concerning who makes such decisions or how the work is organized.

Taro can be planted at any time of year, but it does best if planted in the warm season, especially January into April. After the coffee harvest is completed about September, economic attention turns to preparations for taro planting. If a household decides to expand its taro production, or to replace some terraces currently in use, new terraces are prepared during the last few months of the year. This is heavy work, done by the men. Using a sickle and then a shovel, all the vegetation is removed and the earth stripped bare. Then the surface of the terrace is made level; in an uneven area this can be a backbreaking job. (Often this task is avoided or minimized by renovating a long-abandoned terrace, which is already quite level.) Next the earth is cultivated to a depth of about a foot, and dirt curbs are built around the terrace with passages for the entrance and exit of water. The irrigation ditch is dug and opened, the terrace fills with water, and soon the turned soil is reduced to soft mud about the consistency of thick soup. Now the terrace is ready for planting. If the soil is especially good it will produce a high quality of taro for up to thirty years of continuous cultivation. Rapans feel they have a poor return on the labor invested in making the terrace if it yields good taro for only five or six years. A well-maintained terrace — one kept constantly filled with water and free of weeds — requires little or no preparation before each planting.

Taro propagates itself by sending up peripheral plants around the main one. In a terrace I examined, each central plant was surrounded by from four to fifteen smaller plants. Rapans call the central plant *mīkaka*, and its peripheral offspring *kavake*. The plants of any complex grow independently enough that, when ripe, any one may be removed without damaging the rest.

Throughout most of the year Rapans harvest the larger central plants. The plant is extracted by hand, the corm broken off, and the stalk thrown away. Getting taro is considered to be hard work, and is done by both sexes. Probably the most difficult part of the job is bringing the taro home from those terraces located in the outer bays. One begins to appreciate the physical exertion required of these people when they are seen trudging over the steep ridges, often in a cold drizzle or driving rain, bent double under a sack of taro weighing eighty pounds or more.

In October through December, the time of preparation for taro planting, they harvest mainly the small peripheral plants, or kavake. These have corms about the size of an egg, at most half the size of the mīkaka corm. The corm is broken off for food, but instead of discarding the stalk they remove all the leaves but one and replace it in the terrace. (The leaves are removed to minimize the possibility of the plant, no longer firmly rooted, being blown over by the wind.) After a month or two, the stalk sprouts long tendril roots. By the time the planting season begins in earnest after New Year's, each household has a large number of these stalks taking root in their terraces. Planting taro consists simply of transplanting these stalks, using the correct spacing for optimal production. Each of these stalks in this growing cycle becomes the central plant or mīkaka, producing the large corm and sending off its own peripheral kavake, which in turn will be replanted in the following year.

Rapans regard taro planting as more fun than work. In a good terrace the job is easy and fast. Using the hands, one simply presses the stalk through the foot-thick layer of soft mud until the tendril roots rest on the firmer soil below. The leafed top of the stalk sways about a foot above the water surface. In these hot months it is pleasant to work in the cool water and mud of the taro terraces. Rapans are constantly covered with powdery grey mud, dried on their legs up to the knees, from taro cultivation. And it can be a health measure: if one has an infected sore on the leg, they say the best treatment is to bathe it in taro terrace mud.

Although Rapans do not always take their own advice, they say taro and other plants will grow best if planted in the weeks of the full or new moon. They avoid planting taro during the first two weeks of March. Curiously, the times immediately before and after this period are among the best for planting, but taro planted in early March matures with a hole running through the center of the corm from the bottom, making it inferior in quality and likely to rot in the terrace. They can give no explanation for this, nor for the value of planting according to the phases of the moon.

Taro ripens in about eight months, but there is no special season for the harvest. An admirable trait of the plant is that (unless planted in the first two weeks of March) mature plants can be left in the terrace for up to two years without rotting. Such aging may even improve its quality. Once removed, however, taro spoils in about five days. Therefore the Rapans harvest taro the year around, each time taking only as much as they need for a few days.

Taro in at least one form provides the basis of every meal. Its preparation is the women's work. Sometimes the corms are simply boiled or baked in an earth oven, which turns them a deep blue-grey in color, and are eaten whole. The tastiest preparation is taro paste, called popoi. Most taro is eaten in this form; it is a rare meal that does not include popoi. It is made in several outdoor locations scattered around the villages. These areas consist of a place for a fire, a faucet, and several flat stones about three feet square which are placed in a circle.

The corms are boiled for several hours in a large kettle or a sawed-off oil drum. A young, strong woman of the household vigorously scrubs one of the flat rocks with soap and brush to clean it of chicken droppings and other impurities. This done, she seats herself on a small rock, takes a stone the size of a brick in one hand, a cleaned taro corm in the other, and begins to mash the taro on the table rock. She smashes corm after corm, until she has a rounded mass of sticky paste eighteen inches to two feet in diameter. Then she pokes her fingers into it and scoops water into the depression. She begins to knead the paste with her hands, hits it with her fists, and delivers crashing blows with her pounder from a full arm's length. (This is one of the points where making popoi is very hard work, and why women over forty seldom do it. Jobs like this make it highly desirable to have a youthful [taure'are'a] girl in the household.) During this process she adds a small lump of old popoi to aid the fermentation, and keeps splashing on water until she has the desired consistency. Finally she sets aside her pounder, wipes her brow, and confronts the grey, rubbery blob for a final time. Reaching over it, she cuts into the far side about two inches from the edge with the sides of both hands, scoops it toward her and quickly flips it back over. This process, which takes much practice, traps an air bubble and thus aerates the popoi. After about fifteen minutes of aeration, the popoi is trussed up in leaf bundles exactly the size and shape of punching bags. These are hung in a tree while the popoi ferments, to preserve them from hungry chickens and rats.

In a normal sitting a woman makes enough popoi for about three bundles, in a process requiring around an hour and a half from smashing the first corm to completion. A household prepares popoi two or three times a week. On Saturdays everyone makes it for the Sabbath, and shiny green bundles of popoi decorate trees, roofs of outhouses, and other high places.

As might be imagined, popoi-making is a highy audible process. Daily one hears it emanating from some quarter of the village, and occasionally even late at night. Soon one can tell in which stage of the process a woman is simply by listening — the rapid smacks when the corms are being smashed; the louder reports when water and the bit of old popoi are being mixed in with vigorous blows of the pounder; and the loud slap followed rapidly by a hollow *burump!* as the popoi is flipped and the bubble breaks in the aeration process. Women cock their ears and can often identify who is making popoi by the distinctive sound of her work. There is friendly rivalry among the girls and women as to who makes the best popoi. When many of them prepare it for a large feast, each one scratches her name on a leaf placed on top of the popoi in the bundles she made. Perhaps this is to inform young suitors who among the unmarried girls makes the best popoi, or perhaps it is so people will know whom to chide if it turns out poorly.

Making popoi is fun when done in groups. Five or six young women seat themselves around a circle of table rocks and, when

Top, *a man planting taro;* bottom, *a group of women making popoi—
the aeration process.*

they reach the aeration stage, time their flips to produce a rapid cadence. Occasionally this provokes some old crone to do a lascivious song and dance — the song mentioned earlier about the twins and their great-grandmother who stumbled upon a couple in the act of adultery, is a case in point. Such a performance rapidly draws a large crowd, which dissolves in howls of laughter when she gets to the spiciest part.

After a day or two a bundle of popoi is ready to come down from its tree. Household members watch as the bundle is placed in the center of their eating area and opened. If poorly made, it is sickly grey and runs like heavy soup. Well-made popoi maintains its shape, a glistening white mound filled with tiny air holes. The opened bundle now serves as a common platter, from which household members scoop up portions with two fingers and either eat it directly or dunk it first in water or coffee. While other preparations of taro are heavy, very filling and rather tasteless, popoi is remarkably good. It is a light food, large quantities of it are easily digestible, and the fermentation gives it a tangy taste faintly reminiscent of beer. It is important to eat popoi within about four days of its preparation; older popoi is so badly fermented that it is fit only for pigs. Incidentally, "taro paste" is a highly appropriate translation for popoi. One day a young woman seated with us in the cookhouse was preparing a letter to send to Tahiti via a ship then in port. Finding her envelope was not gummed, she took a bit of popoi, spread it over the flap, and it served her purpose very well.

Rights to cultivate taro terraces belong exclusively to their owners. My figures indicate that about half the taro terraces now under cultivation are owned by individuals. Some of these were made by their current owners, but most were made from one to three generations ago and have been willed to their owners by a parent, foster parent, or some other relative. Individually owned terraces are cultivated by the households to which their owners belong.

The rest of the currently cultivated terraces are owned by ramages. These are never cultivated jointly by the ramage, but by households to which ramage members belong. Thus when a household cultivates a ramage-owned terrace, it is because at least one member of the household belongs to the owning ramage. A ramage has no single manager to look after all its taro terraces. The manager of each terrace is the ramage member whose household cultivates it. (If more than one ramage member belongs to the household, the manager is usually the senior male.) This individual is responsible to the ramage for the terrace; he may modify its size and shape, improve it by adding a new layer of soil, and his household may use it for as long as he wishes. The only restrictions on the manager are that he may not destroy the terrace or alienate it from the ownership of the ramage. When his household ceases to cultivate it, the terrace lies fallow until the household of some other ramage member desires to use it. Then this other ramage member becomes the terrace's new manager.

A household cultivates anywhere from ten to over fifty taro terraces, depending mainly on the size of the household and the size of the terraces. Whether owned individually or by ramages, rights to cultivate the various terraces usually stem from different household members. In the actual work of producing taro, however, these distinctions carry little meaning. All household members cooperate in cultivating all the terraces, and the produce from all of them goes into a common store.

Rapans encounter little difficulty in sorting out who has rights to cultivate which taro terraces. The system operates smoothly and casually, probably because there is no shortage of taro terraces. Many terraces now lie fallow and are available for renovation, and new terraces can be made on unused land. If a household runs short of taro it is due to laziness or poor planning, never to difficulty in finding enough terraces to cultivate.

OTHER CROPS

Compared to coffee and taro, other forms of agriculture are of minor significance. European vegetables grow beautifully in Rapa, and a few gardens are maintained by those gourmets who have acquired a taste for exotic dishes such as lettuce, cabbage, green beans, radishes and tomatoes. As mentioned above, watermelon strikes everyone's fancy as a sweet supplement in the warm season. Oranges fill this role in the cold season, while bananas are enjoyed the year round. In 1964 the French administration introduced the cultivation of potatoes and onions for export to Tahiti, in an attempt to lessen the great proportion of these commodities imported from the United States, Australia, and New Zealand. If the experiment proves profitable, these crops will undoubtedly become important elements in Rapa's economy. Finally, a number of Pride of India trees have been planted for their lumber, valued in making canoes, boats and oars.

Vegetable gardens seldom last more than a few years, and so are owned and used by their individual makers. But groves of trees may persist for generations, and thus are often owned by ramages composed of the descendants of their planters. With reference to oranges and bananas, ramages are casual organizations. Rights to gather the fruit are restricted to ramage members, although others may pick and eat a few oranges or bananas if they are hungry and far from any grove in which they have ownership rights. As far as ramage members are concerned the attitude is that any of them may pick as many oranges or bananas as he desires, whenever he desires. Ideally the senior male of the ramage acts as manager over its orange and banana groves, but since the ramage exercises so little control over these forms of property, the manager has almost nothing to do.

Nevertheless, friction occasionally does arise over property in this category. This may be illustrated by an incident which occurred while I was in Rapa and which, incidentally, provides an insight into Rapan temperament. In the hills above Ha'urei there is an orange grove planted about three generations ago which belongs to a large ramage spanning at least five adult sibling groups. Rua, a senior member of the ramage and a rather aggressive man, informally assumed the duties of manager. In 1964 the grove produced a fine crop, and Rua suggested that no owners take oranges until they were all ripe. Then all would go together to pick them, thus assuring that everyone would get an equal share. So, the trees remained laden with oranges until one day when a French naval vessel called at Rapa. Oranges are not often sold, but the opportunity arose when the captain mentioned he would like to buy some for the ship's mess. Rua and Tere, his cousin and also a member of the ramage which owns the grove, clandestinely picked quite a few of the oranges and sold them to the ship. The other members of the ramage, most of whom were women, got wind of this within a couple of days. Fired with indignation, a group of them went to the orange grove without telling Rua and Tere. They picked all the oranges they could carry, and in spite they tore the great quantity remaining from the trees and left them on the ground to rot and provide food for the rats. The women were incensed because the property of all had been sold for the profit of a few, and especially because Rua had broken the prohibition which he himself had suggested. There was talk of holding a meeting of the ramage to verbalize their anger and to elect an official manager. However, this came to nothing and the furor died down in a few days. From the satanic glee with which the woman who organized the expedition told us of their exploits in taking so many oranges and destroying the rest, it seemed that most of their anger had been worked off by these reprisals. And anyway, these were only oranges. Had it been a more valued type of property like coffee, reverberations of the dispute would most likely have rocked Rapa for months.

FISHING

About 4:30 one chilly June morning I staggered into the cook-house to wash away my sleepiness with coffee and popoi. Already seated on the straw around the kerosene lamp were Te'ura, his cousin Ra'i, and the four other men of our party. As we ate break-fast and checked our gear, I described a dream I had that night. Two Rapan friends and I were rowing in a boat close to the shoreline. Just ahead stood a herd of cattle, some in the water and some on shore. As we passed through them, those in the water began jumping on shore, many of them leaping over the bow of our boat, threatening to upset it. Then men in the cookhouse flashed smiles and murmured approval as I recounted my dream, and Te'ura said, "You should catch many tuna today!" When-ever a man dreams of cattle on the eve of tuna fishing, he ex-

79

plained, it is a sure sign that his luck will be good. Perhaps this interpretation is related to the reference I once heard to tuna — the largest and most prized fish Rapans catch — as the "cattle of the sea."

We walked to the shore and launched Ra'i's whaleboat *June* (named for the month in which its construction was completed), carefully rolling it over oars and large sticks so the bottom would not be damaged on the rocky beach. Like most Rapan whaleboats, the *June* is long and narrow, eighteen to twenty feet by three or four feet. The lines are simple and clean, designed for speed and ease of rowing. Whaleboats are built locally and of native materials except for the imported plank siding. They are the finest example of Rapan craftsmanship.

Seating ourselves one to a thwart, five of the men each took a heavy oar eight or nine feet long, and Ra'i manned the higher stern seat with his steering paddle. As we rowed rapidly east out of Ha'urei Bay, Rapa's hills and peaks began to detach themselves from the night in the first glint of dawn. The stillness was broken only by the rhythmic bumping of the oars in their wooden locks. We stopped near a small beach covered with loose stones that rustled and rolled with the waves, and the men bent over their oars as Ra'i quietly offered a morning prayer. Then the four youths in our party donned face masks and began diving for sea crayfish (clawless lobster) for bait. The rest of us filled the boat's bottom with stones weighing a pound or two, to be used as sinkers.

After this brief pause we rowed east out to sea, following the golden avenue cast by the rising sun across the Pacific. Our destination was a spot two or three miles off shore, excellent for deep sea fishing. Good fishermen know of many such places, most of which seem to be near the point where the island's shelf drops off to the ocean floor. These fishing spots are named just as tracts of land are. They are located by lining up three or more prominent landmarks on the island.

When we arrived each man shipped his oar and began to prepare his line. A Rapan generally follows this procedure to bait his hook. With his teeth, he tears out chunks of flesh from the raw crayfish. These are tied to the hook with thin strips of shredded bark; the baited hook is placed on a sinker stone, and secured by wrapping a few turns of line around the stone. As he prepares his hook, the man chews vigorously on a mouthful of crayfish. Now he spits this on the stone, wraps several more turns of line around it, and fastens it all with a slip knot. Then the lines are let out gently, and the depths measured by counting double-arm spans of line. There is a proper depth for each spot; here it is thirty-five spans, or about 200 feet. At this depth the fisherman jerks his line, undoing the slip knot and allowing the sinker rock to fall away. The chewed crayfish is released and forms a cloud of chum, to attract the fish. The fine morsel concealing the hook floats in the center of the cloud.

As the fisherman and his companions wait, each holds his line lightly in one hand, alert for a bite. A trickster may clandestinely snag a neighbor's line, pull it up and steal the hook, tie a heavy rock to it and then give the line a strong tug. The owner of the line thinks he has a fish, hauls in, and reddens when he discovers the rock and hears his comrades' loud laughter. This and other pranks provide welcome diversion, for bobbing in an open boat all day is boring, and exhausting when the day is hot. The men pass the time chatting about local events of current interest, reminiscing about previous times they had fished at this spot, and exchanging jokes and catcalls with other boats which may be in the area. Suddenly one of the men grunts, jerks his line high overhead and, in the same motion, begins hauling it in hand over hand as fast as he can. The line hums across the gunwale, and the other fishermen peer over the side. Soon the fish appears, a tiny white dot far below the surface. (By the time I could first see it, my Rapan comrades had already identified the species.) It comes up straight and fast, growing larger and spinning rapidly in the water, There is no thought of playing a fish; the idea is to get it in the boat as soon as possible. If the fisherman tires near the end of the long pull the fish may try a few dashes as it nears the surface, but soon it is swung into the boat. A large fish is killed immediately, its exuberant captor beating it with a stout stick or a rock or stabbing it in the head with a knife.

On this day our luck was just fair. We caught one tuna of thirty or forty pounds (this was mine — perhaps because of my dream), four salmon ranging up to about twenty-five pounds, four other large fish and several small ones.

Beyond knowing where to go (which varies with the season and the currents) and the proper depth for each spot, Rapans consider deep-sea fishing to be basically a matter of luck. But in most other methods of fishing they can see their prey, and skill is at a premium. Rapans have an uncanny ability to see fish. Whenever they are in a boat or walking on the shore, their eyes continually rove over the water. One day as we were rowing across a bay, one-eyed Pu exclaimed, *"Matu!"* (a species of fish), and pointed to a spot about thirty yards away. I do not think the fish had jumped; he probably saw it through a wave, as one can learn to do with practice. Pu slipped into the water and returned a moment later with the fish impaled on his spear. Another time Te'ura and I were walking along a ledge about three feet above the water. He stopped abruptly and pointed just below us, where a fish of about three pounds was lying in the shallows. Swiftly he picked up a large rock and dropped it. When the water cleared, he reached in and pulled out the fish, its head neatly smashed.

Most of the time Rapans fish in the bays or within a few hundred yards of shore. Skin diving with face mask, snorkel and spear gun is one favorite method. Another is to use a drop line at a depth of ten or twelve feet. They seed the water with chum, and pound on the bottom of the boat to attract the fish. The fisherman watches through a glass-bottomed wooden box, so he can set the hook at the right instant. If the fish are diffident toward the bait, the skillful fisherman hooks them through the gill, stomach or tail with a deft jerk of his line. In March the *ahore*, silver fish weighing about a pound, run in great numbers. They bite on dark nights, and five or six men fishing with long bamboo poles may bring home 200 or more. Finally, the most picturesque mode of fishing is the *rama*. Two men go out in a boat or canoe on a moonless, perfectly still night. One paddles softly, and the other stands in the bow, a pressure gas lantern in one hand and a pronged spear poised in the other. Fish are attracted by the light and are easily seen and speared through the calm water. Viewed from shore, the lights gliding across Ha'urei Bay create a scene of serenity, while they reveal to the fisherman a vivid panorama of coral banks, undulating seaweed, swimming fish, red-eyed crayfish, and occasionally the menacing form of a large shark.

Whenever Rapans go fishing they divide the catch equally among all the men in the boat. If the owner of the boat is not along, a share may be set aside for him as well. Almost every day that weather permits some boats and canoes go out for fish, but the major expedition occurs on Saturday. On this day nearly every able-bodied man in Rapa goes fishing, principally to provide for the week's major meal at noon Sunday.

Each season has its advantages and disadvantages for fishing. The weather is generally fair in the warm season, so frequent fishing is possible. It is also necessary, for fish are not so abundant and without refrigeration they will spoil in about two days in the warm weather. In the cold season nearly all species of fish are plentiful, and this is the only time tuna, salmon and other large deep-sea fish are taken. Furthermore, fish will keep for about four days, so a man can spend less time fishing. On the other hand, the frequent storms during the cold season make fishing impossible for as much as a week or two at a stretch. In such inclement periods Rapans substitute meat for fish and kill a few chickens, capture some goats from the hills, or butcher a hog.

Fish is eaten raw (usually after being marinated for several hours in sea water and lemon juice), boiled, or fried in oil. One of the best-tasting preparations, and also the simplest, is to roast fish directly on the coals. The fish may be wrapped in a leaf, or thrown on the fire with no covering but its own skin. Large fish such as tuna and salmon may be baked in an earth oven, a process which keeps the fish from spoiling for several days. In cleaning fish, Rapans remove the entrails but usually retain the head, for they relish the eyes and other soft parts.

CASH

A Rapan does not need much money to live, but he must have some to purchase those imported goods which have come to be essential to the standard of living. Purchased goods which everyone counts as necessary are laundry soap, sugar, flour, cooking oil, cooking utensils, matches, kerosene and lamps, flashlights and batteries, tools, nails, fishhooks and lines, and clothes. For most, tobacco is also included in this list. The owners of the ten or twelve outboard motors on the island must also purchase gasoline. A man building a boat must buy planks for siding. Construction of a masonry house usually entails the purchase of cement, corrugated iron for the roof, and perhaps even glass for the windows (although most content themselves with wooden shutters). Finally, those with cash to spare may buy luxury items such as tinned beef, butter and jam, furniture and a radio. The role of cash in the economy will increase in the future as more families strive to raise their level of living and educate children in Tahiti.

Rapans derive income from several sources. The most lucrative enterprise is the sale of coffee, which brings 35¢–40¢[2] per kilogram. The next is public works labor: men are employed by the administration to maintain the paths and public places in the village, and to construct major improvements such as schools, the weather station, the infirmary, the piers, and the network of water pipes throughout the villages. During most of 1964 men were paid $2.00 per day for such labor. The native head of public works arranges a rotation so all men have an equal opportunity for this paid work. Then there are several minor sources of income. Neighbors occasionally buy a few chickens, or pork when a hog is slaughtered. Locally-made baskets are sold to visitors, and goats are occasionally exported to Tahiti. The Cooperative Society (described below) sometimes hires workers, and distributes among its members the proceeds from the sale of cattle. Finally, a few women have sewing machines and earn money by making clothes.

A few individuals hold salaried posts, which in many cases greatly augment their income. The pastor receives a salary from the church headquarters in Tahiti, and the chief, assistant chief, policeman, civil secretary and public works head have government salaries. The Cooperative Society also pays its officers small sal-

[2] The currency of French Polynesia is the Pacific franc. For the reader's convenience, monetary amounts have been translated to U.S. dollars throughout the book.

aries. Most of these are part-time positions which do not greatly reduce the individual's subsistence activities. The highest salaries go to the school teachers, the weatherman, and the infirmary keeper, for they hold full-time positions. Their families live basically in a cash economy, but since all but one of these positions are held by Tahitian functionaries, we shall not consider them further.

The basic consuming unit in the cash economy is the elementary family: a man, his wife, and their children. In households containing more than one elementary family, each shares in the expense of flour, sugar, other purchased foods and cooking utensils. The elementary family, however, buys its own clothes, soap, kerosene, and other manufactured goods. To give a more detailed picture of cash in the Rapan economy, Table 2 presents the annual cash budget of three elementary families. The first two fall somewhere in the "middle class" (some families earn considerably less), while the third is among the most wealthy families on the island, chiefly due to the family head's salary as policeman. Since Rapans are not accustomed to making up annual budgets, these figures are probably not exact, but they do give a general idea of the sources, uses, and importance of cash in the Rapan way of life. These budgets include only recurrent expenses, not infrequent major costs for such items as construction materials.

THE COOPERATIVE

Rapa's financial institution is the Cooperative Society. This organization operates the island's only store, a wooden building located in Ha'urei. The store can be frustrating to a foreigner, as it is almost always closed. It opens briefly three or four times a week, early in the morning, in the evening or, rarely, around noon, and there is little stock to compensate for the irregular hours. Almost lost on the near-empty shelves are a few coils of heavy fish line, some cartons of tobacco and matches, a bolt of cloth or two, a few charcoal-burning irons and kerosene lamps, and some second-hand French comic books. In one back room, piles of coffee beans await export, and in the other are stored sacks of flour and sugar, drums of kerosene, and bars of blue laundry soap. When the interval between supply ships is long, most of these goods must be rationed, and often stock is exhausted altogether.

TABLE 2. ESTIMATED ANNUAL BUDGETS

Teone's Family (7 members)

Income		Expenses	
Coffee sales	$103	Clothes	$ 23
Public works labor	40	Flour	6
Co-op cattle sales	24	Sugar	19
Co-op office salary	6	Other foods	11
Co-op labor	3	Tobacco	4
Pork sales	26	Cooking & eating utensils	4
Goat sales	6	Matches	1
Chicken sales	3	Kerosene	5
Basket sales	6	Soap	11
Taro sales	6	Tools & nails	3
Total	$223	Paint	10
		Fishing supplies	4
		Church donations	11
		Other donations	7
		Furniture	11
		Aid in support of a foster child in Tahiti	1
		Total	$131

Ra'i's Family (6 members)

Income		Expenses	
Coffee sales	$ 69	Clothes	$ 57
Public works labor	60	Flour	18
Co-op cattle sales	10	Sugar	11
Co-op labor	8	Other foods	9
Pork sales	30	Tobacco	3
Goat sales	17	Cooking & eating utensils	11
Chicken sales	4	Kerosene	9
Basket sales	20	Flashlight batteries	3
Total	$218	Soap	17
		Paint & tools	23
		Fishing supplies	17
		Church donations	16
		Other donations	8
		Total	$202

TABLE 2 (*Continued*)

Mera's Family (10 members)

Income		Expenses	
Policeman's salary	$648	Clothes	$115
Coffee sales	69	Flour	24
Co-op office salary	29	Sugar	20
Co-op cattle sales	10	Other foods	27
Pork sales	34	Tobacco	3
Chicken sales	1	Cooking & eating utensils	29
Basket sales	7	Kerosene	6
Taro sales	6	Gasoline (for outboard)	86
Total	$804	Flashlight batteries	2
		Soap	17
		Paint	40
		Tools	3
		Fishing supplies	11
		Church donations	18
		Other donations	28
		Telegrams	6
		Total	$435

The store's finances operate in conjunction with coffee exports. Rapans sell their coffee to the store, where it is weighed and the amount for each person or elementary family recorded. The Cooperative ships all the coffee to its agent in Tahiti, a French merchant. He sells it at a small profit for the Cooperative, and keeps the proceeds in a special fund. Goods for the store are ordered from this agent by wire, and he purchases them and ships them to Rapa, paying the expenses from the coffee-sale fund. People make most of their purchases from the store on their coffee accounts, either against their earnings from the previous harvest or on credit against the next harvest. The only problem is that people spend more at the store than they earn from coffee; thus they are often in debt to the store, and the store's fund in Tahiti frequently runs in the red. Then the French agent extends credit to the Cooperative. Occasionally Rapans make purchases or pay their bills in cash earned from sources other than coffee, so a cash fund for the store accumulates in Rapa. When this becomes sizeable, it is sent to Tahiti by some trustworthy individual (a person often difficult to find), who gives it to the agent to pay off the debts of the store's fund there.

The Co-operative also owns a cattle herd which in 1964 numbered about 200 head. These range wild over the northern side of the island from Akatamiro to Angaira'o Bays. Once each two or three years some 80 to 100 head are exported to Tahiti to be slaughtered for beef. A few times a year one or two cows are sold locally for a special feast. The Cooperative also gives a cow to each ship which brings supplies for the store and carries coffee back to Tahiti. This is a gesture of gratitude, for nearly all ships which visit Rapa are naval or administration vessels and they collect no freight charges. Capturing the cattle is tremendously exciting, the herd stampeding through a funnel of shouting and waving men from the highlands into a corral built on the shore of Tupuaki Bay.

Separate from the records of store goods and coffee exports, a special fund is kept for all income and expenses related to the cattle operation. After a major shipment to Tahiti this fund becomes quite large, and is distributed among the members of the Cooperative. Members are also paid for certain labor the Cooperative requires, such as capturing cattle and loading and unloading ships, at about $1.40 per day. Labor related to cattle is paid from the cattle fund, that involving store goods or coffee from the store fund. Table 2 (pages 86–87) gives an indication of how much families make annually from Cooperative cattle sales and wages.

The Cooperative is much like a corporation with sixty-six shareholders. The shares are indivisible, so when a shareholder dies he wills his share to a single heir — usually a child or foster child, with probable preference for the eldest child. (The Cooperative has been in existence only since about 1930, so there have not been enough inheritances of shares to establish a clear pattern.) All persons, members or not, are treated alike in matters of coffee sales and credit-buying at the store. But when cattle are sold, the profits are divided in just sixty-six equal portions for the shareholders, and they alone have the right to discuss policy and vote in the annual meeting. The Cooperative has ten officers, elected at the annual meeting: the president oversees the entire operation; the storekeeper works behind the counter on those rare occasions when the store is open; two treasurers are entrusted with the cash in the store fund and two more with that in the cattle fund; and four cattle chiefs organize the drives and handle any other matters concerning the cattle.

The annual meeting of the Cooperative Society takes place in early January. The shareholders meet in the store's back room, where they recline on a mound of coffee beans, lounge in the open windows or sit on the grass outside the door. The order of business is to review the past year, then to discuss policy for the coming year, and finally to elect new officers. As people listen to the reports, they jot down figures and add them up (one man lacking paper and pencil scratched numbers on his leg with a nail). The meeting I witnessed in January, 1964, was scarcely an orderly one. People drifted in and out frequently; they seemed to pay little attention to the proceedings. Yet a pattern did emerge, unmistakable in its repetition. The president, a woman, would read a portion of her report and wait for reactions. After a minute or two of silence, a few comments would be made. The speakers began calmly and deliberately, but as the discussion proceeded voices rose and soon two or three were shouting at one another. This would continue at full tilt for about ten minutes, the protagonists looking as if they were about to come to blows. Then the furor would subside and the meeting would go into a sort of recess. People would chat about diverse subjects, or would begin throwing paper wads and coffee beans at each other amid loud laughing and joking. After ten or twenty minutes this too subsided, more of the president's report was read, and the cycle from calm discussion to enraged argument to a respite of horseplay repeated itself. For five days the meeting wore on, lasting one night to one o'clock in the morning. Again and again the cycle recurred, the village air punctuated at alternating intervals with the sound of angry voices and laughter.

CHAPTER FIVE

The Map
of Social
Relations

For the Rapan the world is made up essentially of five kinds of people: strangers, friends, neighbors, lovers, and kinsmen. Some of these categories — especially kinsmen — are further divided. The shape of his interaction with anyone is defined to a certain extent by the category or sub-category to which that person belongs. This chapter attempts to describe this system of social categories and to explain how it channels human relations.

CATEGORIES AND THE SOCIAL ORDER

In an earlier chapter it was suggested that by classing events according to the places where they occur, the Rapan brings a sense of order to what happens in the world, and that through the land he owns, he finds his place in that order. The social categories also lend order to the Rapan world. Through them the individual classifies, and therefore orders, the amorphous mass of people who happen to live in his time and place. And at least as important, the system insures some degree of regularity and predictability in his relations with other people. Since the categories define rules for behavior, the individual has guidelines to determine how he should treat people, and to predict with reasonable certainty how they will react to him.

Although Rapans are perhaps no different in this from anyone else, I was struck by how much they seem to need predictability in their social relations. They appear to be vulnerable in their dealings with others, fearing that something they may say or do will provoke an adverse reaction. Always lurking in the wings, and not infrequently dominating the stage entirely, is the emotion they call *ha'amā*. Often on Rapan lips, this term in its various applications covers states ranging from uneasiness to shame and mortification. A young man inexperienced in the art of oratory is called upon to make a statement at some public gathering. He reddens, laughs awkwardly, shuffles his feet, stammers, and may sit down in the middle of a sentence. He is ha'amā. A young woman sits facing me, surrounded by a crowd of chuckling onlookers, as I pose a set of questions aimed at getting some vital statistics about the society. She stares at the ground, pulls up blades of grass, and cannot bring herself to utter her own name. She is ha'amā. A middle-aged woman spies me coming with a folder in hand, and correctly surmises that I hope to ask these same questions of her. She does not know how to act with this white man, cannot predict his reaction to her. She literally runs away rather than undergo the ordeal for she, too, is ha'amā.

Ha'amā is an intensely uncomfortable state which threatens the ego. Hence the importance of the predictability which the system of categories confers upon social relations. Most of the categories provide a map of behavior, clearly marking those areas of interaction which could generate friction or ha'amā. When two persons have clearly categorized one another their relationship is predictable. They follow the same map, and so the dangerous areas are easily avoided. Unpredictable relationships have no map. One never knows when he might step over the brink of ha'amā.

Strangers represent the category of people for which there is no map. The hallmark of interaction with a stranger is uncertainty. He is a person with no credentials. You are uncertain of his motivations, uncertain of what might embarrass or offend him, fearful that he might offend or embarrass you. One solution to the problem of strangers is to avoid them altogether, even if it means running away from them. But this is hardly a satisfactory solution, for in itself it betrays great ha'amā which might attract ridicule or disapproval from one's companions. Most Rapans are somewhat more urbane. They treat strangers with polite hospitality but marked restraint; often there is an undercurrent of suspicion.

Even in this tiny community of 360 there are strangers. Not total strangers, to be sure, but persons who are unrelated and who have never become well acquainted. In their infrequent interaction, polite reserve is apparent; when they talk about one another, suspicion tinged with hostility is unmistakable. Total strangers are people who visit Rapa from the outside world. The most dangerous are white men. Being from a different culture, they carry a completely different set of maps for social relations, rendering the probability of ha'amā especially high. Furthermore, most white men who visit Rapa are connected with the French administration, and thus are figures of power whom it could be dangerous to offend.

The best example I can give of attitudes toward strangers is our own reception in Rapa. My wife and I knew no one when we arrived, and we had the extra liability of being white and therefore more unpredictable than Polynesian strangers. Although not as potent as administration officials, the fact that we had come all the way from America made us appear important. Happily, however, we were young enough (twenty-three and twenty-four) that they did not rank us so high as to make us unapproachable. We were very hospitably received, but at first they kept up a guard of reserve. This was partly due to difficulties in communication while we were learning Tahitian. But a friend later told us they treated us carefully, even reluctant to ask us for small articles they may have needed (pencils, paper, aspirin, etc.) until they got to know what kind of people we were.

Before our arrival, friends in Tahiti had arranged for us to live in one of the Rapan households. We decided it was essential to share our meals with the members of the household. Given the effect of food in promoting solidarity and intimacy, most casual conversations between Rapans take place at mealtime. By eating with them we could touch their lives more closely. Participating in conversation, we were able to obtain much information of special interest which would have been difficult to elicit in the framework of a formal interview. On a few happy occasions we were even able to stimulate a lively mealtime discussion among them on some topic of special relevance to the study, and there was no richer source of data.

Our design of eating with them met with initial opposition, basically because we were in the category of strangers. Sharing food symbolizes a close relationship, and it is precisely this that one seeks to avoid with strangers. More specifically, Rapans are aware that most white people are accustomed to eating somewhat more elegantly than their own style — sitting on the straw floor of the smoky, dingy cookhouse and using fingers to scoop popoi from a common leaf platter. They are aware, too, that the white man's diet tends to be more varied and more elaborately prepared than their own. Thus enters ha'amā. By allowing white strangers to share their food in the cookhouse, they expose themselves to possible expressions of disapproval, even disgust and outright indignation.

So the battle lines were drawn. To approach the ideal of knowing them as they really are, we were determined to eat with them in the cookhouse. To protect themselves from ha'amā and to avoid having to be in close contact with people who might turn out to be obnoxious, they were determined that we should not. The first few meals were served to us alone at a table (complete with tablecloth and silverware) in the attractive masonry house they had given us for sleeping and working. We endured this for the first day, then protested that it would be far less work for them, and far more enjoyable for us, if we ate in the cookhouse. When mealtime came again, however, we found they had adopted a new tactic. The mistress of the household showed us to a larger table set up in another masonry sleeping house. As a compromise to our desire to eat in the Rapan style, the surroundings here were much dirtier than in the first house and they had dispensed with the tablecloth. Bowing to our desire to share meals with them, she said that most of the other members of the household would leave the cookhouse to eat at this table with us. But we insisted this was still too much trouble for them, and we took our plates, marched into the smoke and gloom of the cookhouse, seated ourselves on the straw and finished the meal there. When she called us for the next meal, we called back, "In the cookhouse?" "Yes," she laughed with resignation, "in the cookhouse." And so the first battle was won.

Even then our presence made mealtime silent and tense. The eating area in that cookhouse was rectangular, about twelve feet long and eight feet at the ends. In the evenings a pressure gas lantern was set on a shelf above one side, so bright light was cast on the opposite side while the area beneath the shelf was in darkness. My wife and I ate alone on the brightly lit side while the fifteen Rapans of the household huddled together in the shadows opposite us. We jokingly likened the situation to a cinema, where we were the actors and they the audience silently watching our every move. It was strange, we said, that we had come to learn about them and in this situation the only observation was theirs of us. The household head laughed and said that next evening they would all sit on the bright side and let us occupy the shadows. Banter such as this helped break the ice and within a week or two all seventeen of us were fairly evenly spaced about the popoi and other food. While I am sure our presence always had some restraining effect, gradually the near silence of the earliest meals was replaced by lively conversation and we came to participate in something approximating normal mealtime behavior.

With time and contact, strangers get to know each other. If their initial contacts are not congenial, they make little effort to deepen the relationship. It remains essentially like that between strangers, characterized by restraint, perhaps suspicion as well, and a low frequency of interaction. They may even develop a positive dislike, in which case they make every effort to avoid one another. Each heaps malicious gossip on the other, and their face-to-face relationship is limited to screaming insults in heated disputes, and perhaps an occasional fistfight for the men or hair-pulling contests for the women. On the other hand, if strangers come to like each other they become friends (*hoa*).

The category of friends is like that of strangers in one respect: here, too, the behavioral map of the relationship is lightly sketched. Beyond the broad precept that friends should manifest mutual affection and consideration at all times, there are few rules governing the shape of their interaction. Unlike the case with strangers, however, the scantily drawn map serves not to restrain but to liberate the relationship. Strangers are unpredictable but friends are the hallmark of certainty. Close friends know one another well, like each other a great deal, and so their mutual trust is complete. There is no need to hedge the relationship with formal rules of conduct since there is no danger that a good friend will put one in the uncomfortable and threatening state of ha'amā. More than with anyone else, a Rapan behaves freely and spontaneously with a friend.

Friends derive great satisfaction from each other. They exchange frequent visits and enjoy working, playing and chatting together. Rapans confide first in their friends. Women, married or not, are secretive about the first stages of pregnancy. They tell their close friends first; only later do their relatives hear about it.

Someone in trouble turns to a friend. One young man had made a girl pregnant. It could have caused a scandal, since they were first cousins and sexual relations between such close kinsmen are despised. He went to his best friend, who came to his aid by claiming that he was the father. Although it is apparently rare,

95

girls sometimes induce abortions. The girl enlists her best friend to help gather necessary herbs for the potion and to administer the massage.

Husbands and wives who are compatible consider themselves to be friends. This, however, is about the only case where strong friendship crosses the sex line. Friendship means being much together, and if a man and woman are often seen together, public opinion automatically assumes they are lovers. Thus in this society, platonic friendship between a man and woman is impossible.

In Rapa, as in many other simple societies, the most important social relations occur between kinsmen. Under these circumstances it may seem curious that Rapans bypass relatives to confide first in friends, and turn first to them in times of trouble. The reason seems to be that in the eyes of society kinsmen are irrevocably associated. Jointly they uphold the honor of the family. A relative is thus an extension of the self; his actions, for good or ill, reflect upon the family and hence upon oneself. One can bask in the glory of a highly respected relative, and one shares the shame of a kinsman who has fallen. Because their own standing is inextricably involved with his, an individual's relatives are deeply concerned that his conduct be respectable and they are particularly harsh when it is not. Therefore, if he has gotten into some potentially embarrassing or shameful situation, he tries to keep his relatives ignorant of it to avoid their condemnation and (since love is an important ingredient in close kinship) to avoid hurting those whom he loves.

Friends are different. Theirs is a personal bond, based purely on mutual affection. This affection makes a friend an interested and trustworthy confidant and someone from whom sympathy and assistance may be expected in times of trouble. Furthermore, one can afford to hear a friend's secret thoughts and can try to help him in his plight with no serious danger of being dragged down himself. The personal nature of friendship means that society does not judge friends by each other's actions to the same extent as with kinsmen. And unlike kinship, friendship is contingent on continuing affection. If a friend commits some enormous sin, one can dissociate himself from it entirely by stating that the affection has ceased and they are friends no longer.

For clarity, pure cases have been used in developing this point. That done, it is necessary to caution against drawing the boundary between kinsman and friends too sharply; in actuality, these categories of the Rapan social world often overlap. The relatives whose own standing is bound up in an individual's behavior are his closest kin: the immediate family; parents-, siblings-, and children-in-law; grandparents and grandchildren; uncles and aunts, nephews and nieces. The involvement decreases greatly with more distant kin. If there is strong mutual affection, the relationship with some of these more remote relatives is often characterized by the tolerance and contingency of friendship. In such cases their relationship is a blend of kinship and friendship, the relative amount of each ingredient depending on the closeness of genealogical connection and degree of affection. Many Rapans are close friends to some of their first cousins, although at this distance the kinship element is invariably strong. With second cousins and more distant relatives, bonds of friendship may far outweigh those of kinship.

KINSMEN

In this small island community everyone can trace, with varying precision, some tie of kinship with most of his fellow Rapans. He interacts more frequently with kinsmen than with any other category of people. Members of his household, with whom he is in intimate daily contact, are invariably relatives. Much of the visiting and mutual economic aid between households is carried out in the idiom of kinship.

One measure of the importance of kinship is the condition of those few people who have no kin in Rapa. A young woman named Marama was born on the island of Rurutu but spent most of her youth in Tahiti. There she met a Rapan boy, married him, and went with him to his native island. They had been in Rapa only a few months when we arrived; she had no relatives on the island and her lot was not a happy one. She was slow in learning the uniquely Rapan feminine skills such as the local way of cooking, of preparing pandanus leaves for roofing, and of making popoi. The instruction in these skills that other women gave Marama was obviously condescending, and she was an object of criticism, gossip and suspicion. After supper the household members would engage in lively conversation, rippling with laughter and marked by a peculiar sing-song inflection, their Tahitian peppered with numerous words from the Rapan dialect. Probably Marama could not understand everything that was being said; obviously she was blocked out of these conversations. She would sit slightly back from the others and in the shadows, silently staring at a piece of straw she shredded between her fingers. Kinless immigrants like Marama live on the fringe of society. Slowly they make breaches in the wall through friendship, but it requires years of residence and especially the establishment of kin ties on the island by having children before they are treated like normal members of society.

Kinsmen, then, represent the largest and most important category of people in Rapan social relations, a category richly differentiated into subdivisions. The remainder of this chapter is devoted to the Rapan way of classing kinsmen and the maps of behavior appropriate for each type.

The term which Rapans use to mark the category of kinsmen in general is *feti'i*. As with the English word *relative*, it can refer to a single kinsman of any type or, as a plural, to any group of kin. Sometimes it is restricted to consanguineal kin; in other usages, affines (relatives by marriage) are included. The meaning is normally clear by the context, and can be more precisely specified by the use of modifying adjectives or phrases.

The Rapan kinship system is thoroughly bilateral: no distinctions in terminology or rules for behavior are drawn between relatives on the father's and mother's sides. The terminology is classificatory. That is, the same terms are used for lineal and collateral relatives. Thus, a single term is used for father and all uncles, another for mother and all aunts, siblings and cousins are included in a single set of terms, nephews and nieces are classed with one's own children in another set, and so on. In the technical lexicon of anthropology, terminologies of this type are called

Hawaiian or generational. Except for a few complications in terms for siblings and cousins, the kinship terminology is extremely simple (see Table 3). In general, people address their consanguineal kinsman of senior generations by the appropriate kinship term, and address kin of their own and junior generations by name. For these latter generations, the kinship term is used only in reference and in contexts where the kinship connection is important.

An individual should follow certain rules of behavior with relatives in each of the above categories, but the intensity of the relationship varies as kinsmen are more or less closely related. For example, although he calls them all pāpā, an individual normally interacts much more frequently and observes the appropriate rules of behavior much more closely with his own father than with his father's or mother's male cousins. With terms such as "first cousin," "second cousin" and so on, the distance of relationship is built into English kinship terminology. This does not work in Rapa, where all cousins, no matter how distant, are called by the same terms as those used for siblings. They determine distance of relationship by counting the number of generations back to the common ancestor of a pair of kinsmen. The extraordinary richness of the terminology in descending generations, where each generation down to great-great-great-grandchildren is distinguished by a separate term, is useful for this purpose. Instead of specifying the distance of relationship by saying that a pair of kinsmen are second cousins, the Rapan expresses the same thing by saying that they are both 'ina (great-grandchildren) of their common ancestor.

As kinsmen are more distantly related, the norms governing their interaction diminish in strength and finally fade out entirely. A good index of this is marriage, for people who should treat one another as relatives are not supposed to marry. One evening I was working with Te'ura on this question of "fadeout." We took hypothetical pairs in the tu'āne–tuahine relationship (brothers and sisters, cousins of opposite sex), and I asked him how they should act as they became more distantly related. As the pairs in the examples passed through the levels of being mo'otua of their

TABLE 3. CONSANGUINEAL KINSHIP TERMINOLOGY

Generation	Terms
+3 and above	*tupuna* (all relatives of great-grandparental generation and above, and their spouses)
+2	*pāpā ru'au* (all males of the grandparental generation, including husbands of females of that generation) *māmā ru'au* (all females of the grandparental generation, including wives of males of that generation)
+1	*metūa tāne* or *pāpā* (all males of the parental generation, including husbands of females of that generation) *metūa vahine* or *māmā* (all females of the parental generation, including wives of males of that generation)
0	*tu'āne* (male siblings and male cousins of a female) *tua'ana* (elder siblings and cousins of same sex as ego) *teina* (younger siblings and cousins of same sex as ego) *tuahine* (female siblings and female cousins of a male)
−1	*tamaiti* (all males of child's generation) *tamahine* (all females of child's generation)
−2	*mo'otua* (all relatives of grandchild's generation)
−3	*'ina* (all relatives of great-grandchild's generation)
−4	*'inarere* (all relatives of great-great-grandchild's generation)
−5	*rere* (all relatives of great-great-great-grandchild's generation)

common ancestor (first cousins to one another), 'ina, and 'inarere, the strength of the norms governing their relationship decreased considerably but ideally remained in effect. When we reached the level of rere of the common ancestor (making the pair fourth cousins), Te'ura said, "They are no longer relatives. They may marry." He explained this limit by saying that an individual may conceivably live long enough to see his 'inarere (great-great grandchildren), but he would certainly have died before the birth of their children, his rere. Any two individuals who were born during this maximal life-span of their common ancestor, he continued, should observe the norms defining their kin relationship in interaction and should not marry.

According to Te'ura, then, the expected rules of behavior between kinsmen apply to persons related out to the range of third cousins, but no further. There is, however, no universal agreement on this span. As Te'ura's statement indicates, Rapans conceive of the limit largely in terms of the prohibition against marriage. Some people defined the limit one degree closer, saying second cousins should not marry but third cousins may; others insisted that no two kinsmen should marry no matter how remote their relationship.

At any rate, precise definition of the limits of effective kinship remains a theoretical matter. There is great individual variation in how relatively distant kinsmen interact, depending largely on the personalities involved. Furthermore, genealogical knowledge is fragmentary enough that people are often not sure whether certain kin are related to them at a distance of second, third, or fourth cousin. These variations recognized, the broad generalization might be drawn that in daily life the rules for behavior based on kin ties are important in defining interaction between kin related within the range of first cousin, of minor importance for those related in the range of second cousin, and of almost no importance for more distant relatives.

Parents and Children. To a Rapan, having children is an essential ingredient in the full and good life. During the quiet hours after supper and on Sunday afternoons small children are fondled and passed from lap to lap while their elders chat. Adults clap their hands, sing gently, and delight in the awkward movements of a toddler learning the gyrating Tahitian hula. They say there is no greater love than that for one's children. Pregnant with our first child, my wife had to leave Rapa a few months before the study ended. It was clear to the Rapans that I missed her very much after she left. "If you think you love your wife," my friends told me, "just wait until the baby is born. Then you'll see how strong love can get."

Children are desired for economic reasons as well. They insure security, for in Rapan reasoning, children are obliged to repay their care in infancy and childhood by supporting their aged parents. There are also indications that people feel an obligation to society to reproduce themselves. Sterility is fairly high in Rapa. (In my sample, representing 86 percent of the total population, 20 percent of the women and 18 percent of the men over the age of twenty-five have no children.) One childless man said half-humorously and half-sadly, "We who have no children are worthless." Those without children are occasionally ridiculed — for example, it was said of one childless old man, "His irrigation ditch is dry." Rapan society recognizes the fertility of its members: the birth of a woman's first child is celebrated by an island-wide feast at which everyone gives gifts to the infant and his parents.

Parents hold strong authority over their children, and receive respect in return. To the age of ten or twelve, children are treated with indulgence and discipline is lax, but later the response to disobedience is often a severe beating. Probably as a result of this change in parental attitude, children in early adolescence often appear sullen and unmanageable. By the late teens, however, most of them seem to have readjusted. In the economy, in disputes with other persons, and in all matters, people feel more obliged to aid and support their parents than they do any other kinsman, with the possible exception of grandparents. Mothers are primarily responsible for the care of children, and they most frequently administer discipline. Both males and females say they feel deeper love and greater obligation toward their mothers than their fathers.

The norms are the same for collateral "parents" and "children." These are quite strong between immediate uncles and aunts,

Rapan children: top, *taking a bath;* bottom, *playing at making popoi.*

nephews and nieces, but lessen greatly in intensity as the relationship is more remote. Authority and discipline, for example, are not often exercised over a first cousin's child, nor does the child feel much of an obligation to support that "parent" in his old age. While in daily life a remote tie means very little, blatant transgressions of expected behavior between distant "parents" and "children" are regarded seriously. Rapans celebrate July 14 (the French National Holiday) with enthusiasm — meaning that most of the young men get roaring drunk. While in this state, one young man struck another who happened to be his "father," a second or third cousin of one of his parents. Another distant "son" immediately sprang to the aid of the "father" and began pummeling the aggressor, who was quickly hustled off to his house by concerned onlookers. Everyone was highly indignant that the young man had raised a hand against his "father."

Grandparents and Grandchildren. To my question about the affection Rapans feel for their grandchildren, a middle-aged woman beamed and said, "Your grandchild is your pearl." Grandparents indulge every whim of their small grandchildren, who may decide to live with their grandparents for several days or even months if they feel a lack of attention at home, or if they need sanctuary against their parents' wrath. As grandchildren enter their teens, the great freedom they enjoyed vis-à-vis their grandparents is transformed into deep respect and solidarity. Grandparents may have even greater authority over the individual than his own parents. Some informants said they would obey their grandparents in preference to their parents, and would support a grandparent in a dispute with a parent. (One man said that any situation in which one would have to choose between a parent and a grandparent would be intensely uncomfortable and should be avoided because of the love and obligation one feels for both parties. If forced to take sides, however, he said he would support the grandparent since he is older, weaker, and therefore needs the help more.)

People feel an obligation to support their aged grandparents economically, as they do their parents. Grandmothers, with no distinction drawn between paternal and maternal sides, are accorded greater affection and authority than grandfathers. Again, between siblings' childrens' children and parents' parents' siblings the norms of the relationship operate with some force, but in more remote relationships they slacken greatly.

More distant lineal relationships, between tupuna and their 'ina and 'inarere, are similar in most respects to that between grandparents and grandchildren. Here, however, the relationship is much less intimate, authority is exercised only rarely, but the respect accorded to a tupuna is even greater. The most remote ancestors are also termed tupuna, and they are regarded with great admiration and respect. When a person lives to see his great-grandchildren he has reached the pinnacle of prestige in this kinship system for he has joined the elite company of the tupuna while still alive.

Tua'ana and Teina. The relationship between siblings and cousins of the same sex is the least restrained consanguineal bond in Rapa. While not required, "strong joking" such as playing pranks or banter about sex, is allowed. A young woman was in labor with her first child, and attending her were two rather distant female cousins. She said she needed to have a bowel movement, and her cousins escorted her outside. They directed her to squat down, and then one peered under her. "Wait! Wait!" she cried excitedly. "This is no bowel movement! It's the baby!" she lied. Making a great show of urgency they told her to keep her dress up and rush to the house. They followed close on her heels, laughing and whipping her bare buttocks with light switches.

Juxtaposed against the joking and lack of restraint in this relationship is the authority of the tua'ana (the elder) over the teina (the younger). A tua'ana may remonstrate with his or her teina and administer some discipline if the latter is misbehaving; a tua'ana's opinion carries weight in such matters as the teina's marriage, and in any joint enterprise the tua'ana takes the directing role. In all these matters, however, the authority of the tua'ana is subordinate to that of parents and grandparents if they are still alive and of clear mind.

Joking and authority verge on incompatibility in the same relationship. In Rapa this difficulty is averted by reference to the distance of relationship of the individuals involved. For full siblings, the aspect of authority is emphasized at the expense of joking. While they do laugh and converse easily together, tua'ana and teina who are full siblings do not indulge in "strong joking." Through first- and second-cousin relationships the joking increases and the authority subsides. The tua'ana does retain a residue of authority which may be exercised if circumstances demand it, but this happens only occasionally between first cousins and rarely for second cousins. For third cousins and beyond, the entire relationship diminishes almost to the vanishing point. There is no real authority and any joking is done more in the idiom of friendship than of kinship.

Tu'āne and Tuahine. In sharp contrast with the relationship between tua'ana and teina is that between brother and sister or cousins of the opposite sex. Beginning at about puberty, their conduct is characterized by a great deal of restraint, especially in all matters pertaining to sex. They should never discuss the subject, and are uncomfortable if it is mentioned when both are present. They should never sit on one another's bed or sleeping mat, and most Rapans prefer to get drenched in the rain or shiver with cold rather than borrow a coat belonging to a tu'āne or tuahine. They are careful to avoid situations in which they might see each other's genitals. On the rare occasions when a woman goes fishing, she never goes in a boat which also carries a tu'āne, for it would be intensely embarrassing should one of them have to urinate over the side. After a birth, I asked if a particular man especially skilled as a midwife had attended. "Of course not!" I was told in shocked tones, for he is a tu'āne of the mother, her second or third cousin.

The aim of all these prohibitions, of course, is to avoid any situation where their passions could be aroused and which might lead them to sleep together. Sexual contact between full brother and sister is a heinous act. In the one case I know, the couple left Rapa in self-imposed exile, probably because they could not bear the shame. Telling me about this case, an indignant old man threatened that if they ever returned to Rapa he personally would kill them both. Sexual relations between cousins are also disapproved, although not so strongly. Most Rapans are careful to observe the restrictions relating to sexual matters even when the relationship is as distant as second and third cousins. This observance is by no means universal, however. Although much condemned, and in spite of the idea held by some persons that in punishment the partners and their children will contract leprosy, there are currently two cases of first cousins living together openly.

These restrictions not withstanding, affection is strong between tu'āne and tuahine, stronger than between tua'ana and teina. A tu'āne has some authority over his tuahine, and often considers himself to be her protector — he is willing and anxious to help her in any time of need. The elements of protectiveness and authority are most intense between full brother and sister, carry some weight between first cousins, and are virtually nonexistent in more remote relationships.

The Sibling Group. The sibling group, termed *'ōpū ho'e* ("one abdomen"), is a highly solidary unit. By the system of descent, full siblings normally share ownership in a considerable amount of property, and the sentiments of affection and mutual obligation binding them to one another and to their parents enhance their common interest. As a result, much of the economic cooperation between households is based on ties between full siblings. As their parents grow old, authority over the other siblings and over the parents themselves devolves usually upon the *matahiapo*, the first-born. For this reason Rapans prefer that the first born be male; the feast honoring a first-born child is a more elaborate affair for a son than for a daughter. Should the matahiapo be female, she may still exercise authority over her siblings if she has strong will and capability. Otherwise the eldest brother assumes leadership.

Parents expect most from the first child and often give him some authority over his siblings while still young. In contrast, they lavish the greatest love and attention on the *hope'a*, the last-born. I did not uncover any resentment on the part of the older siblings against the hope'a. On the contrary, I was told that they too reserve special love for their youngest sibling and treat him like their own child. This is especially true if the hope'a is a child

107

of the parents' later years, after the others are grown. In a sense, then, the sibling group contains within itself all the consanguineal relationships of the elementary family, for the matahiapo is like a parent to the group, and the hope'a is like its child.

Relations between half-siblings are often strained. The elder set of siblings may think that their stepparent treats them unjustly, and they resent sharing the love and property of their common parent with his new children. The tension is less in cases of levirate or sororate (see pages 131–32).

KIN BY MARRIAGE

Yet to be considered is the affinal side of the kinship system: the set of relationships between relatives by marriage. It will be recalled that the Rapan kinship terminology is classificatory: aunts are included with mother under one term, nephews with sons under another, and so on. For simplicity and clarity I shall use English terms in defining the affinal kin terms, but when they are enclosed in single quotation marks they are to be understood in the classificatory, Rapan sense. (See Table 3.) For example, 'brother' refers to male cousins as well as brothers, and 'father'-in-law refers to the spouse's father and uncles. Affines address each other by name, never by kinship terms. Affinal terms are used only in reference, and then only in situations where the kin connection is important to the context.

TABLE 4. AFFINAL KINSHIP TERMINOLOGY

Generation	Terms	
+1	*metūa ho'ovai tāne* ('father'-in-law)	*metūa ho'ovai vahine* ('mother'-in-law)
0	*tāne* (husband, theoretically also 'brother'-in-law of a female)	*vahine* (wife, theoretically also 'sister'-in-law of a male)
	tau'ate ('brother'-in-law of a male, 'sister'-in-law of a female)	
−1	*huno'a tāne* ('son'-in-law)	*huno'a vahine* ('daughter'-in-law)

The intensity of affinal relationships seems in general to taper off more quickly with increasing genealogical distance than is the case with consanguineal ties. With the spouse's own parents and siblings, the norms are usually followed closely, but with the aunts, uncles and first cousins of the spouse, the rules often diminish sharply. Beyond this range, affinal ties are seldom effective determinants of daily interaction. The major exceptions to this generalization are cases where a person belongs to the same household as the spouse's aunt, uncle, or cousins. In such an event, he is in frequent contact with these affines and tends to follow the rules of conduct defining his relationship with them rather closely.

Spouses and Lovers. Only a bare skeleton of the relationships between spouses and lovers is given here, for in the following chapter romance, courtship and marriage will be depicted in many of their intricacies. The relationship between husband and wife is one of considerable freedom: they may joke together, and they live under no special restrictions. While they should consult together on important matters, the husband has authority over his wife. Each has exclusive rights over the sexual activity of the other, and adultery by either is met with moral indignation from society at large. The terms tāne and vahine are used for unmarried cohabiting couples as well, and their relationship is broadly similar to that of man and wife. Here, however, the authority of the male is less clearly defined, and while infidelity usually leads to the termination of the relationship, this is a matter between the individuals involved and of no concern to society.

'Siblings'-in-Law. There are two distinct types of relationship between 'siblings'-in-law. One is between 'siblings'-in-law of the opposite sex: a man and his 'sister'-in-law, a woman and her 'brother'-in-law. As noted above, theoretically they may refer to one another as tāne and vahine, although this seems not to occur in practice — usually they refer to each other by name. If their kinship is being stressed they may use the general term "relative" (feti'i), or may specify the precise connection in a descriptive phrase, as "my wife's sister." This relationship is quite free and easy, it being permissible to play pranks and even to make jokes

about each other's sex life. The other relationship is that between 'siblings'-in-law of the same sex (tau'ate): a man and his 'brother'-in-law, a woman and her 'sister'-in-law. The tau'ate relationship is hedged with restraint, and they are often quite uncomfortable together. No pranking is allowed, and joking about sexual matters is especially prohibited. It would be unthinkable for a man to discuss his personal sex life with, or in the presence of, his wife's 'brother.'

At this point we may note an interesting arrangement of inverse symmetry in the Rapan kinship system. It will be recalled that among consanguineal kin of the same generation, the relationship between 'siblings' of the same sex (tua'ana and teina) is free, while that between 'siblings' of the opposite sex (tu'āne and tuahine) is characterized by restraint. Exactly the opposite occurs among affines of the same generation. Here freedom marks the behavior between 'siblings'-in-law of the *opposite* sex, while those of the *same* sex (tau'ate) treat each other with restraint.

As noted earlier, strong affection and a sense of protectiveness exists between brother and sister, and brothers hold authority over their sisters. When a woman marries, her husband assumes responsibility for her welfare and authority over her. However, her relationship with her brother does not cease. Thus there are now two persons who are interested in her well-being and who hold authority over her. This is a delicate situation which could lead to serious friction. The brother might believe that the husband is mistreating his sister and may be moved to interfere on her behalf. The husband might become irritated with the brother's watching him so narrowly and angry that he cannot be master in his own house. Perhaps another element of possible rancor on the part of the brother is that this woman, whom he has always viewed almost as a sacred object of total sexual avoidance, is freely accessible to her husband. The situation is potentially dangerous, for if friction between brothers-in-law becomes serious enough it could disrupt the marriage. (For this reason women usually silently endure the occasional beatings some husbands administer, for to cry out might bring an enraged brother to her aid and then real trouble would ensue.)

In Rapa the way of dealing with relationships which could engender open friction is to keep a lid on them. The attitude is that if brothers-in-law are required to maintain social distance, to treat one another with general restraint and particularly to avoid dangerous subjects of conversation, the chances of an explosion are minimized (see Radcliffe-Brown 1952:92).

The restraint between tau'ate is much the strongest in the case of immediate brothers-in-law, because a man feels by far the most concern for his full sister. Since his sentiments about a female cousin are much less intense, more distant 'brothers'-in-law can normally interact somewhat more freely, although a tinge of restraint is still present. Female tau'ate ('sisters'-in-law) are also restrained and tend to be catty behind each other's backs, but the relationship is less tense than between 'brothers'-in-law, probably because 'sisters' do not feel as protective about their 'brothers.'

What of the contrasting free and easy conduct between 'siblings'-in-law of the opposite sex? Again, this appears to be tied to the relationship between 'siblings,' this time 'siblings' of the same sex (tua'ana and teina). Rapans tend not to be so strongly attached to their tua'ana and teina as they are to 'siblings' of the opposite sex, nor do they feel nearly the same sense of protectiveness for them. They seem to think that 'siblings' of their own sex can take care of themselves. Therefore they are not so quick to make critical judgments of the spouses of such 'siblings.' Hence the potential friction is lacking in the relationship between opposite sexed 'siblings'-in-law, so there is no reason for them to behave with restraint. More will be said of this relationship in the next chapter.

'Parents'-in-Law. When I asked Te'ura how a Rapan feels toward his 'parents'-in-law, he screwed up his face in distaste and said, "You don't even want to talk to those people." Like that between 'siblings'-in-law of the same sex (tau'ate), the relationship between 'parents'-in-law and 'children'-in-law (metūa ho'ovai and huno'a) is characterized by restraint, tension and discomfort. The reason is probably the same: both parties have strong interest in the same individual (one as a 'parent,' the other as a spouse), and

111

restrained behavior serves to keep the latent hostility between them from breaking into open conflict. All reference to sexual matters is forbidden in this relationship. Rapans say it would be *hupehupe* (filthy — the strongest word they know in this context) for an individual to have sexual relations with a 'parent'-in-law or a 'child'-in-law. 'Parents'-in-law have authority over their 'children'-in-law, although this is not nearly as strong as that of 'parents' over their 'children.' This notwithstanding, and although one often loses little love or concern for his 'parents'-in-law, if requested he will help them in some job more quickly than he would his own parents. The reason is that the relationship with his parents is cemented by strong affection and mutual interest, and it can therefore easily withstand postponement of assistance. Due to the tension inherent in the relationship with 'parents'-in-law, however, no one wishes to give the slightest opportunity for the latent friction to break into the open.

Of the five major categories of people mentioned at the beginning of this chapter — strangers, friends, kinsmen, neighbors and lovers — the last two have thus far received scant attention. The next chapter is devoted to lovers, while we shall encounter neighbors at various points in Chapters 7 and 8.

FREEDOM AND CONFORMITY

Reading about these norms, one might get the impression that Rapans are people sapped of spontaneity — slaves to custom, mechanically classifying each other in categories and then acting in dull conformity with the appropriate, preordained rules of behavior. Nothing could be further from the truth. A few individuals deviate sharply from the expected patterns of action. Tara, for example, is a *mahū*: a man who in some context plays the role of a woman. He wears shorts or pants as men do, although he usually ties a bright sash around his waist and occasionally dons earrings. His voice is high-pitched, his gait and gestures are effeminate, and he prefers the company of women. With interests identical to theirs, he fits in comfortably with the women's gossip sessions and they accept him as one of themselves. He prefers women's work. On Saturdays, when the men all go fishing, Tara often remains in the village making popoi, baking bread, and joining the women in other tasks of food preparation. In the quiet hours before sunset he enjoys sitting in front of his house mending clothes. Tara is not homosexual. He has a wife and several children, and my informants insisted that he does not engage in sexual relations with men. He simply prefers the work, company and manners of women.

Then there is Miti, the nonconformist. He is never seen at church functions and only rarely at other large gatherings. He loves to cook and is highly skilled at it. His major contribution to the community is serving as cook for large feasts. Miti withholds wholesale acceptance of his society. He appears consciously to evaluate all its activities, and participates only in those he finds personally appealing. The badge of Miti's nonconformity is his hair. Unlike all other men, he allows it to grow down to his shoulders. Habitually he ties a bandanna around his head, looking for all the world like a pirate. Rapan society has room for people like Tara and Miti. They are neither ridiculed nor despised, but simply accepted on their own terms. It is not likely that they will ever attain prominent positions of leadership, but equally unlikely that they harbor ambitions in this direction.

Nor do the norms of behavior significantly curtail the freedom of the vast majority of Rapans who do not qualify as deviants. The rules are most specific for relations between kinsmen, but even here they merely lay down broad guidelines rather than rigidly defining every facet of interaction. Between very close kinsmen the elements of authority and restraint in some of the relationships are essential to the smooth running of society. Beyond this, however, the norms of kinship are often bent, and actual behavior between two persons depends at least as much on the specific circumstances and the personalities involved.

The major value of the norms, I believe, is to define how kinsmen should act in unfamiliar situations, or in cases where they do not know one another well. In familiar situations and for relatives who are well acquainted, the experience of their past interaction largely determines how they behave. If they trust each other and get along well they may joke and act with considerable freedom though the norms of their kin relationship call for restraint; if they find they are incompatible, they may avoid interaction and be restrained and sullen in one another's company, although by the norms of kinship their solidarity should be high and their relationship free. For example, the restraint of the relationships between same sexed 'siblings'-in-law or 'parents'- and 'children'-in-law is strongest when they are new. It can continue indefinitely if the persons involved do not get along well, but if they find themselves compatible, the tension and restraint relax greatly. One man who is especially fond of his mother-in-law said they treat one another more as mother and son than as metūa ho'ovai and huno'a.

Even when people do conform closely to the rules for a given relationship, they are not necessarily sacrificing their freedom. At several points in this chapter I have likened the norms defining interpersonal relationships to maps. I think the metaphor is appropriate to the problem of conformity and freedom. When someone plans a motor tour he consults a road map. The map does not determine his destination; he has freely chosen this already. The map does tell him the best route to follow to that destination. To disregard the map and set out blindly on his own may have a ring of impulsive spontaneity about it, but if he is at all serious about reaching his destination it is less an act of freedom than an act of idiocy. Conceivably he could go so hopelessly astray that he is no longer able — and therefore no longer free — to reach the destination. It is much the same in human relations. Normally when people interact they have destinations or goals in mind. The goal may be as specific as asking, granting, or refusing a favor; as general as maintaining a harmonious relationship. Each relationship has a map indicating the routes or channels of behavior to follow for the various goals in mind. Unless one knows the other person well enough to predict his reactions in all circumstances, to deviate from the expected channel of behavior could disorient or offend him to the point that it would no longer be possible to reach the goal. Thus to follow the norms governing a particular relationship is not to submerge one's freedom in conformity; it is often the only way one can retain freedom to achieve a desired end.[1]

Finally, to reiterate the point made at the outset of this chapter, the norms of behavior governing human relationships endow interaction with predictability. Probably all men share the Rapans' vulnerability in contact with others, their fear of being embarrassed or emotionally injured. Rules of behavior provide a sanctuary from this fear, for they allow people to predict the general course of interaction. Were there no rules, it is not likely that human relations would become warmer and more spontaneous — probably they would become more restrained, more guarded and perhaps they would have difficulty continuing at all.

[1] For more detailed discussions of the problem of freedom and conformity, see Lee (1959) and Bidney (1963).

CHAPTER SIX

Courtship
and Marriage

Norms governing many important social relationships in Rapa have been mapped out, but these provide only the bare outlines of expected behavior. They neither delineate each detail, nor are they observed with mechanical precision. Rapans adhere to them like a vessel to the shipping lanes in a broad swath of ocean, not like a train confined to its rails. In this and the following two chapters are numerous examples of how Rapans observe, bend, or controvert these norms.

PRELUDE TO MARRIAGE

Most people in Rapa retire by eight or nine o'clock, leaving behind a scene of stillness and beauty. The Southern Cross and other stars of the Austral skies are brilliant, and moonlight silvers the sleeping village. The silence is complete, shattered only rarely by a dog's bark or the startlingly loud braying of a bull. While children and adults sleep, the darkness shrouds scenes of excitement and passionate adventure for the youths. During the day young lovers have arranged their rendezvous in a furtive conversation, by means of a note, or through a trusted intermediary. At night a girl slips outside to meet her waiting lover and goes with him to his house or to the woods. Under the cover of darkness a young man paddles his canoe across the bay to the other village to spend the night with his mistress. (If they are so bold as to meet in her house he must be sure to make no noise and to be gone before dawn, for if discovered he risks a severe drubbing from her enraged father. Early risers of his own village who see him return will greet his embarrassed smile with jokes and laughter.) An unattached girl goes out late at night to relieve herself, and a rustle nearby causes her heart to quicken. An admirer, lurking near the house in hopes of just this opportunity, pounces on her and carries her off. She struggles at first, but is careful not to call out or awaken anyone. For her, too, the rape is thrilling.

So begins the exciting period of experimentation with love and learning about living together, which will culminate eventually in a family and stable marriage. There are many variations, but the sex life normally begins in the late teens and formal marriage comes anywhere from the middle twenties to the early thirties. The years in between are the taure'are'a years described previously — the time for the irresponsible gaiety of youth.

At first, youths seem motivated by the sheer joy of being taure'are'a. They relish the independence they gradually gain from parental control and discipline, and they give vent to their exuberance in the sports, singing and dancing that mark the taure'are'a way of life. Most of all they delight in sex, that newly discovered dimension in their lives. Not that they are promiscuous: the relationship with one lover is normally cut off when a new one is taken. But many of them seem to change partners fairly frequently, so their experience with age-mates of the opposite sex becomes quite broad.

Not all of a youth's age-mates are potential sex partners. A young man often numbers several tuahine (sisters or female cousins) among the crop of nubile girls, and these are forbidden to him by the rules of kinship. It will be recalled that 'brothers' and 'sisters' should never talk of sex, or both be present when the subject is mentioned. The youths take advantage of this in their banter, mercilessly kidding a young man about his sex life when his 'sister' is present. The poor fellow is unable to retort in kind, and must take the ribbing in embarrassed silence. Again, one's previous liaisons may have an effect on the choice of future lovers. Even if the premarital affairs are short and casual, it is considered despicable to sleep with a 'parent' or 'child' of a previous lover, no matter how distant their kin connection might be. (It is acceptable, however, to sleep with a previous lover's 'sibling.')

Even with these limitations the field of potential spouses is fairly large, and after a few years most youths find partners whom they come to love. At this stage the casual liaisons take on a more permanent character, although the lovers continue to meet only at night behind a veil of secrecy. A critical point in the relationship comes when the girl gets pregnant. If they are not serious about one another the pregnancy and birth usually lead them to break up. Should they remain together during this period, it is likely that they will eventually marry — although usually not for a few more years.

THE FIRST STEP

For those couples that survive it, pregnancy and the birth of their first child signal a new phase in their relationship. Until now their affair had been officially secret. (In a community as small as Rapa there are few true secrets and everyone in fact knew about it, but it was "unofficial knowledge." For example, I could learn of these "secret" liaisons from private conversation with my close friends, but the youths in question and other people I knew less well would not acknowledge them to me.) Now the facade of secrecy is dropped. They no longer sneak away after everyone is asleep and return to their own houses before the village awakens. They allow themselves to be seen entering the same house in the evening and leaving it in the morning.

Here we encounter one of the oblique ways human beings communicate in delicate situations. By allowing themselves to be seen in these circumstances the young couple brings their relationship into the realm of public recognition. They are making an announcement which they would be embarrassed and unwilling to say in words. Now that they are introducing a new member to society in their child, they communicate their intention to care for that child. Furthermore, their message reads that they feel a certain affection for, and commitment to, each other, and therefore they will probably get married some day.

The delicacy of the situation calls for indirect communication by acts rather than a verbal announcement. There are two points to make here. First, courtship poses a contradiction in Rapan culture. As Protestant Christians, they have been taught that premarital sex is sinful. They pay verbal tribute to this precept, but they do not practice it (see Hoebel 1960:175). As in other Polynesian societies, sex is and always has been an integral part of courtship for almost all youths. Rapan culture seems unprepared to give up either the precept or the practice. The one is deemed important to the Christian image they seek to present to the world, while the other is explained as an inevitable part of imperfect human nature. Were an unmarried couple to say openly that they are sleeping together, this would flagrantly flaunt the stated rules of conduct. The contradiction between precept and practice would be clarified — would demand resolution more urgently because both sides would be brought onto the verbal plane. The contradiction is less sharply drawn, and therefore more livable, if one side is kept on the level of words and the other restricted to the level of action.[1]

The second element of delicacy in this situation is that everything remains tentative. Each partner retains his option to dissolve the relationship. In this sense, overt cohabitation is analogous to an engagement in the United States, although the Rapan form is less binding in that the couple communicates only the likelihood that they will marry eventually, not a firm intention to do so on a particular date. Until an explicit decision is made, the future lives of the couple and of their child or children hang in the balance. These, of course, are of utmost importance to the

---

[1] Compare the attitude I have heard expressed by an older person concerning the furor over "sex on the campus" in American society: "We did the same things in our day, only we didn't *talk* about it."

people directly involved, to the parents of the pair and to society at large. With the stakes so high, a verbal statement would be intolerable. It would be unwise, even dangerous, for the young man to tell the father of his mistress, "I think I will marry your daughter, but I plan to live with her a few more years to make sure." Nor would he be well advised to announce to the community: "I have fathered a child. Currently I plan to provide for its welfare and make it my heir, but if its mother and I separate I may change my mind." Yet precisely these messages are communicated, with far less danger of unpleasant confrontations, when a couple drops the shroud of secrecy from their relationship.

From the perspective of the youths involved, overt cohabitation is a means of resolving a number of conflicting obligations and desires. With the birth of a child, society expects some assurance of parental responsibility, and most youths are willing and anxious to give this assurance. At the same time, they are still taure'are'a. Although the transition has begun, they are not tired of the revelry and freedom of youth; they are not ready to shoulder the full responsibility and adopt the sober demeanor of adulthood. In brief, since marriage is a sign that one is ready to enter adulthood, they are not ready to marry. Through overt cohabitation they take the first tentative step to adulthood. They acknowledge contingent responsibility to each other and to their offspring, while retaining the right of continued participation in the taure-'are'a way of life.

Economic obligations are also involved. Youths do most of the heavy labor in the Rapan economy, and often a youth supports a parent, grandparent, or other aged kinsman. In the Rapan view, this is his means of discharging the debt of support and upbringing that he incurred as a child. Upon marriage, spouses invariably belong to the same household, and primary economic responsibility shifts to one's mate and children. Not rarely, youths otherwise ready to marry defer the wedding until a dependent senior kinsman dies or a younger sibling grows old enough to take over the responsibility of support. Overtly cohabiting couples often do not belong to the same household, primarily for the economic reason that neither the young man nor woman is willing to deprive his household of his labor. Again, overt cohabitation provides a resolution whereby a youth may discharge his economic obligation to elder dependents by day while deepening the relationship with his probable spouse by night.

Consonant with the precept that premarital sex is sinful, parents generally maintain an attitude of official disapproval throughout courtship. Some parents try to delay their children's transition from childhood to youth by keeping them from the evening sessions when youths gather to sing and dance. Attendance here marks an inevitable prelude to the beginning of sex life. The first signs of flirting and sneaking out at night may be met with harsh parental scolding and perhaps a beating. Parents try to control their daughters considerably more than their sons. Thus, especially for girls, entrance into the taure'are'a years may be somewhat traumatic.

Later, parents usually remain aloof from their child's romances, unless they are adamantly opposed to his or her lover. In this event, more scoldings and beatings may be applied in an effort to terminate the affair. One man went so far as to send his daughter to Tahiti with instructions to find a husband there, to get her away from her Rapan lover. Parents unwilling to take such drastic measures find their control limited: if they press their case too strongly, their angered child might leave the household.[2] Given the important role of youths in the economy, this could leave a serious gap in the household's labor force. At least as important, few parents would welcome the rupture with a beloved child that such a departure would signify.

In fact, if their child's mate is diligent, of good character and family, parents often approve of the relationship. As for its sexual dimension, while most parents maintain public opposition to premarital sex, their private attitudes are not so rigid. "Premarital sex is a sin," adults would tell me, "but it is only a small sin." After mouthing some mild castigations against the youths for

---

[2] In such a case, the youth might form a new household with his or her lover, or join the household of a near kinsman.

their sinful ways, adults would smile and reminisce about the delicious excitement of their own taure'are'a years and the devices they used to deceive their parents to keep illicit rendezvous.

Just as they are limited in discouraging their children's courtship activities, however, parents can do little to encourage them. The relationship between parents and children-in-law is always marked by tension and restraint, and this situation is heightened when the young couple is not married. Any relations parents might have with their child's lover could compromise the outcome of the affair, so the only way they can show their encouragement is to do nothing. Incidentally, this indicates a reason, beyond the economic one, why overtly cohabiting couples seldom belong to the same household. This would place the parents and their child's lover in close daily contact: an uncomfortable position for both sides. The parents would find it difficult to maintain their official disapproval of their child's affair in these circumstances, and could therefore be embarrassed before the community. The parents might get the idea that their child's lover is not serious about eventual marriage, and friction over this or a number of other problems could easily break out, leading to the termination of a relationship that might otherwise have culminated in marriage. In such a delicate situation, it is best if the lovers have as little as possible to do with each other's parents until a firm and explicit decision to marry is made.

MAKING THE DECISION

Even after a few years of overt cohabitation and one or more children, young Rapan couples seldom formalize their union by marriage without goading from the outside. Their delay stems from economic obligations felt by each partner toward his own household or, more often, a reluctance to leave the carefree taure'are'a way of life.

Perhaps the most frequent and certainly the most intriguing means of pressuring young couples to marry is the *pererina*, or "pilgrimage." This is a church institution, largely under the auspices of the deacons' wives, who are responsible for keeping track of the state of the community. On their recommendation, deputations or "pilgrimages" are sent to visit the sick, to comfort those in mourning, and to encourage and admonish those who are lax in church attendance and other aspects of the Christian life.

The deacons' wives keep an eye on the youths who are cohabiting openly. If a couple has been living together for some time in a happy and stable relationship, but shows no sign of planning a wedding, the deacons' wives decide to encourage them with a pilgrimage. Toward midnight the deacons, their wives, and perhaps a few other married church members steal quietly into the house where the couple is sleeping. They station themselves around the bed, light a lamp, then rouse the pair and ask, in a most dignified manner, if they might pray. During the ensuing prayer, usually one of great length, the young lovers clutch their sheet about them, redden with embarrassment, and rack their brains for a way to evade the questions to come. After the amen, the head of the deputation turns to the young man and asks when he plans to marry. Those Rapans who have gone through this ordeal describe it with rich laughter, mimicking the grimaces and whining explanations: "We're too young, we're not sure of ourselves, we're not ready to settle down." An especially rattled young man might plead that he must step outside to urinate, upon which he promptly runs away, leaving his hapless mistress to face the inquisition alone.

Usually nothing conclusive is established in the first pilgrimage. But the lovers know they are a marked pair and can expect further visits. They may adopt evasive tactics, varying their place of sleeping so the pilgrims cannot find them. But the visitors have their sources of information, and it is not long before the fugitives are located. For their part, the pilgrims closely guard the secret of the time and victims of their visits. Should this information reach the young couple in question, the deputation would surely find an empty bed.

These visits occur at random intervals over several weeks or months. Life becomes uncomfortable for a marked couple, as it is disconcerting to go to sleep never knowing whether one will be awakened to a row of kindly but serious faces ranged around the bed. If the lovers are not truly serious about each other, this ordeal may be enough to end their relationship. But the pilgrims choose as targets only those persons who appear ready for marriage, and usually after several visits the couple agrees to wed. A marriage contracted in this manner is termed *fa'aipoipo na te pererina*, or "marriage of the pilgrimage." The pilgrimage suggests that Rapan society tolerates the carefree taure'are'a way of life only to a point. Eventually society steps in, acting through the instrument of the church, and demands that the responsibilities of adulthood be shouldered.

THE WEDDING

Once the couple has decided upon marriage their parents play an active role in the arrangements. The young man discusses his plans with his parents, and if they approve, they pay an evening visit to the parents of the prospective bride. After a few pleasantries the boy's parents suggest the marriage. The girl's parents give no direct answer on the first visit. This tactic forestalls the impression that they are anxious to marry off a worthless daughter, and gives her parents the chance to determine how strongly the groom's side desires the match. The visits continue each evening, although if a positive answer is not given by the third or fourth time it is a sign that the girl's family is strongly opposed, and the boy's parents cease coming. If the girl's parents do agree, there are a few more visits, now with the betrothed present, to set the date and to plan the wedding feast.

If the couple has been openly cohabiting for some time, and especially if they have children, it is most unlikely that the parents of either would attempt to block the marriage. In such cases their discussions bear the marks of a hollow formality. In one sort of marriage, however, the parental negotiations are of utmost importance. This is the *fa'aipoipo ti'a mā*, or virgin marriage.

Some persons never go through the taure'are'a stage of life. They pass directly from childhood to adulthood because they show no taste for the revelry of the youths, they stay home at night, and they marry as virgins. As might be expected from the fact that

124

parents control daughters more closely than sons, far more girls marry as virgins than boys. To my knowledge only one man in Rapa married without previous sex experience, while four women married as virgins and two more girls are likely to do so. Although some Rapans view them as a little strange, many think that virgins make especially good wives. Usually they are serious and sober girls, far more obedient and dutiful to their parents than the average. The expectation is that they will behave in much the same way toward their husbands. It is scarcely possible for a young man to court such a girl, however, for by definition Rapan courtship entails sexual relations. This explains the importance of negotiations between parents.

The young man suggests the match to his parents. If they agree, they visit the parents of the prospective bride. Negotiations proceed as described above, only her parents may hold out a bit longer and his may press the affair more earnestly since both sides think she is a special prize. The girl herself may know nothing of the matter until her parents tell her of their visitors. Her own wishes have more or less weight depending on the nature of her relationship with her parents. They would be reluctant to force a match that she adamantly opposes, but at the same time her uncommon obedience means they could be very persuasive in getting her to accept the man whom they think is best for her.

Prolonged virginity may signify virtue, but Rapans believe it can also endanger the health. Tehina, a virgin of about twenty, was having trouble with her menstruation and was feeling poorly in general. A friend told me that the French military doctor who visits Rapa periodically had examined her, and had said the trouble would probably take care of itself when she married. My informant was in enthusiastic agreement, one of the few times I heard a Rapan express strong approval of Western medical practice. Rapans view semen much as we think of vitamin pills: it gives women strength and vitality. One man made this point by saying, "Look at those women who have recently lost a husband or lover. They mope around all the time, have no energy, can't work well. But when they get a new man, they perk up right away." So Rapans make love to their women not only for purposes of procreation or pleasure, but also to keep them strong and healthy.

Be it a virgin marriage or the more usual form, the wedding generally occurs about a month after the conclusion of parental negotiations. During this interval the betrothed are the darlings of the community, especially of the married adults. The previous posture of official disapproval because of their illicit sex life is replaced by benevolent encouragement. The young couple is showered with gifts of money and goods; everything possible is done to make them feel welcome among the adults — the married communicant church members — whose ranks they are about to join. In the past the betrothed were forbidden to sleep together during this period, on pain of cancellation of the marriage. About ten years ago, however, this restriction was relaxed.

Unfortunately I can give no detailed description of a Rapan wedding. During the eleven months of the study only one wedding took place. This was the day after our arrival, so I had no foundation of understanding on which to make meaningful observations. Briefly, then, there are two ceremonies. The first is a civil ceremony, conducted in the small government building. Having acknowledged Caesar, the bridal party parades through the village to the church. Only the bridal party attends the two services. The rest watch the procession, and then return to work preparing the feast. The church service, like the civil ceremony, lasts only about fifteen minutes. Following this the feast begins.

One important element of the feast is the conferring of the marriage name. This is usually done in an elaborate oration by an older man from either the bride's or groom's family, and the name itself may be for one of the ancestors of that family. Both spouses retain their family names, but after the wedding their given names are no longer used and they are henceforth called by the marriage name. Thus, when Ara'i Pukoki took Teitia Ma'ihuri as his bride, they were given the marriage name Fa'atu. Since then everyone has called him Fa'atu Tāne (the best translation would be "Fa'atu the husband") or simply Fa'atu, and she is called Fa'atu Vahine ("Fa'atu the wife").

126

Usually two, three or more couples marry simultaneously; probably this is one reason weddings only occur at long intervals in Rapa. All couples ready to marry do so at one time, and then a year or more passes in waiting for the next group. Rapans give an economic reason for multiple weddings. Although many people make small gifts of money or food, the wedding feast is costly because most of the population attends. The expenses are shared equally by the families of the bride and groom, so if several couples marry simultaneously, the cost of the feast can be split several ways, making a lighter burden for each family. It may also be that the youths themselves prefer joint weddings; they tend to be shy on public occasions and are embarrassed if attention focuses on them. An almost pathetic element of the wedding mentioned above, for example, was the intense discomfort (ha'amā) of the bride and groom throughout the entire affair. Probably it is easier for the young people if they share the stage with several companions.

Occasionally these joint weddings include pairs of spouses who marry by sister-exchange. Ten or fifteen years ago, for example, Tu married the sister of Tohu and, in the same ceremony, Tohu married Tu's sister. This was especially interesting to me because in some societies sister-exchange is a preferred form signifying a close alliance between two groups of kin. I was surprised, then, when an informant explained, "It's a matter of revenge." In the preceding chapter we noted that men tend to feel great affection and a sense of protectiveness for their sisters, especially their younger sisters. Because of this, my informant explained, a young man is often angry when his sister takes a lover. He may join their parents in scolding and perhaps beating her, but he is especially anxious to wreak vengeance on her lover. It would cause the brother great embarrassment to confront the lover directly, but he may try to repay him in kind. The sweetest revenge is to take the lover's youngest (and therefore most beloved) sister, deflower her, and then drop her. Occasionally, however, both unions result in marriage, that is, marriage by sister-exchange. Interestingly, a double marriage where a pair of brothers from one family marries a pair of sisters of another never seems to happen, and Rapans to whom I put the possibility thought it would be most undesirable. I could discover no satisfactory reason why they oppose this form of marriage but not the other.

After marriage the couple always takes up residence in the same household. This may be the parental household of one of the spouses, or a household of their own. All other things being equal, Rapans prefer that the wife move to join her husband. A man should have authority over his wife and children, and this can be difficult if they live with or near her family. In actuality, however, other factors often outweigh this preference. Most important is the decision whether the husband's parents or the wife's have more need of the economic assistance of the young couple. Of Rapa's thirty-seven married pairs, sixteen reside in or near the parental household of the husband, sixteen in or near that of the wife, four have established households in new neighborhoods, and I have no information for the final pair.

THE MARRIAGE CONTRACT

A Rapan wedding seals a contract. The tentative agreement which the young couple first communicated to society by allowing themselves to be seen entering and leaving the same house is now formalized in words — the marriage vows — before the State, God, and society. One part of the covenant is between the two spouses. By marrying they commit themselves to permanent partnership in every area of life: to live together in fidelity, to work together for their common welfare and that of their children, and to support each other in all things. Greater authority rests with the husband, but as in all true partnerships, decisions should be motivated by common interest and made jointly.

At least as important, the marriage contract involves an agreement between the couple and society. The couple pledges to remain together and to help perpetuate a stable society by bearing and responsibly rearing children. They also promise a change in their own way of life: henceforth they will abandon the carefree revelry of the taure'are'a and become sober adults. Although the transition to adulthood usually has been developing over a few years with a gradual change in state of mind, the critical point of

128

marriage may still be difficult. This, incidentally, may suggest another reason for the occurrence of multiple weddings in Rapa. The change of general conduct which marriage signifies may be easier to accomplish if a group of age-mates and friends make it together.

The couple may begin to fulfill its contract with society in the civil marriage ceremoney. If they have children who were not legally recognized at birth by one or both of them, they are often recognized then. This makes both parents legally responsible and insures the children's rights of inheritance, thus representing a formal provision for their present and future welfare.

Newlyweds fulfill the agreement to change their way of life under the auspices of the church, the most important and active instrument of society at large. Shortly after the wedding they become part of the *Pupu 'Imi* or "Searching Group" which meets with the pastor each week to study the Bible, catechism and church organization, and to be admonished about the puritanical rules of conduct that communicants are expected to observe. These rules include no drunkenness, no participation in the evening song and dance fests of the taure'are'a, active participation in church activities, and no sex outside of marriage. After a couple of months the aspirants are presented for a public examination conducted by the deacons; having passed this, they take their first communion and become *etaretia* — communicant church members. A few young married persons — especially men — lose their communicant status after a few months or years. They find the sobriety and community responsibility required of them confining, and revert to the carefree taure'are'a way of life in many of its aspects (although they do appear to remain faithful to their spouses). For most people, however, marriage and the assumption of communicant membership mark the shift to adulthood and responsible citizenship.

For its part of the contract, society places its stamp of recognition and approval on the marriage partnership, to the extent that the couple becomes more like one social unit than two individuals. The clearest symbol of this merger is the calling of both husband and wife by the same marriage name. Society also pledges its full opposition to anyone or anything that threatens to dissolve the union.

The weight of society's sanction is distinctly seen in the question of sexual infidelity. Except for efforts to bring a couple to marriage through the Pilgrimage, society gives no official recognition to liaisons not legitimized by marriage. Should one of the partners desert the other for a new lover, it is the concern of no one but the individuals involved. But adultery on the part of married persons is very much a public matter. One of the spouses has broken the contract with society, and society takes punitive action. A common step is moral indignation, which may attain the point of ostracism. For example, the song about the old woman and her great-grandchildren who discovered a couple in the act of adultery, mentioned above, ridicules the couple and is thus a form of social condemnation. In this case the couple was so shamed they left Rapa for good. In other words, the sanctions of ridicule and indignation can be strong enough to expel wrongdoers from society.

In dealing with adultery, society often brings in reinforcements from the Divinity. Some years ago a congregating point for crews of ships calling at Rapa was the house of a government functionary. A young married woman used to go there when a ship was in the harbor to make, she said, a little money washing and ironing the seamen's clothes; in fact, her earnings came not from laundry but from prostitution. This flagrant violation of the sanctity of marriage is thought to have caused her death. Her abdomen began to swell, much like a pregnancy. She became seriously ill as the swelling continued until, horribly bloated, she died. Her last words were a confession of her sin. The pastor recalled that she had taken communion shortly before she fell ill. "This is God's work!" he cried. "He caused the communion bread to swell inside her and kill her in punishment for her sin."

The marriage contract is taken seriously, and Rapan unions tend to be stable. Within the memory of my informants there has never been a divorce in Rapa, although this is more an index of their disinclination to go through the complicated and costly legal process of divorce than it is of the stability of marriage. When

130

marriages break up, the spouses simply separate permanently, but this is a rare occurrence. Of the forty marriages where at least one spouse currently resides in Rapa, only three have been broken by separation, and one of these involved an American who deserted his Rapan wife and left the island within a year after their marriage. The period of premarital cohabitation probably insures that incompatible mates seldom marry.

SECONDARY UNIONS

Death is the one predator against which all the safeguards upholding the marriage contract are of no avail. Death of the spouse appears to carry more finality for women than for men. Thus, of the thirteen widows in my sample, nine have remained celibate, while all but one of the seven widowers have remarried or are living with concubines. This situation is due chiefly to a preponderance of women in the population.[3] Females may have a longer life expectancy than males, and more important, men tend to take jobs as sailors or to emigrate to Tahiti in search of the paid labor and greater excitement found there. Only one man over forty-five is currently living without a wife or concubine, while at least eighteen women in that age category are celibate.

A widower or widow is normally supported by his or her children. But if the individual has no mature children living in Rapa, life can be hard. The tasks required for subsistence are numerous enough, and the sexual division of labor sharp enough, that a single man or woman is economically incomplete, having neither the time nor the skills to do all jobs. Furthermore, a person desires companionship, and if not elderly, craves the fulfillment of having children and a normal sex life. For all these reasons, after the year of mourning demanded by custom, the widowed individual often seeks a new mate.

The proper remarriage for a widower is to marry his wife's sister, and for a widow to marry her husband's brother. Remar-

[3] Since my sample (86 percent of the population) is not complete, I cannot give the exact proportions of the sexes in the population of 1964. In 1956, however, the official census shows Rapa's population of 279 to have been composed of 116 males and 163 females.

riages of this sort are known as sororate and levirate. Only two widowed individuals in the sample have remarried, one by levirate and the other by sororate. Five other widowers and three widows are currently cohabiting in unions not formalized by marriage. My information is not complete on this point, but I believe that in few (if any) of these cases is the new mate a brother or sister of the deceased spouse.

In discussing the preference for levirate and sororate, one informant characterized these forms of marriage as a "sacrifice." She explained how a woman, approaching death, might call an unmarried sister to her side and ask that she marry her husband. In doing so, this informant said, the new wife makes a sacrifice for the welfare of her deceased sister's children. Other informants did not mention the element of sacrifice, but nearly all of them stressed that sororate and levirate are for the sake of the children. Rapans say that the relationship between stepparents and stepchildren is potentially filled with unhappiness. Unlike the Western view (if folktales like "Cinderella" are any indication), the difficulty stems not so much from cruelty by the stepparent as from the hostility and resentment of the stepchildren. Sororate and levirate are the ideal forms of remarriage because this difficulty is avoided. From the children's point of view, if their father marries their deceased mother's sister, he does not bring a stranger into the home as their stepmother. He brings someone whom, by their classificatory kinship system, they have always called "mother" and whom they have always loved and treated very much like their own mother. The situation is the same for levirate — when their widowed mother marries their father's brother.

Rapan expectations of difficulty between stepparents and stepchildren are borne out by the following episode. One afternoon loud screaming erupted in one part of the village. I ran quickly over and saw Hina, a young woman in her mid-twenties, lying on the grass sobbing, her face streaked with tears and dirt, her long hair disheveled. People were streaming in from all directions to see what was happening. She was crying, "Papa! Papa!" and saying something about his "new woman." This went on for a few minutes, until her boyfriend gently helped her up and led her away, still sobbing. I was told later that her mother had died about five years ago, and her father had taken a concubine shortly thereafter. This woman is not a close relative of the deceased wife, and Hina had never gotten along with her. One of their family arguments had occurred that afternoon, and apparently Hina broke down because her father had struck her. As a result of this episode, Hina left her father's household.[4] During the course of the study she changed her household membership several times, leaving her father's household when relations with his concubine deteriorated to the breaking point and returning when their anger cooled.

[4] Hina formed a new household with her cousin, a young woman with a similar problem in that she could not get along with her widowed mother's lover.

CHAPTER SEVEN

Social Dynamics
of the Household

Most simply stated, the Rapan household is a group of kinsmen who have banded together for the joint production and consumption of food. This statement is full of implications, many of which have been pursued already. The production of food implies a series of economic tasks allocated among certain kinds of people (males, females, young, old, etc.) and carried out by certain techniques. The fact that household members are kinsmen implies that they are expected to treat one another in certain ways. The broadest implication of all is that within the economic purpose and the kinship structure of the household live real people, coexisting in intimate daily contact.

HOUSEHOLD COMPOSITION

Rapans define the household as the group of people who habitually eat in the same cookhouse. The work of household members is coordinated by its head, who is usually the senior active male.

The population of 362 is distributed among 54 households, for an average of 6.7 persons per household. The island's smallest household contains a pair of spouses; the largest has 15 members. Many households consist of a single elementary family, while others are composed of extended families. Some of the extended family households have an elementary family as the core, with a parent, sibling, or other kinsman of one of the spouses attached. The larger ones consist basically of two or three elementary families linked by ties of kinship. Representatives of most basic types of extended family households found in Rapa are diagrammed in Figure 4.

Rapans much prefer large extended family households containing several adults and youths. People pointed to Parima's household (diagrammed in Figure 4) as the ideal. This is the largest household on the island, and eight of its fifteen members are over the age of eighteen. The reason for this preference is that one eats better in a large household than in a small one.

Why this is so is partly — but only partly — an economic matter. As will be recalled from the discussion of subsistence economy and technology, the tasks required to keep a household fed are many and varied: taro must be cultivated, firewood cut, oranges and bananas occasionally gathered. Since distant treks over the mountains are often necessary, any one of these jobs can take a a day. Fish spoil within two to four days, depending on the season, so men try to go fishing several times a week. An elementary family household simply does not have the personnel to do all these jobs at once, especially when someone is temporarily ill, or if the wife is tied down caring for infants and small children. Some tasks must be postponed, which means that occasionally the household is short of food. Normally enough taro is kept on hand, but there are days when fish is lacking. Since fish is the most prized of all foods, to be without it is deplorable, and more fortunate people sometimes refer to those households that lack fish frequently as *veve*, "poverty-stricken."

Large households work more efficiently. To return to Parima's household, in it there are four males and four females available for full-time subsistence work. With a labor force of this size, one or

FIGURE 4   SOME EXTENDED FAMILY HOUSEHOLDS*

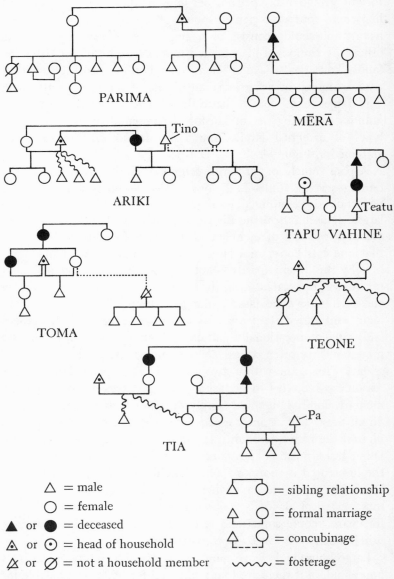

PARIMA

MĒRĀ

Tino

ARIKI

TAPU VAHINE

Teatu

TOMA

TEONE

TIA

Pa

△ = male   △   ○ = sibling relationship

○ = female

▲ or ● = deceased   △   ○ = formal marriage

⊿ or ⊙ = head of household   △___○ = concubinage

⊘ or ⊘ = not a household member   〰〰〰 = fosterage

*The name of the household head appears in capitals under each diagram.

136

two women can be at home to look after the infants, wash clothes, and prepare the meals; others can work in the taro terraces; one or two men can join them, or gather firewood, or go fishing; and a couple of men are free to engage in paid public-works labor or to work on building a new canoe, boat, or house. Thus large households can easily secure enough fish and other food for their needs, and are far better equipped to take on special jobs as well.

Having enough food is only part of eating well. The meaning of food was discussed in Chapter 4: how the Rapan image of the good life is painted in terms of food; how they are most relaxed and jovial in its presence. If food uplifts their spirits, it is axiomatic that the more people who share it, the greater their pleasure. A large household is not only more efficient than a small one, but it is also more fun. As one woman explained, "The food tastes better when many people eat together." In the cookhouse, the focal point of the household, its members find their greatest pleasure in one another. The most satisfying hour of the day is after the evening meal, when their work is finished and they are *pa'ia* (full). They sit on the straw floor in the glow of a kerosene lamp, smoke cigarettes, and recount the day's experiences, dwelling with rich laughter on the humorous incidents. Small children are passed from lap to lap, or urged to dance to the clapping of hands and mirth of their elders. These periods are particularly satisfying in large households. Walking through the village in the evening one hears only a quiet murmur of voices from the small cookhouses, and their occupants hope some visitor will stop in and add a little variety. In large households there is lively conversation and outbursts of laughter. When Rapans express their preference for large households, they refer at least as much to occasions such as these as to their efficiency.

However, large extended family households are in the definite minority. Working at cross-purposes to the advantages of a large household is the primary commitment to one's own elementary family. The first concern of youths, who do most of the heavy labor, is for their own parents and siblings, as opposed to cousins, aunts and uncles who may also belong to the household. As they grow older, youths who would accept orders gladly from a parent begin to chafe under the authority of an aunt or uncle. The ties of the elementary family itself loosen with the passage of time. Those with parents remain always strong, but when youths begin families of their own, the bonds between siblings weaken as primary concern shifts to their spouses and children. When the spouse of a young household member joins the group, the seeds of discord are often sown. The spouse is tau'ate (same sex sibling-in-law) to some members of the household and child-in-law to others, and these relationships are problematic. Conflicts of interest between the in-marrying spouse and his or her affines can push their distant and restrained relationship (which is uncomfortable in itself) into outright hostility. Seeking to achieve the Rapan expectation that a man is master of his family, a young husband wants to make the decisions concerning how he, his wife and their children shall live. If they reside with his own family this can at times be difficult; if living with his wife's family, he feels his authority and initiative are usurped daily and he resents it. An in-marrying wife is anxious that her husband devote his attention more to her and their children than to his parents and siblings. For such reasons, as a household moves through time, cleavages between its component elementary families develop and deepen. Once suspicion sets in that one elementary family is benefiting at the expense of another, the resentment and friction intensify and become self-perpetuating. Directives of the household head are followed grudgingly if at all, cooperation evaporates, and petty quarrels flare up easily. Economic efficiency is replaced by disorganization, and pleasure in one another's company gives way to irritation. When a household reaches this point it usually splits.

FISSION AND FUSION

Since these tensions develop over time, household fission is a process rather than an event. While the moment they cease eating together can be taken as the critical point, the entire process may take several years. Several of the households diagrammed in Figure 4 are in various stages of fission. Young in-marrying husbands live in both Tia's and Tapu Vahine's households. Men

138

often feel their authority over wife and children is compromised when they live with their wives' families, and this is producing fission in these two households. Pā was building a new cookhouse for his family when I left Rapa, so the split in Tia's household was imminent. In Tapu Vahine's household, Teatu and his wife were expecting their first child and making vague plans to move to his home village. Teatu supports his decrepit 'grandmother,' who is nearly blind, and brought her with him to Tapu Vahine's household after his marriage. (When I entered their house one day, the old woman chuckled mischievously and said, "I smell a white man." Perhaps she can see better than she admits.) When they move, Teatu will take her with them. Finally, there is friction in Ariki's household. The widower Tino has recently brought a new mistress and her three children into the household, which has occasioned general indignation since she and Tino are first cousins. Relations between Tino and Ariki have deteriorated as a result — relations already tenuous because the men are doubly linked in the difficult tau'ate (brother-in-law) relationship due to a sister-exchange marriage. Probably Tino will either have to get rid of his mistress, or take her and form a new household.

Household fission does not always mean one household splits into two or more new households. A single individual may join another household, as often happens when a member marries and becomes a part of his or her spouse's household. Even if an elementary family leaves, they may join another household rather than founding a new one. Relations may have become strained in one household, but because of the preference for large extended family households, the family hopes to make a better go of it with someone else. Therefore, when considering the dynamics of the Rapan household, fusion must be taken into account as well as fission. To give an idea of the frequency of inter-household movements, 22 percent of the people over the age of five in my sample changed their household affiliations at least once during the five years preceding the study.

To come close to the realities of household dynamics, we shall trace how fission and fusion intertwined the histories of several Ha'urei households during the latter half of 1964. This story has no proper beginning or end; it is simply a slice lifted arbitrarily from the continuous stream of Rapan social life. Some of the circumstances and motivations leading to household fission are typical and tend to recur, while others are rare or even unique. Like almost any aspect of life in Rapa, this story cannot be understood without a knowledge of the kinship ties involved. The various households are diagrammed in Figure 5 as they were about May 1964, immediately before the movements to be described. It will be remembered that married persons are called by their marriage name: Parima's wife is Parima Vahine, Manu's wife is Manu Vahine, and so on.

The first shift occurred about June, when the young couple Teva and Teva Vahine left Rua's household to join that of Amo. Teva is from the island of Rimatara, like Rapa a member of the Austral chain. He met and married his wife in Tahiti a year before. (Teva Vahine is the girl whose father sent her to Tahiti expressly to find a husband, in order to prevent her marriage to the Rapan boy Noa, of whom he disapproved.) Since their return to Rapa they had lived in the household of her parents, Rua and Rua Vahine. In spite of the norm that the relationship between parents and children should be the most solidary and affectionate of all, Teva Vahine had many violent arguments with her parents. This discord and the decision to leave were probably due in large measure to recurrent rumors that her father was engaged in an incestuous affair with her sister. Teva is a distant kinsman of Amo through the latter's maternal grandmother who was from Rimatara, and on this basis they joined his household. This case of fusion was only temporary since Teva Vahine is the school teacher in 'Area; they moved to that village in August in preparation for the beginning of the school year. (Mere, another of Rua's daughters, also left his household because of the rumored incest. She joined the household of Tini, the kin connection being that Tini Vahine is Mere's mother's half-sister's daughter.)

Amo's and Manu's households were originally merged; Amo and his wife lived virilocally (the wife moved to join the husband), while Manu and his wife lived uxorilocally (the husband

FIGURE 5   HOUSEHOLD DYNAMICS*

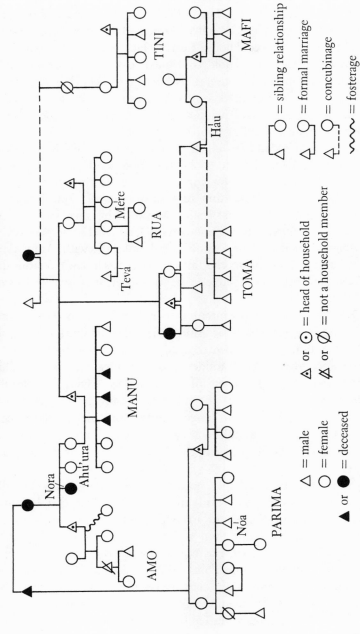

= sibling relationship
= formal marriage
= concubinage
= fosterage

△ = male
○ = female
▲ or ● = deceased

△ or ⊙ = head of household
⧄ or ⊘ = not a household member

*The name of the household head appears in capitals under each diagram.

141

moved to join the wife). The critical point of fission had occurred six or seven years earlier when Amo and his elementary family established a new cookhouse nearby. However, up to June 1964, members of each household continued to sleep in separate rooms of the same masonry house. This house had been built by Amo's father, and was inherited jointly by Amo and his sisters. A few years before, Amo had made a cement floor in his room, while Manu's room had a dirt floor covered with straw. In late August one of Manu's children fell ill, so the members of his household decided to sleep in their cookhouse in order to keep the child warm near the fire and for convenience in heating medicines for him during the night. Amo took advantage of their temporary absence and, without first telling Manu or his own sister, Manu Vahine, he filled Manu's room with large rocks, preparatory to laying a concrete floor. Manu could not talk with Amo about this because they are in the tau'ate (brothers-in-law) relationship which demands considerable restraint, especially in situations such as this.

But to Manu, Amo's intent was unmistakable. As one woman told me, "It was just as if Amo had said, 'Get out!' " Although Manu Vahine is part owner of the house, consistent with the preference for virilocal residence is the idea that sons should have prior use rights over inherited houses. Living uxorilocally, Manu was a stranger in the house and now he was convinced that his wife's brother no longer wanted him there. Manu began to make plans to establish a new household for his family in his own neighborhood, near the households of his brother and sister.

About this time, Manu's household was enlarged by the addition of his sister's son Hau and his wife. This couple moves frequently from household to household, unable to get along with anyone for more than a year but unwilling to set up a household of their own. For much of 1963 they had belonged to Toma's household, for Toma Vahine is Hau's mother. Hau Vahine was unhappy there, largely because Hau's four sons by a previous mistress are members of that household. As is often true of such relationships, a mutual dislike exists between Hau Vahine and her four stepsons. This was the main reason why, in early 1964, Hau and his wife left Toma's household for that of Mafi, Hau Vahine's brother and the local head of public works. With her own kinsmen, Hau Vahine was happy enough, but Hau found himself surrounded by affines, and his life became more complicated. Hau's relations with his brother-in-law Mafi had always been strained, as is common between tau'ate, and in July they reached the breaking point. At this time the construction of a more elaborate weather station was begun in Rapa to be used, among other things, in connection with the French nuclear tests at Mururoa. A few members of the Foreign Legion arrived to supervise the construction, and they needed a native foreman to act as translator, to arrange worker-rotation so that all would have an equal opportunity for this paid labor, and to help as paymaster. Mafi was anxious to secure the extra salary accompanying this position and thought that as public works head he should have it, although he speaks no French. But the job went to Hau, who speaks some French and shows intelligence. Mafi's jealousy and resentment accelerated the process of fission in his household, and in August Hau and his wife joined Manu's household.

Thus, at the beginning of September, affairs stood as follows: Amo was still making his cement floor in Manu's sleeping room; Teva and his wife had moved from Amo's household to 'Area for the opening of school; Hau and his wife had recently joined Manu's household, which was still located in Manu Vahine's neighborhood and whose members were sleeping in their cookhouse, but planning to relocate the household in Manu's neighborhood. On September 14 the worst hurricane in memory struck Rapa and raged for the greater part of a week. 'Area was relatively sheltered in the lee of a ridge, but Ha'urei took the storm's full force. One pandanus cookhouse was crushed by a falling tree, and a few others caved in. Most hazardous are corrugated iron roofs which may be ripped from the houses and can cause considerable damage. During the storm, food ran short and the people were literally paralyzed with fear. They huddled together in large groups in the best-built houses. Several families left the village altogether, trekking across the rain-swept mountains to the outer bays where they waited out the gale safe from the flying debris of the village. Among these were the families of Amo and Manu. Returning to Ha'urei after the hurricane, Amo and Manu found that both their cookhouses had been nearly destroyed. With no place to eat, both of them temporarily fused their households with that of Parima, a first cousin of Amo and Manu Vahine. (Parima's household was already the largest in Rapa with fifteen members. These additions increased it to an unheard of twenty-seven.) However, Hau and his wife did not go with Manu's household to Parima's, perhaps because neither was closely related to any member of that household. They ate in the ruins of Manu's cookhouse and slept in the masonry house belonging to Amo and Manu Vahine, in a small room where the new floor had been finished.

The terror Rapans confessed having during the hurricane was replaced by numb immobility in its aftermath. Only the arrival of a French ship carrying medicine, food, clothing, blankets and building materials caused them slowly to turn to the task of reconstruction. The destroyed houses were rebuilt by large cooperative work groups organized by the District Council, and gradually, in a process not totally completed upon my departure two months after the hurricane, life returned to normal.

Amo's family left Parima's household in October. One reason was that Teva and his wife (the 'Area schoolteacher) desired to return to Ha'urei and stay in Amo's household during the period that school was disrupted after the hurricane, and later for weekends and vacations. This return was not possible while Amo's family was in Parima's household because Teva Vahine's previous lover Noa belonged to that household. Moreover, the episode of the concrete floor made it difficult for Amo and Manu to live in the same household. Finally, Amo Vahine became cantankerous while they were in Parima's household, and complained to her husband that they always associate more with his relatives than hers. After about a month of nagging, Amo reluctantly agreed to leave Parima's household and move in with his wife's sister. However, he then accelerated repairs on their own cookhouse, and in a week or two they returned to their own household.

The hurricane was catastrophic for Manu's family. On their flight from the village at the height of the storm, their only surviving son, a child of about two, caught pneumonia and died. The blow was doubly crushing because in November 1963 they had lost two other sons within the space of a week during an epidemic started by a visiting ship. At the funeral of his last son, Manu impressed me as a man of immense courage. After the burial the mourners gathered in Parima's house for coffee, hymn singing and a Bible discussion; the verse chosen for interpretation was John 14:15 — "If you love me, you will keep my commandments." The closest kin of the deceased are usually too overcome with grief to speak on these occasions. But after several persons had grappled with the verse, Manu rose . . . Manu, whose house lay in ruins and who had buried that day the last of his four sons. He said that man is weak, a sinner, that we do not keep God's commandments precisely because we do not love him, but that God loves us so much that, despite our sins, he saves us by his mercy and grace. I do not think he was merely parroting the pat phrases of his Protestant upbringing. These struck me as the words of a man with profound faith in a God of love and goodness, faith so strong that even the loss of his four sons, three of them within the space of a single year, could not shake it. That night I noted in my journal that Manu is a Rapan Job.

However, their son's death had drained much vitality from Manu and his wife, who went listlessly, mechanically, about their daily tasks. Although their new house had been built in late September, when I left in mid-November they were still living in Parima's household and seemed to lack the strength to establish their new home. Meanwhile, Hau and his wife were eating in the ruins of Manu's former cookhouse, waiting to fuse with Manu's household when he should decide to move.

To complete this story of household dynamics a few words must be said about the two middle-aged sisters of Amo and Manu Vahine: Ahu'ura and Nora. Neither had married. Nora was a total cripple and had no children; Ahu'ura's one son, about twenty, lived in Tahiti, and his father had long since left her. When Amo made his separate cookhouse, these two sisters remained in Manu's household. In her grief at the death of her two sons in 1963, Manu Vahine somehow concluded that her sister Ahu'ura had wanted the boys to die. Finding life intolerable in Manu's household, Ahu'ura joined Amo's household. Then, in April 1964, her crippled sister Nora died. Her funeral was the briefest and least elaborate possible; the only expression of regret I heard was that now Manu Vahine would have to iron her family's clothes herself. As Manu Vahine's unjust accusation against Ahu'ura had been forgotten by then, she returned to Manu's household to help with the funeral preparations and to take up the slack in labor left by Nora's death.

After the hurricane, Ahu'ura came with Manu's family to Parima's household. In accordance with his intention to relocate in a virilocal setting, Manu's new house was built in a neighborhood inhabited by his own close kinsmen. Ahu'ura and her sister Manu Vahine were distracted at the prospect of leaving their own neighborhood and kinsmen for a strange place where they would be surrounded by affines. Although the new site was no more than a hundred yards from their former residence, they wept and grieved as if they were to be taken to the ends of the earth. Manu Vahine argued, cajoled, and pleaded with her husband to change his mind, and even Amo expressed sadness that his sister was being taken away. All this fell on deaf ears. Manu had not forgotten Amo's behavior in the episode of the cement floor, and furthermore he confessed that their previous residence reminded him too acutely of his lost sons. Angered at her insistence, he told his wife that she could live where she pleased, but he would never return to their former neighborhood. Manu Vahine was not prepared to see her marriage destroyed, and since a husband has authority over his wife and children, she had no choice but to comply with his decision. Ahu'ura was not so irrevocably committed to Manu's elementary family. In Manu's neighborhood she would be only the sister of an inmarrying wife, and this distant tie would not lead most persons to feel any special affection or responsibility for her. Therefore, consulting with her 'brother' Parima, she decided that when Manu and his family left for their new residence she would remain in her own neighborhood among her own people as a member of Parima's household.

Persons of middle age or older such as Ahu'ura and Nora live tenuously in Rapa. Lacking spouses and children to be concerned for their welfare, they are simply appendages to the household. As attention turns more to children and descendents, the bond between siblings loosens, so no one feels strong responsibility for childless adults. Especially as they grow older they are taken into a household more as a favor than because of the benefits derived from their membership. Such individuals act almost servile to more firmly entrenched household members, even to children, and they take a considerable amount of abuse. As in Manu Vahine's treatment of Ahu'ura upon the death of the former's sons, childless adults may serve as convenient scapegoats with little power of retribution. Hence they move rather frequently from one household to another, seeking to better their condition.

FOSTERAGE

Childless persons are not automatically doomed to the fate of Nora and Ahu'ura. As young adults they usually take foster children, partly as an insurance measure against want in old age. Rapans call a foster child *tamari'i fa'a'amu*, or "feeding child." (Here is further evidence of the significance of food in this culture. We normally say foster parents *raise* a child; Rapans say they *feed* him.) Fosterage is frequent in Rapa: 52 percent of the individuals in the sample have foster parents.

Before, or immediately after, the birth of a child an individual or couple may ask its parents for rights of fosterage. If the request is granted, the child is taken to its foster home upon weaning, which may occur anywhere from about ten months to two years. Ideally, the child is raised to adulthood in its foster household. The foster parents love, care for, and in daily life have authority over the child as if he were their own, and the child behaves toward them as to his own parents. Ultimate authority over the child, however, remains with his parents. They may dissolve the relationship and take the child back if they have reason to believe he is being mistreated. Foster parents do not legally

147

recognize the child; therefore the child affiliates to property-owning ramages through his parents (provided they have recognized him), but not through his foster parents. If the relationship has been a satisfactory one, Rapans usually leave a few taro terraces and/or coffee groves from their personal estate to foster children, but are under no obligation to do so.

Nearly always one of the foster parents is a close kinsman of one of the biological parents, such as a sibling or parent. People often foster children of their favorite relatives; to foster a child is one means of expressing special fondness for his parent. One minor element in fosterage, then, is the alliance between parents and foster parents. This, however, usually intensifies a relationship that is already strong, rather than establishing a new one.

Fosterage is a direct bond between foster parents and children; the relationship does not extend collaterally. Should foster parents also have children of their own, for example, no new relationship is created between them and their parents' foster children (who are often resented by the biological children, since they dislike sharing parental affection and property with them). After the parents have died, children on a few occasions have confiscated property left to foster children. Judicious persons usually transfer ownership of those taro terraces and coffee groves destined for foster children long before death is anticipated. This allows the foster children to become firmly entrenched in ownership and minimizes the chance of confiscation by the children.

The first reasons Rapans give when asked why they foster children are those of sentiment. Since they derive great pleasure from the presence of children, fosterage allows childless couples to fill this void in their lives. Older people miss small children, and their desire to bring them back into the household, coupled with their indulgent affection for grandchildren, explains in large part the frequent fosterage of grandchildren. Some couples have so many children that they have difficulty caring for them. Less fertile kinsmen with greater resources foster some of them, both out of sympathy for the parents and concern for the children's welfare.

Beyond these considerations, fosterage is an economic contract. The foster parents assume the obligation to raise the child, and the child is thereby placed under the reciprocal obligation to support his foster parents in their old age. Rapans who were raised in a foster household accept this obligation as fully as they do that to support their own aged parents. Largely for this reason, childless couples such as Teone and his wife (see Figure 4, page 136) are especially active in establishing fosterage relationships. To foster grandchildren also has economic value, for occasionally an individual outlives all his children. If one has fostered grandchildren, their obligation of support is doubled. For example, the old woman in Mērā's household (also diagrammed in Figure 4) is supported by her grandson, whom she fostered, now that all her own children are dead.

The strength of the obligation on persons to support their aged foster parents depends on how much of their childhood was actually spent in the foster household. Ideally they remain there permanently after weaning, but in fact there is a great deal of movement on the part of children between parental and foster households. Children who do not especially like their foster parents spend little time in their household, and later feel little responsibility to support them. Therefore childless couples usually foster five or six children to be sure of keeping one or two long enough to insure the security of their later years.

An intriguing aspect of fosterage is that the child himself decides where he will live. Should he get tired of his foster household he goes to live with his parents for a few weeks, months, or years. Then, on a new whim, he returns to his foster home. Referring to Figure 5, page 141, Parima's elder daughter, a little girl of about eight years, is a foster child of Amo. During 1964 she moved between the two households twice. It is considered proper that a child remain in the foster household, and both parents and foster parents often urge him to do so. But the final decision is the child's. It is amusing to watch foster parents — and sometimes parents if they sorely miss him — entice a small child of two or three with promises of all sorts of good things to eat and perhaps even balloons to play with if he comes to live with them. Very likely, leaving the decision to the child serves to avert friction between parents and foster parents.

RELATIONS BETWEEN HOUSEHOLDS

While the household is the primary economic unit, on numerous occasions members of different households band together in co-operative ventures. One idiom expressing such joint effort is kinship. Should a household be in economic difficulty, or be engaged in building a new house or boat, close kinsmen from other households come to lend a hand. Spatial proximity is another basis for inter-household cooperation. Whether linked by close ties of kinship or not, Rapans say that households in the same neighborhood should freely aid one another when needed.

When discussing relations between households, it is necessary to distinguish between 'Area and Ha'urei. 'Area is much the smaller of Rapa's two villages, with a population of 100 as opposed to 260 for Ha'urei. Village solidarity and pride are markedly stronger in 'Area. Should someone in Ha'urei build a new house or boat, for example, only close kinsmen, neighbors and friends come to help; in 'Area every man in the village devotes as much time to the project as he can. Briefly stated, in Ha'urei cooperation between households is sporadic; in 'Area it is a way of life.

Except for Ariki's fourteen-member operation (see Figure 4), 'Area's sixteen households are small. Each is limited to a single elementary family, sometimes including a parent or foster parent of one of the spouses. The lack of efficiency of small households is overcome in 'Area by formal cooperation between households, structured on a village-wide basis and according to subdivisions. The backbone of cooperation in 'Area is the *pupu:* a work group within which the participating units are households. In some years, all households in the village band together in a single work group; in other years there are two, or three, as in 1964. All but three 'Area households belong to one or another of these three groups. Ideally, each participating household contributes two members to the group — one man and one woman. The entire group works one day, in rotation, for each of its member house-

Top, *shaping the hull for an outrigger canoe;* bottom, *launching a new whaleboat — a momentous occasion.*

holds. The man from that household directs the group for that day and it does any job he desires, such as planting taro, gathering coffee, bringing in firewood, bananas or oranges, and so on. Often he will divide the group into sections for different jobs. Sometimes the men are engaged in special work, e.g., when a house or boat is being built in the village, or when the Public Works undertakes some large project (such as building a school) which involves paid labor. On such occasions the female portion of the work group continues the cycle alone.

The 'Area work groups function from mid-January to mid-December. The last few weeks of one year and the first week of the next are filled with preparing for and holding the elaborate church New Year's festival, and the annual meetings held by the Rapa Cooperative Society and various voluntary associations. Some groups work five days a week, Monday through Friday, while others are organized on the basis of a four-day week and do not function on Fridays. Friday is a special day in the weekly cycle, devoted to bringing taro and firewood into the household for the weekend. Those groups which work on Fridays try to stop around noon to free their members for these tasks. It should be noted, incidentally, that most households arrange it so there is at least one worker who is not involved in these groups, who is free at all times to do any jobs the household may require.

The three work groups in 'Area were defined geographically and termed the *pupu 'i tai* (seaward), *pupu 'i rōpū* (central), and *pupu 'i 'uta* (inland). The orientation refers not to Ha'urei Bay but to the open sea, located about a half-mile east of the village. Kinship ties link a number of the households in the seaward and inland groups, but Rapans say these work groups are organized on a geographical basis. The inland group includes five households located in the western half of the village, and the seaward group consists of five households in the eastern half. The central work group is composed of three households located in the middle of 'Area, plus three more from Ha'urei. This group is organized more in terms of kinship than geography. Briefly, two of the households in this group are headed by a pair of elderly sisters;

152

their grown sons and daughters head the other four households of the work group.

As noted previously, one of the major problems in a small household is to maintain a steady supply of fish. In the warm season when they spoil rapidly a man would have to go fishing every day or two if his household were to eat fish daily — an impossibility in a small household where the one or two male workers have too many other jobs they must perform. In 'Area the work groups solve this problem. Almost every day that the group works, it sends one or two men fishing. Their catch is divided among the participating households, and shares are also given to the three 'Area households which do not belong to work groups. In line with the intense rivalry between the two villages, the people of 'Area relish comparing their generosity in fish-sharing with the selfish habits of Ha'urei. Even if only one or two 'Area men go fishing on a particular day, they told me, the catch is distributed among all the households in the village. Their idea is that if anyone in the village has fish, everyone should have it. Informants emphasized that the fisherman does not first take all the fish his own household can use, but that the distribution is equal among all households even if each receives but half of a fish. (I did observe a very equitable and far-reaching fish distribution in 'Area, striking in its contrast to the situation in Ha'urei. Yet, in describing some of the most generous and finest points of this system, my informants may have stretched the truth somewhat in their eagerness to impress me with the merits of life in 'Area.)

In Ha'urei, cooperation between households consists largely of aid in difficult periods, sharing fish, assistance in house- or boat-building for the men, and groups of women who make popoi together or cooperate in baking in a single earth oven. As in 'Area, such forms of mutual aid rest on the principles of kinship and the neighborhood. Households most closely connected by kinship are often in the same neighborhood because siblings and other close kin tend to live near each other. Yet, since close ties are retained with near kinsmen who have moved away to join their spouses, a household often cooperates with others well outside its neighborhood.

Village solidarity and mutual aid between households are not nearly as pronounced in Ha'urei as in 'Area. A good index of the general difference, both in attitude and in practice, is found in fish-sharing. There is no idea in Ha'urei that fish should be distributed throughout the village. A Ha'urei man first extracts from his catch all the fish his own household can use before they spoil, and then he distributes the excess among other households, the number of households included depending on the size of the catch. He ranks these households in priority, those at the top receiving fish from him frequently and those at the bottom only when he has a great many extra fish. The ranking in fish exchange is diagnostic of the general strength of cooperative ties between Ha'urei households. I studied the fish-sharing hierarchy of five or six households in Ha'urei, and found that each exchanges excess fish with from three to eight other households. Invariably, nearby households belonging to close kinsmen are at the top of the list. After these, some informants gave preference to unrelated neighbors, and others listed close kin residing some distance away. This variation can be explained largely in terms of how well members of the relevant households get along.

Mutual aid between households need not be strictly symmetrical. Successful households often take the responsibility of aiding those in their neighborhoods and/or of their kinsmen which, for reasons of lack of adequate personnel in the labor force, have difficulty securing their subsistence. In such cases there is no expectation of full reciprocity. However, hardship cases such as these are usually placed low on the priority list for fish distribution, and presumably other forms of assistance are not frequent either.

Pupu occasionally operate in Ha'urei. They are organized like the 'Area groups: each participating household ideally contributes two members, and the whole group works a day for each of these households in turn. Ha'urei groups are usually organized among three to five households which aid one another informally in matters such as fish exchange. Whereas membership in a work group is the normal state of affairs for an 'Area household, it is somewhat of a novelty for households in Ha'urei. Here the motivation seems to be to infuse a little variety into economic life: to have the fun of working in a larger group and to be able to order people around on the day when the group works for one's own household. Many work groups in Ha'urei dissolve after a few months' operation. While they appear to come and go in fads, probably no more than one-fourth or one-fifth of the households in Ha'urei are involved in work groups at most times.

The work groups discussed thus far are general-purpose groups; they do any jobs required by the household whose day it happens to be. Occasionally special-purpose work groups are formed. In 1956 or 1957 Rapa enjoyed a bumper coffee crop, exceeding by several times the normal yield. Many households in Ha'urei banded together in a pupu that totaled thirty-eight members — the largest work group in memory. This group did nothing but harvest coffee. Four foremen were elected in the organizational meeting, and each evening they consulted with the group member who was to benefit from the morrow's work. The entire group might work together, or be divided into as many as four subgroups (each under a foreman) to work in different groves. The person for whom the group worked decided which groves were to be harvested on his day, but the actual work was under the supervision of the elected foremen.

The major value of this work group was that it was great fun. Rapans say in general that work is lighter and more fun when done in groups. The sight of so much coffee (representing a great increase over their normal cash income) put them in high spirits, and harvesting it in a large company redoubled their pleasure. The group swept through a grove like an army of ants, picking up every coffee bean in sight. People competed for the reputation of being the fastest worker. Joking remarks were shouted back and forth that so-and-so was loafing or perhaps had crept off for a few moments of dalliance with one of the women. The foremen stalked along the line urging greater speed; one woman laughingly told me when someone wanted to smoke a cigarette he had to keep it in his lips all the time or the foreman would pelt him with sticks and pebbles for not working with both hands. One needed to be alert, for the tricksters would pour beans from someone else's bag into their own and then crow about how much more coffee they had gathered. This fondly-remembered work group operated for over two months, devoting two days work to each of its members.

Although solidarity runs high on special occasions such as this, in general, village and neighborhood cooperation is weaker in Ha'urei than in 'Area. One result is that small households find life harder in the larger village. If no one from the household goes fishing, it is probable that their supper will be limited to taro and coffee. Outside assistance in the construction of a house or boat is somewhat less likely to be forthcoming. An 'Area man proudly told me, "In our village we do everything together." By comparison, in Ha'urei each household essentially goes it alone.

CHAPTER EIGHT

The Village and the Island Community

VILLAGE RIVALRY, JULY 14, AND THE YOUTH CLUBS

One morning the news flashed through Ha'urei that a cow belonging to a woman of that village had been stabbed and was near death. It was found near some taro terraces cultivated by 'Area households. (Cattle sometimes get into taro terraces and tear them up badly, causing hot disputes between terrace owners and cattle owners.) The immediate conclusion reached by some in Ha'urei was that an 'Area man had found the cow in or near his terrace and had stabbed it in anger. "Isn't that just like an 'Area man?" opined some of my informants in Ha'urei. "Rapa would be a very nice place," they continued, "were it not for those scoundrels and thieves who live in 'Area."

Similarly, the iniquities of Ha'urei are a constant topic of conversation in 'Area. They rejoice in comparing their own customs of inter-household cooperation in work groups and fish-sharing with the Ha'urei practice of every household fending for itself.

Ha'urei people are depicted as mean and antisocial, unwilling to lift a finger unless it is of direct benefit to themselves.

Village rivalry attains its zenith on July 14, the French national holiday and Rapa's major secular festival. The most active organizations at this time are the *Pupu Taure'are'a,* or Youth Clubs; these are voluntary associations organized along village lines. For almost a week preceding July 14 the youths of Ha'urei defer work for their households and band together to prepare the holiday feast. The 13th is a flurry of activity. Under the direction of the club's elected officers firewood is stockpiled; taro is brought in and cooked; groups of young men bring strings of fish and crayfish; pigs, chickens and a cow are butchered; and the school is decorated for the feast. All of these activities are paralleled in 'Area, where the youths of that village prepare their rival feast.

Festivities begin in earnest the night of July 13. The youths disappear immediately after supper, and small children run to and fro scarcely able to contain their excitement. About 7:30 P.M. youths file from the schoolhouse, all wearing flower wreaths and the girls dressed in bright sarongs or grass skirts from Tahiti. Carrying colored Japanese lanterns and surrounded by a crowd of yelping children and smiling adults, the youths march to the house of the island chief. They circle the house two or three times, chanting and singing, and then group themselves before the front door. When the chief and other members of his household appear, the youths produce their guitars and drums and soon the densely packed area is filled with swaying bodies of dancers alternating between the gyrating Tahitian hula and the equally energetic Twist. After a few dances one of the Youth Club officers approaches the door with a hat and the chief makes a contribution ranging anywhere from two or three to ten or fifteen dollars. Glasses and a wine-filled pitcher are brought from within the house and the youths refresh themselves. With shouts of "Thank you, chief!" they form ranks and march away. From house to house they go, visiting the salaried functionaries (who can be expected to make substantial gifts) and community leaders. Each householder visited gives money, and wine if he has it. A sense of competition enlivens the evening, for a similar group of troubadors rows over from 'Area. The groups never dance at the same house simultaneously, but one often follows the other's heels. Each tries to outdo the other and draw away its crowd of spectators, who evaluate the two groups, comparing their dress and energy in dancing.

As the evening wears on, the ranks of the Youth Clubs become ragged. The strenuous dancing is exhausting, especially since their patrons like to make them work for the money. Instead of giving the cash in one lump they often give a dollar or so, and then call the youths back with another donation just as they are leaving. Each gift requires another dance in thanks, and the more mischievous donors evoke laughter from the spectators and groans from the youths when they call them back two or three times to dance for contributions as small as twenty or twenty-five cents. The boys had fortified themselves with homemade orange beer before beginning, and this plus the wine they are served takes its effect, augmenting the progressive disarray. By the end of the evening most of the boys have glazed eyes, garble their songs, and straggle behind the main group, snatching draughts from coffee pots filled with orange beer.

The morning of July 14 is devoted to athletic contests: boat and canoe races, foot races, and tugs of war for both men and women. To stimulate the observance of the national holiday, the French administration sends about a hundred dollars as prize money for these contests. Here competition is clearly drawn along village lines, and for several days preceding the 14th people discuss which village is likely to win the most prize money. Anticipating some of the underhanded tricks the 'Area people were likely to pull, one old Ha'urei woman called them *cochons* (pigs), one of her few French words. During the contests people cheer avidly for competitors from their village, and occasionally tempers flare and fistfights break out between rival participants and spectators.

The members of Ha'urei's Youth Club eat together around noon. In the early afternoon they call their guests to the lavish feast they have prepared. Numbering thirty-five or forty, the guests include the chief and members of the District Council, the pastor and church officials, school teachers and other salaried persons, and recognized community leaders. A similar feast is held in 'Area later in the afternoon, with much the same guest list. The Youth Clubs give their feasts as an expression of thanks to the community leaders, and speeches are made to this effect. Perhaps one might interpret this as gratitude on the part of the youths for being allowed to pursue their carefree and irresponsible way of life while the community leaders shoulder the burden of planning for the future and holding the society together.

During the afternoon there is also a soccer game between teams from the two villages, but most of the players are ineffectual because they are drunk. After the feast, members of the Youth Club clean up and remain in the schoolhouse until late at night, singing, dancing and consuming large quantities of orange beer. The festival ends on July 15, a day devoted to games and contests for the children.

The Youth Clubs are organized differently in the two villages, and these differences provide another example of 'Area's greater village solidarity. In Ha'urei the Youth Club is made up of most of that village's people who are in the taure'are'a stage of life. Members of the club form the group of troubadors who perform on the night of July 13, and they use the donations received then to pay for the cow and other expenses of the feast they give on the 14th. The situation is more complex in 'Area. That village has two separate Youth Clubs: the Youth Club — Everyone (*Pupu Taure'are'a — Hui Ra'atira*) and the Youth Club — Feast (*Pupu Taure'are'a — Tāma'ara'a*). The various activities connected with July 14 are divided between these two organizations.

The Youth Club — Everyone is the prime example of 'Area's village unity. Its name stems from the fact that virtually everyone in 'Area — adults and children as well as youths — belongs to it. Officers are normally adult village leaders rather than youths. This organization, which has no counterpart in Ha'urei, might have more aptly been named the 'Area Advancement Association, since its goal is simply to promote well-being in the village. Stated rather callously, beyond the fun it provides, the realists of 'Area view the July 14 festival as an opportunity to make some money.

160

They decided that this money could be used to benefit 'Area as a whole, and so the Youth Club — Everyone was founded largely to profit as much as possible from the national holiday. The two sources of cash in the festival are the donations for dancing on the night of July 13 and the prize money for contests on the 14th. This organization directs 'Area's efforts in both of these enterprises. The money earned by the dancers goes into the club's treasury; so does the prize money won by 'Area contestants. (Competitors from Ha'urei keep their prizes for themselves.) Moreover, 'Area makes every effort to ensure the greatest possible winnings: contestants in the various events do not participate in the preceding evening's revelry. They get a good night's sleep while their opponents from Ha'urei are up half the night and then run or row with hangovers (or are drunk with the free-flowing wine and beer of the 14th). The biggest prize money is awarded for the boat races, and 'Area devotes special preparations to these. Ha'urei people make up their crews immediately before the races, but 'Area crews are chosen beforehand for strength and balance and they train for several days before the race. In a rowing race, the boat itself makes a great deal of difference and the fastest boats had been in Ha'urei. In 1963, 'Area's Youth Club — Everyone turned the tables by building a new boat designed specifically for the July 14 races and used for little else. It belongs to the club, and is the narrowest, shortest and fastest boat on the island. After 'Area swept the men's and women's races, a Ha'urei man ruefully remarked the 'Area boat should have been entered in the canoe races.

The treasury of this Youth Club provides a source of capital to be borrowed by members in need of cash. If a sizable sum accumulates, a cash dividend is distributed among all members. Most frequently, however, the money is used to buy flour, sugar and other essentials directly from Tahiti, the goods being resold to 'Area people for prices lower than those charged by the Cooperative store.

'Area's Youth Club — Feast is in charge of the July 14 feast given in 'Area. Some adults and children also belong to this organization, but it is made up largely of youths and its officers are generally elected from this group. The expenses of the 'Area feast are met by dues collected from club members and contributions from the guests. The other function of this club is to aid in funerals. About three times a year each member contributes around twenty-five cents to the club's funeral fund, and whenever someone in a member's family dies, the club contributes about eight dollars to help defray expenses for the coffin and the dinner following the burial. In Ha'urei, a separate club exists for the sole purpose of maintaining a funeral fund.

ISLAND UNITY, NEW YEAR'S, AND THE CHURCH

At the opposite end of the calendar from July 14 stands New Year's — Rapa's other major festival. New Year's presents a contrast with July 14 in almost every respect. July 14 is secular, it belongs essentially to the youths, and it stimulates rivalry between the villages. New Year's is religious, it is basically the province of adults, and it puts stress on harmony between the villages. To understand New Year's in particular and the more harmonious aspects of the Rapan community in general, we must first learn more about the church.

The first missionaries who settled in Rapa in 1826 were Protestant, and today everyone on the island except three or four Roman Catholics adheres to Protestant Christianity. The Rapan church consists of two parishes, representing the two villages. Each parish has a church building for worship services, a meeting house for Bible discussions, and an eating house for Sunday dinners. Nearly everyone is listed on the rolls of one or the other parish. This parish allegiance, rather than place of residence, is the most accurate sign of whether a person considers that he belongs to Ha'urei or to 'Area. A number of families have moved from 'Area to Ha'urei, usually because of a child in school ('Area's school serves only the lower grades). Yet their names remain in the 'Area parish, they consider themselves to be 'Area people and their sentiments rest staunchly with 'Area in all competition between the villages.

One ordained minister (a native Rapan) and a chief deacon serve both parishes. The pastor conducts the major worship

162

services, sometimes in Ha'urei and sometimes in 'Area, and administers the sacraments. He is paid about $700 annually by the church's central office in Tahiti. This is the only salaried church position, and beyond the full-time functionaries (school teachers, etc.), it is the highest salary in Rapa. When the pastor is preaching in one village, the chief deacon often conducts worship services in the other.

Each parish has two deacons and an assistant deacon. The deacons organize the services and Bible discussions in their parish, teach church school, and occasionally call and supervise work groups for maintenance of the church buildings and grounds. The assistant deacon takes care of such tasks as ringing the bell before worship services and blowing the conch to call people to Bible discussions. His most picturesque duty is to prowl the aisles with a long bamboo pole during the sermon, rapping restless children and prodding dozing adults.

The pastor, chief deacon and four deacons form the church's governing council, which meets monthly. The pastor presides, and the council deliberates such matters as the date an offering should be collected (there are only two or three a year), the acceptance of new communicant members, and the warning and perhaps expulsion of members who are not conducting themselves properly. Immediately after their meeting, the bell is rung and all communicants come to hear what was decided in the council meeting.

In addition to the ability to make sound decisions, church officials and all others in positions of leadership are accorded respect and prestige to the extent that they are *marū* — kindly, generous, easy-going. The marū individual is strong-minded but persuasive, using quiet and reasonable arguments. (A volatile and baldly ambitious man commands little respect in Rapa.)

All church officials are elected, and all members of both parishes over the age of eighteen, communicant members or not, vote in church elections. When a pastor gets old, he calls a special meeting to elect his successor. The chosen man, a fairly young communicant member of promise, is sent to Tahiti for four years of seminary and two years of internship, after which he returns as

Rapa's new pastor. The other officials are elected for five-year terms, and popular men are usually returned for two or more terms. Men usually rise through the ranks of the church hierarchy, beginning as assistant deacon, then becoming deacon and finally, for the most successful, chief deacon. Although deacons and assistant deacons represent the separate parishes, they are chosen in a single election. Parishioners from both villages meet together and each writes the names of five men, from either or both parishes, on his ballot. All votes are tabulated, the order in which they are listed carrying no weight. The man with the most votes is the chief deacon. The three men from the Ha'urei parish with the most votes become the deacons and assistant deacon for that village, and the same holds for the three highest vote-getters from 'Area. Although there are two separate parishes, then, in most matters of church government (council meetings and election of officials) they join together as a single unit.

The highest mark of general prestige in Rapa is church office; this is especially true of the pastor. If he is personally liked and respected, he is more influential than any other man in Rapa, including the chief, in matters secular as well as religious.

It would be difficult to exaggerate the significance of the church in this culture. The church touches — and in many cases directs — the lives of Rapans at every step. An infant is formally introduced to society by baptism. He is a child as long as he attends church school and sits with other boys and girls in the front pews during services. The mark of his transition to becoming a youth is that he stops attending church school and during services sits further back where people are segregated by sex. His decision to marry may be speeded by surprise nocturnal visits from the pilgrims, a church group. The most discernible signs of his transition to adulthood are formal marriage (where one of the two ceremonies is a church wedding) and communicant church membership. If he becomes a man who commands respect and prestige, his high status in the community is most clearly reflected in his election to church office. When he is sick or troubled, deputations from the church visit him. When he mourns a loved one, people rally round him, comfort him and slowly draw him back into the

Top, *the women's boat race on July 14 — the victorious 'Area racing boat in the background;* bottom, *an assistant deacon silencing the children during a Sunday morning church service.*

165

world of the living through hymn-singing and Bible discussions. (These meetings, attended by up to fifty persons, may occur every evening for a week or more following the death.) Finally, when he himself dies, it is with the funeral rites and blessing of the church.

The church is important in the educational as well as religious and social realms. All instruction in government schools is in French, a language never used in daily discourse, and almost no one, whether they have attended school or not, can speak or understand it. But through the study of the Bible in church school, nearly every Rapan is literate in Tahitian. Except for bits of local lore gleaned from their elders, the Rapans' main fund of historical knowledge concerns ancient Palestine, learned from Bible reading and listening to sermons and stories told by the deacons and pastor in church school.

An indication of the significance of the church in this society is that there are no fewer than eleven church functions each week. Brief matins services are held on Monday and Friday. Church school meets early Thursday morning and there is a Bible discussion that evening. Sunday is totally given over to church activities: the day begins with a brief morning service at about 6 o'clock; Church school meets again from 9:00 to 10:30; and from 10:30 to 11:30 is the major service of the week, not unlike an American Protestant service; the female communicant members remain in church for about an hour for a Bible discussion; the male communicants eat dinner together in the small church eating house, and their wives eat together after they have finished; around 1:00 or 2:00 P.M. there is another Bible discussion with a brief afternoon service immediately following; finally, there is still another Bible discussion after supper Sunday evening. Although scarcely anyone attends all these events, looking at this schedule one can appreciate the joking remark one man made to to me: "In Rapa we spend more time discussing the Bible than cultivating taro!"

To my mind the most important of the many church activities is the *tuāro'i,* or Bible discussion. The people gather for these four times a week, usually in the church meeting house (a sep-

166

arate building from the church); each communicant member takes his turn as discussion leader. The people seat themselves on pandanus mats covering the concrete floor. The leader says a prayer, reads the verse to be discussed and makes a brief opening statement about it. A hymn follows, sung in the native Polynesian style of choral music. Then someone stands up to give his interpretation of the verse — connecting it with other biblical passages and specifying its relevance to their daily lives. Then another hymn, and for about two hours hymns alternate with speakers rising to give an exegesis. Finally the leader rises again and delivers a brief sermon presenting his own interpretation of the verse, which ideally is the most sagacious of the evening. Then he concludes the meeting with another Bible passage especially relevant to his interpretation.

The preceding chapter's description of the funeral of Manu's son is one example of the sort of things Rapans say when they discuss the Bible. They write down their best interpretations, and although it means stepping briefly into the "spirit side" of life, a translation of one of these will give a better idea of what happens in the Bible discussions and will show more of how Rapans think. The following is an outline of a brief sermon given by the discussion leader at the end of the meeting; in actual delivery it is considerably expanded and embellished. This interpretation is especially interesting because it illustrates two points stressed in this book: the emphasis on food in Rapan culture and the division of life into two "sides." The passage under discussion in Genesis 41:56–57 — "So when the famine had spread over all the land, Joseph opened all the storehouses, and sold to the Egyptians, for the famine was severe in the land of Egypt. Moreover, all the earth came to Egypt to Joseph to buy grain, because the famine was severe over all the earth." The interpretation follows.[1]

Friends, this account took place at the time and in the day when the great famine had fallen over the land of Egypt and over all other countries, in accordance with Pharaoh's dream. Joseph had told the

[1] I am grateful to Rev. Alan Tyree, missionary to French Polynesia for the Reorganized Church of Latter Day Saints, for help in translating this text.

true meaning of this dream, that there would be seven years of plenty followed by seven years of famine. Because the years of plenty were finished, the years of famine were beginning, according to our verse, and Joseph opened the storehouses of food which had been gathered by him during the years of plenty.

I. The conditions under which Joseph opened the storehouses of food.

It was done in the authority of the Pharaoh's name. Let us look at the situation of this young man Joseph in the days when he was released from bondage. Here are the words of the king to him: "You shall be over my house, and all my people shall order themselves as you command; only as regards the throne will I be greater than you." [Genesis 41:40] He became governor over the land of Egypt, to gather together the food of that nation to be used for the survival of all the people. He did not open the storehouses in his own name and of his own authority as governor, but in the name and authority of the king alone. Yet Joseph could properly distribute the food to all who came to him to buy it. Friends, there is an analogy between God the Father and his Son on the one hand, and the Pharaoh and Joseph on the other. As Joseph, in the name and authority of the king, accumulated the food and opened the storehouses for the salvation of all the people on the body side, so also our Lord Jesus Christ gathers together spiritual food and opens His storehouses for the spiritual salvation of this world in the almighty and glorious name of God the Father, as is written in John 14:13–14. What are other differences in this analogy? The food that Joseph gathered is consumable but that of Jesus Christ will never pass away, as is written in Matthew 24:35, Mark 9:14, 17. Consider how Jesus miraculously fed 5,000 with five small loaves and two small fish, and behold, there was more than plenty for 5,000 people and the food remaining filled twelve large baskets. This is a sign to us that the food of Jesus Christ is truly never depleted.

II. The time when Joseph opened the storehouses of food.

It was a time of famine. Friends, the famine occurred in the land of Egypt and the neighboring countries, and even spread to distant countries. And behold, Joseph opened the storehouses of Egypt, and the Egyptians themselves came, and those of the neighboring countries, and even those from far-off lands, to buy food that they might live during that great famine. So it came to pass that, on the body side, Joseph became as a savior to all the people, whereby he was called Joseph, which means "savior." Thus also did our Lord do. In time of famine He also opened the storehouses of spiritual food. What was that famine? A famine of the word of God. Listen to what is written in the book of the prophet Amos, 8:11–12. [" 'Behold, the days are coming,' says the Lord God, 'when I will send a famine on the land; not a famine of bread, nor a thirst for water, but of hearing the words of the Lord. They shall wander from sea to sea, and from north to east; they shall run to and fro, to seek the word of the Lord, but they shall not find it.' "] Mankind lacked the word of God because of faithlessness and evil deeds in the sight of Jehovah. And because this famine occurred, there was no man anywhere to be found except Jesus, the glorious Son of God, who could open the storehouses of spiritual food which exist in his Kingdom.

1. As in the case of the Samaritan woman of the time of Jesus.
2. As in the case of Matthias, chosen just before Pentecost. [See Acts 1:26.]
3. As in the case of the first disciples of Jesus; similarly we, the church of today, let us also seek the spiritual food in Jesus, who abides in life henceforth and forever.

Concluding verse: John 7:37–38. ["On the last day of the feast, the great day, Jesus stood up and proclaimed, 'If any one thirst, let him come to me and drink. He who believes in me, as the scripture has said, "Out of his heart shall flow rivers of living water." ' "]

These Bible discussions provide an opportunity for people to express their Christian faith and to exhort one another to better lives, but they do much more. They represent the main setting for polished oratory, a well-developed and much appreciated art in Rapa. Further, they provide about the only opportunity to exercise the critical and conceptual powers of the mind. Perhaps most important, Bible discussions are a form of entertainment. Communicant church members are prevented from joining the revelry of youths by a rather puritanical code of conduct, and church meetings are one of the few forms of recreation they have. The choral singing is rapture to them, evidenced by the way they rock to and fro with the rhythm, close their eyes and lose themselves in their music. The discussion itself is viewed as a game of matching wits, each participant striving to recall the most relevant verses and to come up with the most appealing analogies and applications. Women discussion leaders are highly secretive about the verses they have chosen, announcing them only at the beginning of the meeting. Fa'atu told me women are afraid that if they make a previous announcement, someone will embarrass them by thinking up a better interpretation than their own. He continued that men usually announce the verse a few days beforehand, to allow people to think about it. Since men are smarter than women, he said, they are less concerned about being upstaged. Although new interpretations are often conceived, many of the favorites are written down in books and passed through the generations to be used again and again. Rapans keep these books hidden, as they are a prime target for thieves. The trick is to steal a man's books and learn his repertoire of interpretations; then when he leads a discussion, one can stand up early in the meeting and reel off exactly what the leader plans to say at the end. Disarming the leader in this manner is the sweetest victory in the Bible discussion game.

The unified system of church government, whereby a single Deacon's Council oversees both parishes and whereby elections for church officials are held jointly, is one aspect of the church's promotion of harmony and unity between Rapa's two villages. The church knits the villages together in a number of other ways as well. One is a pattern of Sunday visits between the two villages. In all its intricacies the system is complex, but in general the idea is that on about half the Sundays of the month a group of communicants from 'Area attends church in Ha'urei, while a group from Ha'urei goes to 'Area. These guests are honored, so much so that they are placed in charge of most of the church functions in the host village. Furthermore, on Communion Sunday all church-goers on the island meet together in one village. The locale for communion, held the first Sunday of each month, alternates. Although some people do not go at all and others return to their home village on Sunday afternoon, the ideal is for Communion Sunday visitors to remain in the host village for all church functions on Sunday, spend the night, and return home after the Monday matins service. The two parishes also meet together for worship services on the four "minor" religious holidays of the year: Good Friday, Easter, Ascension Day, and Pentecost. Again, the two villages alternate as hosts for these services.

The church's greatest contribution to island unity is the religious festival which fills the last two weeks of one year and the first week or two of the next. One high point of this period is Christmas, but the heart of the festival is New Year's. Worship services are held on Christmas Day, New Year's Eve and New

Year's Day. Again the locales alternate, so that one year the Christmas service is in 'Area and both New Year's services are in Ha'urei, and the next year the pattern is reversed.

About the middle of December the normal tempo of life in Rapa stops. Evening Bible discussions cease, inter-household work groups suspend operation, and major jobs of house- or boat-construction are set aside. During the days, household members devote their time to getting food, and every evening the people of each parish gather in their meeting house to practice hymns. Rapans compose most of their own hymns, using stock Polynesian tunes but setting new words to them, taken from the Bible. Night after night there is singing in the meeting houses; someone introduces a hymn he has made up, it is tried, improved, and practiced to perfection. Each village is secretive about their hymns, for they are to be sung in good natured competition during the New Year's services. The chief deacon, an excellent composer and judge of hymns, shuttles across the bay aiding both parishes in their rehearsals. A few new hymns deal with Christ's birth and are sung at Christmas, but most are for New Year's. The New Year's festival commemorates no specific event in Christ's life or in church history. Its general theme is renewal and rededication — it is a time to take moral stock of the year just past and to revitalize faith for the year to come. New Year's hymns come from any part of the Bible, but deal primarily with topics appropriate to the theme of the festival.

At 7:15 P.M. on December 31, the church bell rings inviting the people to spend the last hours of the year together in worship and song. Parishioners from 'Area take their seats on one side of the center aisle and those from Ha'urei on the other. The people wear their finest attire: white or printed cotton dresses and straw hats for the women; shirts that must have once been white, and threadbare, ill-fitting suit jackets with mismated trousers for the older men; a loud sport shirt, a white belt four inches wide, and dark glasses for one of the more stylish youths (he was one of the few worshippers who wore shoes, and displayed them by fastening his trouser legs at mid-calf with metal clips). The service begins with several baptisms, this being considered the ideal time for that sacrament. The bulk of the evening is devoted to about fifteen short sermons, each lasting around a quarter of an hour, delivered by the male communicants. These are interspersed with hymns, beyond any doubt the high points of the service. Parishioners from the two villages alternate in singing the hymns they have composed and rehearsed. Friendly competition is unmistakable, each parish trying to outsing the other.

As the evening wears on, most of the congregation goes to sleep. The interminable series of sermons is interrupted occasionally by a loud thud as a sleeping child falls from his pew. The men lean over the pews in front of them and the women drape themselves over each other's shoulders or laps; they wake up for the hymns and then doze off again during the sermons. Finally, at about 11:30, the pastor mounts the high pulpit for his sermon. Everyone awakes and watches the clock as the hands crawl toward midnight. In the service we attended, an assistant deacon moved to the bell rope about five minutes before twelve. At precisely midnight he began to ring the bell violently, cutting off the pastor in the middle of a sentence. When the bell stopped, the pastor rapidly drew the sermon to a close, chagrined at his poor timing. Then all stood for a final hymn and benediction. They filed slowly out of church, shaking hands with one another with especially warm greetings, the first of the new year.

New Year's Day sees a late morning service much like a major Sunday service, and then church activity halts until Sunday. This, the first Sunday of the month and of the year, includes an especially important communion service. Throughout the rest of the first full week of the new year, church activities reach their peak with a service every evening, Monday through Saturday. These last about an hour, and consist of the male communicants urging their compatriots to greater faith and better living during the year. As always, the favorite part of the service is the singing, where the parishes present still more new hymns they have composed for the festival. This week of services is always in Ha'urei, perhaps because many people spend their days attending the annual meeting of the Cooperative Society, which takes place in Ha'urei during the same week.

172

Three large feasts occur during these festival weeks which are under the auspices of a special organization called the *Amuira'a*, or "Gathering." Each parish has a Gathering; around half the members of the Ha'urei parish belong to the group, and the proportion may be somewhat higher for that of 'Area. The two Gatherings exist solely to feast each other at Christmas and New Year's. The group in the village where the church services are to be held prepares food for its guests, the Gathering of the opposite village. One feast occurs after church on Christmas Day, and there are two feasts in the other village for New Year's — one before the New Year's Eve service and the other after church on New Year's Day. Members of each Gathering pay a dollar or two in annual dues to cover costs of purchasing pork and beef, and they work together seven or eight days a year cultivating their taro terraces (special ones devoted to raising food for the feasts) and preparing the dinners. A Gathering feast is always a jolly affair; the guests seat themselves at long lines of banana leaves spread along the ground and are served great quantities of food. One year both Gatherings tried eating together, but this was unsatisfactory since the host group felt it could not properly honor the guests. Now the host Gathering eats first, and then devotes full time to serving the guests.

After the weeks of hymn rehearsals, the services and feasts of Christmas and New Year's, and the nightly services during the first full week of January, the church's annual festival draws to a close. Rapans then say they are tired of the noise and crowds and the busy activity of this period, so most of them desert the villages and disperse to the outer bays in small family groups to spend a few weeks planting taro in peace.

As with the Youth Clubs and July 14, in terms of the church and its New Year's festival the Rapan community is divided into two villages or parishes. The effect of this division, however, is precisely the opposite of the Youth Clubs and July 14, which set the villages against each other in fierce rivalry and split the society into hostile camps. The church, with its schedule of visits and joint services, the New Year's festival and the Gathering feasts, stresses harmonious cooperation between the villages. Some competition does exist, but its spirit is always friendly. Whereas on July 14 people of the rival village are criticized and defiled, at New Year's and on other church occasions they are welcomed as honored guests. Among its many other benefits, then, the church creates complementary ties between Rapa's two villages and forges them into a unified society.

THE DISTRICT COUNCIL AND POLITICS

Village distinctions are not recognized in the island's formal political structure. Local government is based on a single District Council, elected at five-year intervals by all Rapans of voting age. The District Council consists of seven members, including a chief and assistant chief. The Council meets monthly in the small building where government records are kept, normally on the Saturday evening preceding Communion Sunday.

The District Council has little power. Essentially it is a liaison between the Rapan people and the Administrator, an official appointed by the Governor of French Polynesia and charged with the administration of the Austral Islands. The Council might address recommendations and petitions to the Administrator, but major decisions (like the construction of a school and other public improvements) rest with the Administrator and other officials of the central government. The relative authority of the District Council and the Administrator was vividly portrayed in the aftermath of the devastating hurricane of 1964. When the winds subsided, much of Ha'urei lay in ruins and Rapan society was immobilized until the Administrator arrived. He surveyed the damage, heard the report and recommendations of the Council, and then decided how the food and other relief supplies that had arrived from Tahiti would be distributed and how reconstruction would proceed. He found it necessary to issue stern rebukes to one or two members of the Council who vigorously disagreed with him, and the Council was reduced to the status of an agency which carried out his decisions. After his departure a few problems arose, and the Council responded to these by saying a decision would have to await the Administrator's return.

On its own initiative, the District Council has codified some of the finer points of Rapa's system of property ownership. A military doctor assigned to the Australs visits Rapa each two or three months, and usually on his recommendations the Council has passed local ordinances dealing with sanitation, like that requiring each household to have an outhouse and the one forbidding the tethering of pigs within village limits. (The result of the latter is that pigs are tethered just outside, surrounding the village with a moat of mud.) Every few months the Council makes a formal inspection tour, noting any infractions of these sanitation laws for warnings and possible fines. The Council also mobilizes the people for eight or nine community work days each year, usually to gather food and prepare feasts for visiting government vessels. In case of a disaster like a hurricane, all the men of the island band together to rebuild damaged houses under the direction of the District Council. Activities on July 14 are planned and directed by the Council, which also decides how the prize money received from Tahiti shall be distributed among the various contests. Finally, the District Council occasionally mediates a dispute.

Rapan disputes are highly entertaining affairs. Those between members of the same household normally take place privately indoors, but others are decidedly public. The battle usually flares early in the morning, around noon, or in the early evening — all times when many people are in the village. The antagonists confront each other outside, and yell at the top of their lungs. An angry voice immediately draws a large crowd: children whoop and come running, men saunter over, and old women carrying babies on their backs scurry to the scene with eyes alight. The crowd stands at a small distance; some look concerned but most smile and joke with one another while a few of the more verbal spectators encourage or ridicule the participants with catcalls. Usually the argument is over the theft of some article like a sickle, flashlight or bedspread, or concerns a coffee grove.

Showmanship is essential in a good fight and women can usually outdo the men. They stride up and down glaring at one another, never pausing in their string of maledictions. Gesturing toward the spectators, one disputant asks the other if he is not ashamed to be spouting such lies before all these people. Their vituperations as often concern past misdemeanors or the illicit sex life of the opponent's relatives as the matter at issue. In a really hot dispute, close kinsmen may jump in on either side until five or six are shouting at once. After ten or fifteen minutes, if things have not yet calmed down, the spectators begin to protest that it is enough and the end comes when one of the parties strides indignantly back to his house. Tranquility then returns, each household having a new topic to enliven mealtime conversation.

While tempers blaze during disputes and protagonists may harbor their anger for weeks, violence is rare. Probably the public nature of disputes forestalls it. Often arguments occur in even more rigorously controlled circumstances. The proper place to air grievances is in the church meeting house, immediately before a Bible discussion. Heated disputes may erupt here, but they are controlled not only by being held in public, but by the common knowledge that they occur in a semi-sacred environment. Tempers cool more quickly than disputes held outside because they are followed by religious discussion and hymn-singing, an occasion when solidarity attains its zenith.

In the heat of argument, people make boisterous threats to take the matter to the French Circuit Court, the highest tribunal. But such threats are usually empty and the difference is healed by the passage of time. An especially serious dispute may be taken before the District Council. For example, the Council has been called upon fairly frequently to effect the division of hotly contested coffee groves. In disputes, the District Council is a mediating body only, with no power to enforce its decision. If one or both disputants demand it, the matter may be brought before the French Circuit Court which calls at Rapa once every year or two. Such an appeal is rare, however. If possible, the Court ratifies the decision recommended by the District Council; when it does not, it operates according to a code the Rapans do not fully understand and therefore, in their eyes, its judgments sometimes appear capricious. In general, Rapans try to avoid involvement with

176

the Circuit Court, for the turn of events can quickly get out of their control and the result may be unwelcome.

The chief presides over District Council meetings, organizes crews for workdays called by the Council, performs ceremonies such as civil weddings, and acts as Rapa's official representative to foreigners. The administration pays him an annual salary of $550. The assistant chief aids the chief in any way needed and assumes the duties of the chief if he is ill or absent from Rapa; his annual salary is $225. The other members of the Council are not paid.

Rapans take a decidedly negative attitude toward everything political. On evenings when the District Council meets, people cock their heads toward the government building, snicker, and muse about what new idiocy is being discussed in the "insane asylum." One evening I attended a meeting of one of Rapa's political parties, the only such meeting held during the eleven months of the study. It was called to elect a replacement for the deceased local president. As I walked to the meeting people called out from their cookhouses, "Are you going to the meeting of the madmen?"

This negative attitude stems basically from a problem which is no stranger to Western politics: the conflict between general and particular interest. In Rapa the conflict is fixed in a pair of opposed values concerning social responsibility. On the one hand, Rapans say anyone in a position of leadership and authority should place the interest of the community above his own or those of any individual or faction within it. On the other hand, a Rapan's first duty is to his kinsmen, neighbors and friends. He should freely share his good fortune with them, and he has no special obligation to strangers and slight acquaintances, whom he treats with caution tinged with mistrust. A person holding office is torn, therefore, between the demand of the body politic that he place community interest first, and the expectation of his friends and kinsmen that he use his office on their behalf. While those allied with an officeholder praise him highly, people who can expect no special favors evaluate him harshly. They assume

177

he acts with the motive of favoring friends and kin (largely because they would do so were they in his place), but judge him according to the ideal of fair and equal treatment for all. Under these circumstances his chances of gaining the respect and loyalty of the community are almost nil.

Although some past and present local officials are admiringly reputed to place community interest above partisanship, many are explicitly motivated by opportunities for personal gain. They seek the office of chief not out of a desire to serve Rapa (restrictions on the chief's authority provide little opportunity for this anyway), but because of the salary. Although political parties have chapters in Rapa, the major issues (labor benefits, more positions of responsibility for natives and the nature of the territory's relationship with France) are far more relevant to conditions in Tahiti than in Rapa. When I asked one member of the District Council what value lies in party membership, he replied, "It can help you to become chief." A chief and assistant chief are elected by the seven members of the new Council in a meeting called by the Administrator when he visits the island. These elections often require several ballots. Since each man wants these salaried positions, on the first ballot or two each member usually receives just one vote — his own.

Once elected, as often as not a chief uses his office to advance his own interests and those of his closest associates. One chief tried to convince the Administrator to give him the lucrative job of public-works foreman. Failing in this, he turned his efforts toward having one of Rapa's school teachers removed so that this position and its high salary might go to his daughter.

Occasionally the District Council as a whole is accused of partisan politics. Antagonism here is usually drawn along village lines: if most members of the Council come from one village, people of the other claim its actions heavily favor the village of the majority. For example, 'Area people speak resentfully of the fact that public improvements such as piped water throughout the village come first to Ha'urei and only later, if at all, to 'Area.

The affair of the sheep is a good example of District Council partisanship. A few years ago the administration gave a flock of sheep to the people of Rapa, and the sheep were set free in the highlands in two groups: one above Ha'urei and the other above 'Area. The flock above Ha'urei multiplied, but that above 'Area dwindled drastically. Rumors flew about Ha'urei that those scoundrels from 'Area were clandestinely killing the sheep for food. The District Council, dominated by Ha'urei men, decreed that henceforth the fine flock above Ha'urei belonged exclusively to the people of that village, while the people of 'Area owned the few sheep above their village.

In 1963 a new District Council was elected, and it was composed almost entirely of 'Area men. Shortly after the election the new Council returned all the sheep to the ownership of the Rapan people as a whole, a move benefiting 'Area to the detriment of Ha'urei. The Council planned to organize an expedition of men to shear the sheep early in 1964. Shortly before the shearing, Tetua (an 'Area man, who told me this story) was drinking with a group of men after a wedding feast. The alcohol loosened the tongue of a man from Ha'urei, who said mysteriously that perhaps the sheep would not be found when the day came to shear them. And so it happened. The men sent to shear the sheep returned saying that those above Ha'urei had disappeared. Tetua told me he thought a group of blackguards from Ha'urei, angered when the new Council returned the sheep to the ownership of the whole population, had probably driven the flock over a high cliff into the sea.

After this Rapa had very few sheep, but there were more near 'Area than Ha'urei. So the 'Area-dominated Council determined to split the ownership of the sheep between the villages once more. However, at this juncture the somewhat exasperated Administrator intervened. "There is only one body politic in Rapa," he said, "and so the sheep will remain the property of the total population." This ended the matter. Its pettiness is incredible. No significant profits had ever been realized from the sale of wool or mutton, and it is likely that none of any value ever would. In terms of benefits received by anyone, whether the sheep were owned separately by the villages or in common would make no appreciable difference. The whole affair seems to be solely an expression of antagonism between the two villages.

Each of the above examples of partisan or personal motivations in political activity is related to some benefit received from the French administration, be it salaried positions, public improvements, or a gift of sheep. The administration takes a somewhat paternalistic attitude toward Rapa. The schools and teachers, infirmary and medical practitioner, public buildings, water pipelines, piers, the wages to build and maintain these improvements, and the food and other relief materials sent following disasters are all supplied without any form of direct taxation. In the absence of burning local issues, and given the limitations placed on native initiative and authority in political life, the game of politics in Rapa consists essentially of jockeying for places close to the influx of French benefits in order to put one in the best position to siphon off some of the flow for oneself and one's relatives and friends.

A chief is fairly well placed for this purpose. In addition to the salary his office provides, he is the primary official liaison with the Administrator and other government officials who visit the island. As shown earlier, a chief may attempt to use this connection to further his interests and those of his associates.

Best placed of all, however, is the head school teacher. A new head teacher came to Rapa in 1963; she and her predecessor are women, and although neither is a native Rapan, they both have kinship ties there. While the chief is Rapa's official host, administration officials tend to congregate at the home of the head teacher. She has a guest room where visiting dignitaries often stay. Her education in Tahiti coupled with her substantial salary mean that her manner, the furnishings of her house, and the meals she serves are all more familiar and pleasing to Frenchmen than anything a typical native can supply. Furthermore she speaks French, a skill few Rapan chiefs have mastered, and acts as official interpreter, since French officials who know Tahitian are rare.

For all these reasons, the head teacher is in most frequent

contact with visiting administration officials. Therefore they get much of their information concerning local conditions and personalities from her, and she often learns of projects planned for Rapa before they are announced publicly. Perhaps her views have some effect on government policy for the island. Her informal reports can materially enhance or deteriorate an individual's standing with the administration, and she is ideally situated to suggest people for lucrative positions should a change be contemplated or a new post be established. Her warmest recommendations are reserved for her relatives and friends. For example, Rapa's public-works foreman used to be the husband of the former head teacher, and his successor was one of her close friends. About a year after the teacher was replaced, the job of foreman was given to the husband of the new head teacher. The number two man in public works was the new teacher's brother-in-law, and when the change came, he retained his position with increased responsibilities and a substantial raise in pay. When potatoes and onions were introduced in 1964, the school teacher's husband was again given the salaried position of overseeing cultivation and coordinating preparations for export (although in this case his agricultural skill made him clearly the most qualified for the job).

The influence of the head teacher may be felt in other ways. After the hurricane of 1964 she was given the task of distributing clothing and blankets donated by the administration. A set formula stated how much each household should receive, based on the number of its members. But according to an informant who could expect no favors from her, those persons who "smell good" to her received more than their share and items of the best quality, while those who "smell bad" to her ended up with moth-eaten materials.

As might be expected, local feelings about the head school teacher tend to be strong. Her allies support her staunchly while those who "smell bad" to her refer to her as a "devil woman." Sentiment ran so high against the former head teacher that she was forced to resign and leave Rapa. Although the new one had been in Rapa only fifteen months, at the time of my departure factions for and against her had begun to crystallize and people were beginning to question how long *she* would last.

Informal political life in Rapa is essentially a story of factions lining up for and against individuals in position of influence with the administration. The currents swirl most violently around the head school teacher, but other functionaries and officials such as the medical practitioner, chief, assistant chief, policeman, and public-works foreman may have their pools of allies and enemies. The pastor and deacons may also be centers of factionalism, although with them more purely local issues are at stake. The factions are difficult to see — they have no internal organization and undertake no joint activities. They are only series of people who ally themselves more or less closely with focal individuals in the hopes of obtaining special benefits from the administration. The factions are constantly shifting, for people exercise now one and now another tie of kinship or friendship in the effort to maximize their interests. Finally, factions are usually submerged. They rise to the surface briefly in the hue and cry over some new outrage of favoritism. But the administration is far from this lonely island, the stream of its benefits flows only sporadically, and for the most part daily life proceeds unruffled by problems of politics.

CHAPTER NINE

The
Changing
Society

Since European discovery of the island in 1791, Rapan society has undergone a process of decentralization. In ancient times nearly all aspects of social life were closely tied to one focal organization: the ramage. Today the ramage still exists, in modified form, but its activities and jurisdictions have been reduced to the ownership and administration of property. Patterns of residence, standing in the community, channels of authority, social control and political behavior are now to be understood in terms of a series of separate organizations and institutions, such as the village, the church, the kinship system, the District Council, and political factions. This is what the term "decentralization" means here. This chapter discusses how and why some of these changes occurred.

The most useful theoretical perspective for analyzing social change in Rapa is that which Marshall Sahlins has labeled "specific evolution" (Sahlins and Service 1960:12–44). The essential idea underlying specific evolution is that the historical development of a society is a process of adaptation to its particular human and nonhuman environment. Furthermore, Harding and Kaplan have pointed out that as a culture becomes well adapted to its environment it tends to stabilize, even to resist change (Sahlins and Service 1960:53–68, 80, 87). It is unlikely that a culture ever becomes perfectly adapted and hence ceases to change altogether. Vicissitudes in the environment and man's relationship to it, such as variations in rainfall and changes in population size, require constant social and cultural modifications. We are justified in postulating, however, that a well adapted culture changes relatively slowly, while a poorly adapted one is likely to change more rapidly.[1]

From this theoretical stance, our analysis of Rapan history takes this general form: at the time of Vancouver's discovery, the social system was well adapted to its environment, but the circumstances produced by contact with the outside world drastically modified the relationship between the social system and its environment. No longer well adapted, the society entered a period of rapid change in the direction of readaptation to the new environmental conditions. After several decades, a satisfactory new adaptation had been achieved, and the social system entered an era of gradual change which persists to the present.

The theory of change by adaptation provides a highly useful framework within which social change may be explained. For a satisfactory analysis of change in any particular society, however, the theory must be wedded with history. Thus, poor adaptation makes a social system highly *susceptible* to change, but change does not therefore occur automatically. The impetus of events —

---

[1] Exceptions may be cultures which, having become highly specialized through previous adaptation, lose the flexibility to change should they become poorly adapted (see Sahlins and Service 1960:93–122). This possibility does not appear to be relevant to the Rapan case.

events with which the system in its current form cannot cope — is required to push the system over the brink of change. Furthermore, the relationship between society and environment is not so rigid that only one social form can be adaptive. Kaplan has argued, for example, that subsistence based on either hunting and gathering or agriculture would have formed a satisfactory adaptation to the environment of aboriginal California (Sahlins and Service 1960:77–80). Our theory of change as a process of adaptation leaves unanswered the question of why a society changes as it does, rather than following the path to some other satisfactory adaptation. Other factors will be considered later, but part of the answer is that the specific events occurring during a period of social change propel the system and to some extent determine the direction of change.

Any attempt to make a historically detailed analysis of change in all elements of Rapan culture must be frustrated because sources of Rapan history are few, and those dealing with the internal state of the society are rare indeed. Two aspects of change, however, do seem susceptible to reconstruction and analysis. One is the structure of the ramage, especially its transformation from a discrete to a nondiscrete cognatic descent group. The other is the ramage's loss of all political significance and the development of the modern political system based on the elected District Council. The remainder of this analysis will be limited to change in these areas.

THE HISTORY OF CHANGE

The pre-European social system, which rested squarely on the ramage, has been characterized as well adapted to its environment. As discussed in Chapter 2, the most salient aspect of ecology in pre-European Rapa was heavy population pressure on limited territorial resources. In the political sphere this produced competition for land, competition played out between ramages. The ramage was well adapted to these conditions, where the retention of its territory and perhaps even the survival of its personnel depended ultimately upon its ability to wage war. Ramage localization and discreteness assured that members were close at hand in case of surprise attack, and that their allegiance was not diluted by equal commitments to other ramages. Judging from the size and design of the mountain forts, a great deal of effort and planning was devoted to their construction. This suggests that military strategy and tactics were fairly well developed, and further implies that the ramage included a clearly defined network of authority, enabling effective operation in large-scale construction and military enterprises (Mulloy 1965:58). This authority network was provided by the system of stratification within the ramage.

If Rapan society at the outset of the nineteenth century was well adapted, this soon changed radically. The general cause was increased contact with the outside world; most specifically it was extreme depopulation. Missionaries arriving in 1826 were the first to speak of "a great mortality among the people" (Davies 1961:280). By 1829 epidemics brought by foreigners had already claimed from two-thirds to three-quarters of the population, and by the latter part of the century it had been reduced to scarcely one-tenth of its precontact level (see Table 1, page 30). By about 1830, then, population pressure on territorial resources had been effectively removed. From that time to this, ecology in Rapa has been characterized by the reverse condition of abundant resources easily capable of supporting several times the number of the island's inhabitants. Depopulation also introduced major changes in the political situation. In the new conditions of abundant resources, the ramage had no reason to expand its holdings by conquest and, conversely, no necessity to defend its territory against the encroachments of neighbors.

With ecological and political conditions after 1830 nearly the opposite of what they were before European contact, the ramage-based social system lost its adaptive value. It therefore entered a period of relatively rapid change, in the direction of readaptation to the new environment. We turn now to the history of this period, focussing first on changes in ramage structure.

When the *Latouche-Tréville* arrived in 1867, to bring Rapa under the protection of France, Captain Quentin (1867:90) reported: "All or nearly all the inhabitants are land owners. . . . Some among them are truly great land owners, and they are called district chiefs. . . . These great vassals are six in number, representing five districts around the coast and one in the interior." Méry, also of the *Latouche-Tréville*, mentions the six districts but indicates that in his time these had little meaning and probably were only survivals of an earlier period (Méry 1867:126–127).

In reality, the island is divided in twelve parts, each belonging to a landlord. This individual is master and chief over the extent of the territory which belongs to him, and the natives who live on his land are placed under his immediate authority: their obligations vis-à-vis this chief consist of cultivating the land, and furnishing him with its produce. They are not subjects . . . but tenants who, on the conditions indicated, acquire the right to inhabit and make their living on the part of the island which they have chosen.

The king is placed in about the same conditions relative to the entire population; in addition he has the right to render justice, a right which he shares either with a judge or the minister when, as currently, the position of judge is vacant (Méry 1867:127).[2]

The reports of both Quentin and Méry suggest that the basic unit of society in 1867 was still the ramage. The district chiefs or landlords probably represent ramage chiefs, while the small landowners or tenants presumably were ramage members who cultivated portions of its territory. Méry's report indicates that the system of "taxation," whereby in ancient times ramage members contributed a part of their harvest to the ramage chief (Caillot 1932:29) was still in effect at this time.

In my opinion, however, by 1867 the ramage had changed from a discrete and localized cognatic descent group to one that was nondiscrete and no longer formed an isolated local unit. The argument rests on population movements following European contact. Sometime prior to 1830 inter-ramage warfare ceased, and the Rapans shifted their residence from the fortified mountain villages to a number of villages along the coast (Stokes 1930: 668, Caillot 1910:446–447). This change may be viewed as an adaptive measure allowing for a more efficient exploitation of the environment. After warfare ceased and the danger of surprise

---

[2] This passage would suggest that in 1867 the Rapans resided in twelve different parts of the island, but such was not the case. Méry himself states that at the time of his visit the people lived in five villages, and he gives the population of each (Méry 1867:126–127).

attack disappeared, villages in the lowlands provided far more convenient access to taro terraces and to the sea for fishing. It is not certain how many coastal villages existed in this period, but there must have been several for in 1826 Paulding (1831:252) saw two or three on the north coast alone. This assumption is further supported by the fact that by 1831 the four Tahitian missionaries who arrived in 1826 had established four stations at widely separated points around the island (Davies 1961:281). Caillot identifies ten villages which were presumably inhabited at one time or another during the nineteenth century (1932:19).[3]

The initial shift of residence from the highlands to the coast was followed by a second movement, wherein the diminishing population coalesced into a smaller number of villages. Missionary reports indicate that only two villages were inhabited in the latter part of the 1830s: Tukou (located at the head of Hau'urei Bay) and Ha'urei (Pritchard 1835, Darling 1836, Heath 1840). Tukou was originally more important, boasting in 1836 the residence of the king and a population of 293 to Ha'urei's 160 (Darling 1836). As the century progressed, however, nature and history conspired to make Ha'urei Rapa's major village. Like Tukou, Ha'urei's location on a broad plain provides space for taro terraces easily accessible to its inhabitants. Ha'urei has the further advantage of bordering the best anchorage for visiting ships, making it likely that recruiting and trading vessels carried out the bulk of their business in that village. Especially in the 1840s commerce was brisk, due mainly to the Rapans' reputation as the best pearl divers in the eastern Pacific (Lucett 1851 I:305). The pearler Lucett called to sign on divers and to buy taro for them in February, 1843, again in June of that year, and finally in February, 1845. He notes that between his last two visits three other vessels had called to recruit divers and had stopped again to return them (Lucett 1851 I:306, 341; II:43). Thus there were

---

[3] I fear, however, that Caillot's count is not reliable. Although he gives no references, his sources appear to be the reports of Quentin and Méry, who visited Rapa in 1867. Both of these authors mention six districts, and they list their names (Quentin 1867:91, Méry 1867:126–127). However, the district names they give correspond in only one case: "Ahurei" (Ha'urei). Caillot's list of ten village names is simply the sum of all the different district names provided by Quentin and Méry, minus "Tuou" (Tukou), which Méry states was uninhabited.

at least nine visits by pearlers between February, 1843 and February, 1845. The opportunity for paid labor and trade was probably a primary magnet drawing the population to Ha'urei.

Ha'urei also became Rapa's religious center. Due partly to its location facing the anchorage, English missionaries invariably stopped at Ha'urei first, and occasionally had no time to call at any other village. Moreover, visiting missionaries paid special attention to Ha'urei because the most effective resident Tahitian missionary, named Hape, was stationed there. (Hota, his colleague at Tukou, was discredited by 1836 for numerous sins, including his marriage to a Rapan woman while his Tahitian wife — who was with him in Rapa — was still living [Darling 1836].)

In 1867 Méry lists five inhabited villages.[4] Tukou was abandoned by this time, the king had moved his residence to Ha'urei, and its seventy inhabitants formed a majority of the population of 120 (Méry 1867:126–127). Thus by 1867 Ha'urei was firmly established as Rapa's commercial, religious and political capital and the center of the island's population.[5] The shift of population toward Ha'urei may also be viewed as an adaptive change. In this case adaptation was to a new element of the environment: the outside world, with its initial impact being most significant in the areas of religion and commerce.

What was the effect of the population movements just described on the structure of the ramage and specifically on its shift from a discrete to a nondiscrete social unit? The available historical sources are silent on this point. More than one interpretation could probably be advanced, but the following appears most satisfactory. The ancient ramage was discrete because it was localized, or residentially restricted. An individual exercised active rights of membership only in the ramage which held

---

[4] The minor villages were Tupuaki with twenty-five inhabitants, Hiri with fifteen, Mua with ten and 'Area, "almost abandoned" (Méry 1867:126–127). 'Area was at its modern location, Tupuaki and Hiri were on the bays of those names, and the location of Mua is uncertain.

[5] To bring this thread of history to the present, in 1868 there were just three villages: Ha'urei, 'Area and Tupuaki (Caillet 1886/87:286). These three, with Ha'urei the most important, were still inhabited in 1887 (Lacascade 1887b). By 1912 the entire population resided in Ha'urei, although a few people spent short periods in 'Area (Caillot 1932:19). 'Area was resettled permanently around 1930, but has never rivaled Ha'urei in importance.

the land where he lived and cultivated. His rights in other ramages in which he traced cognatic descent were latent. The initial movement from the highlands to the coast was probably a simple change of residence within ramage territory. That is, each village represented a single pre-European ramage (or perhaps two or more closely related ramages which fused after depopulation drastically reduced their personnel) which had shifted its residential center from its mountain fort to a location in the coastal area of its domains. The territory surrounding each village belonged to the ramage it represented, and probably its inhabitants cultivated that and only that land. In part, this restriction would have been due to the old idea that only resident members have the right to cultivate ramage land. Also it would have been a matter of convenience: these were the lands cultivated by the village occupants immediately prior to their move from the highlands; they were close to their new homes; and as yet there was no reason to change the arrangement. Therefore, the first change of residence probably did not affect the discrete and localized nature of the ramage.

But there followed another shift of residence: the concentration of population in a fewer number of villages. These villages, especially Ha'urei, must have attracted immigrants from several different ramages. In my judgment this migration, coupled with the nature of Rapan taro agriculture and the demographic and political conditions after 1830, removed the restriction that only resident members might cultivate ramage land. Instead, it became possible for people to cultivate simultaneously lands belonging to two or more ramages in which they traced descent, and this transformed the ramage from a discrete to a nondiscrete social unit.

Depending on the nature of the soil, taro terraces may continually produce crops of high quality for as long as thirty years or they may be exhausted after only four or five years. The individual was of course anxious to maximize his personal interests, and in the agricultural realm this was to produce the most taro of the best grade with the least effort. During much of the nineteenth century taro had significance in the cash economy as well as subsistence, since it was sold to pearlers as food for their divers and was later exported to the Tuamotu atolls (Lucett 1851 I:308, Caillot 1932:76). Assured of a good yield without undue labor of cultivation, those people who moved to Ha'urei probably desired to retain their best terraces in their areas of former residence. At the same time, as their inferior terraces wore out they doubtless sought to replace them with new terraces nearer Ha'urei: in the plain adjacent to the village, at Tukou, and at Anatakuri. The individual, in determining where he would cultivate taro, was concerned with the quality of soil and ease of access to his home, and certainly he could best serve these interests were he free to choose among possible sites belonging to any ramage in which he traced descent, rather than being forced to restrict his activity to the lands of just one. The adaptive nature of such an arrangement is clear, in that it allows a more efficient agricultural exploitation of the environment.

The ramage, for its part, had no reason to deny families which had moved to Ha'urei the right to continue cultivating terraces on its land. In the new political conditions of peace, it did not require their proximity and undivided loyalty because it was never called upon to defend its territory. Nor did the members still in residence need those terraces for their subsistence, because depopulation had assured that the ramage had more than enough land for their requirements. For the same reasons, there was no cause for the ramages which owned territory near Ha'urei to deny persons who traced descent in them the opportunity to cultivate their unused lands, regardless of whether these persons continued to use land belonging to other ramages.

Thus residence in the ramage's territory ceased to be a requirement for active ramage membership. The criteria for active membership were probably cultivation of ramage land and donation of a part of the produce to the ramage chief — the form of "taxation" that existed in ancient times (Caillot 1932:29), and was still in effect as late as 1867 (Méry 1867:127). By these criteria an individual could be an active member of several ramages simultaneously, and thus the ramage became a nondiscrete unit. If this reconstruction is accurate, the process of change in structure from ramage discreteness to nondiscreteness began in the 1830s with the concentration of population into a smaller number of villages.

The second change to be analyzed is the shift of political functions from the ramage to the elected District Council. In connection with this, there is a surprising report by Caillet, the French resident agent who lived in Rapa during 1868, the year following the visit of the *Latouche-Tréville*. He depicts a political system remarkably different from that described by Quentin and Méry for the previous year.

In 1868 each village was commanded by a chief and administered by a municipal council, the members of which were elected by the Huiraatiras (land owners, notables, family heads), and named for three years. This council met weekly.

Each month the municipal counsellors of the three villages assembled under the presidency of the principal chief or King, to consider the general affairs of the country.

There were two judges of extended competence: one for Ahurei [Ha'urei] and Area and the other for Tubuai [Tupuaki].

Serious affairs were brought before the King's council, which made the final decisions (Caillet 1886/87:286).

It will be recalled that Quentin and Méry in 1867 place authority in the hands of the district chiefs or landlords, who seem to be ramage chiefs. The following year Caillet describes a government based on elected municipal councils. How to reconcile these reports? Assuming the descriptions are accurate there are two alternatives, each with its complications. It may be that these are simply different aspects of the same social system: that the remarks of Quentin and Méry were limited to the system of land ownership and use, while Caillet was talking about a different subject — political organization. It seems curious, however, that Quentin and Méry — whose mission to Rapa was the political one of bringing the island under a French protectorate — would have failed to mention the municipal councils and other aspects of local government if these existed at the time of their visit. Especially so, since Méry does touch on the king's judicial functions (see page 187), a subject also mentioned by Caillet but this time in terms of the king's council.

The second alternative is that during the brief interval between 1867 and 1868 Rapan society underwent a major reorganization wherein the political powers of the ramage chiefs were taken over by a system of elected village councils. This, however, is a rather drastic change to take place within the space of a single year. It would also be an extraordinary stroke of luck if, deprived of relevant information for any other time between 1843 and 1887, we should have two reports made immediately before and after Rapa's most important political development of the nineteenth century.[6]

Whichever of these alternatives is correct, it seems clear that by 1868 the decentralization of Rapan society was well underway, for the basis of political and judicial organization had shifted from the ramages and their chiefs to the villages and their elected councils.[7] A major reason for this change seems to be that during the decades preceding 1868 the authority of ramage chiefs deteriorated considerably, rendering the ramage an ineffective political organization. Judging from the experience of the trader Lucett, this authority was still fairly strong in 1843 when he called at Rapa to sign on pearl divers. He found many men willing to work at the wage he offered, but they were prevented from

---

[6] If such a reorganization did occur in 1867–68, the advice of foreigners may have played a role since this was a period of fairly intense contact with the outside world. In addition to the continuing influence of missionaries, Quentin and Méry established the French Protectorate in 1867, Caillet resided on the island during 1868 as the representative of France, a British agent lived there during the same period to oversee a coal depot, and British steamers called at monthly intervals for refueling (see pages 33–35).

[7] Caillet's description includes some unclarities. He states that each village had a chief and a council. Was the position of village chief elective, like the council members, or hereditary, like the king? If the latter, then the village chiefs may have been ramage chiefs, and thus one might infer that the ramage retained more political significance than I have attributed to it. But Caillet tells us that there were just three villages in 1868, while Méry and Quentin report at least six ramages, more likely twelve, for this period. Therefore only a few of the ramage chiefs (probably those of ramages which owned the land on which the villages were located) could have been village chiefs. Furthermore, it is clear from Caillet that village chiefs and councils governed entire villages, and we have already established that certainly Ha'urei, and possibly other villages of this period, contained members of more than one ramage. Therefore, while granting the possibility that in 1868 village chiefs were ramage chiefs, I maintain the point that by this time the village had replaced the ramage as Rapa's political unit.

signing by their chiefs, who demanded that they be paid wages that Lucett considered exorbitant. Eventually he was forced to accede to the chiefs' terms in order to secure his divers. Lucett summarized political conditions in Rapa thus: "The common people are restrained from doing their will by fear of their chiefs" (1851 I:309). Less than twenty years later, however, nearly every visitor remarked how little authority the king and chiefs exercised. Méry writes that the king was a "model of benevolence," compares him to "a patriarch among his children" (1867:140), but indicates that his authority was sharply limited (1867:127). According to Quentin, the district chiefs "in reality have no authority over the others. The king himself . . . seems scarcely to have any" (1867:90). Hall records much the same impression (1868: 81).

A number of factors appear to have contributed to the decay of chiefly authority. One was conversion of Rapans to Christianity and the growing influence of the missionaries and the church. Some of the missionaries examined candidates for Communion and refused to administer the sacrament to persons whose conduct had been less than righteous (Pritchard 1835, Platt and Krause 1845). It is probable, then, that if ramage chiefs had ever been concerned with the ethical conduct of their members, they lost much of this responsibility to the church soon after conversion. Again, visiting English missionaries often advised the Rapans on political matters, and this may have helped dilute the authority of the chiefs. In 1835 the king resolved to establish in his own island some of the laws he had encountered on a recent trip to Tahiti. The meeting for this purpose was held during Pritchard's visit, and he opened it with appropriate prayers and exhortations (Pritchard 1835). Shortly thereafter the king took the wife of another man. A number of the chiefs accused the king of breaking the laws, and demanded that he be dethroned. In 1836 the missionary David Darling found Rapa bitterly split over the issue and on the verge of conflict. At the king's request he called and presided over a meeting to settle the matter. "At last through my reasoning with them, and persuading them to try the old king again; it was agreed to, and carried by a show of hands that

194

Teraau should still be king as long as he behaved himself, and acted according to the laws." Darling also advised the king and chiefs how to proceed should the much-feared arrival of Catholic missionaries materialize, and urged them to follow the Tahitian example of outlawing "the buying and drinking of spirits" (Darling 1836). Finally, in 1852,

the people surrounded us, asking questions on, to them, difficult passages of Scripture, especially those which the mormons have wrested to suit their turn [Mormon missionaries had just visited Rapa]. They also asked with regard to their policy, and grievances from the people of vessels touching there. Some of the missionaries ought to reside among them six or eight months to train them a little and put them in order, that they may proceed themselves in regular discipline (Platt 1852).

As representatives of the English missionaries, it is not unlikely that the resident Tahitian teachers also wielded some political influence, further usurping the authority of the ramage chiefs.

The growth of commerce also may have contributed to the decreasing authority of the chiefs. The missionary Davies felt that work as pearl divers would injure the Rapans spiritually and morally by exposing them "to the example of the sailors." He reported: "I have written repeatedly to the teachers and the chiefs to endeavor to keep the people at home, but they say it is not in their power, the foreigners offer temptations of property which they cannot resist" (Davies 1835).[8] Before the advent of inter-island trade, Rapa's primary economic resource was the land. Since the land was owned by ramages, the ramage chiefs were well placed to exercise control over the economic sector of life, and this buttressed their authority over the people. Work as divers, sailors and whalers opened up new sources of income not based on the ramage, and this measure of economic independence most likely served to weaken the general influence of the chiefs.

In addition to their general effect of drastically altering ecological and political conditions, the virulent epidemics may have directly eroded the ramage authority system. Since by mid-century about 90 percent of the pre-European population had perished,

[8] But see page 194.

it is possible that in a number of ramages the ruling line and entire chiefly class had died out. This could have caused confusion over succession, and perhaps when a new chief did emerge, others in the ramage were resentful and reluctant to obey someone who shortly before had been only slightly their better. Again, the frightful decimation of population must have produced some degree of social anomie. Lucett wrote in 1843: "There has been great mortality amongst them of late, and they seem to entertain the most melancholy forebodings, hinting that in five years they believed there would not be one of them left alive upon the island" (Lucett 1851 I:342). Their forebodings were not without justification, for the epidemic of 1863–64 swept away at least a third of the population within about a year. At this time "the people . . . were scattered all over the island thro' fear of the disease" (Green 1864b). Terror was the companion of each new epidemic and listless apathy its aftermath. Doubtless in such periods all joint action ground to a halt while leader and follower alike became totally concerned with the survival of his family and grief over the losses sustained. The system of ramage stratification and authority must have weakened with each successive disaster.

Finally, shifts in residence and changes in ramage structure after 1830 probably contributed to the decay of chiefly authority. If the migrations were by a family or two at a time rather than entire ramages moving *en masse*, many ramages would have been divided residentially, some members still in the home area and others in Ha'urei or some other village. Such a situation would have lessened the authority of the ramage chiefs because they could not maintain close control over those members living at some distance. Probably another factor was the change in ramage structure to nondiscreteness. Strong and general authority cannot persist in nondiscrete ramages, since the individual may be faced with conflicting commands from the chiefs of the various ramages to which he belongs. Therefore the authority system would be undermined because people could retain membership although they occasionally ignored the commands of the chief.

All these factors — conversion to Christianity and the influence of the missionaries, inter-island commerce, epidemics, and population movements toward a few villages with resultant changes in ramage structure — conspired to reduce the authority of the ramage chiefs. In the 1860s the ramage must have been a hollow structure as far as internal and external political matters were concerned. By 1868 the village had replaced the ramage as Rapa's political unit, with administrative and legal affairs in the hands of municipal councils and judges. To phrase this in terms of the theory of specific evolution, in the adapted state of the ancient society the political unit was the ramage, at that time a discrete and local unit. By the 1860s the political organization based on the ramage was poorly adapted to social and economic conditions, one reason for this being that the ramage was no longer discrete. Shifting political functions from the ramage to the village was an adaptive change in the sense that the political unit of society became once again a discrete and local group.

The Rapan polity was again reorganized in 1887 when Lacascade, the Governor of French Oceania, forcefully intervened in the island's internal affairs. He abolished the monarchy and replaced local laws with the French code. In other changes introduced by Lacascade, the municipal councils were replaced by a single District Council composed of seven members; five of these were elected from Ha'urei and one each from the subdistricts of 'Area and Tupuaki.[9] The Governor or his representative gained authority to appoint a chief and assistant chief from among the seven elected counsellors. All acts of the council required the approval of the French resident agent, who replaced the king as the most powerful individual in the political organization. The native judges were retained, but they and the entire administrative

9 The imposed change from councils for each village to a single council may have been nonadaptive. In effect, this redefined the political unit as the entire population rather than the village. This is even more true today, when all counsellors are elected by the entire population rather than Lacascade's plan of each village having its representatives. In Chapter 8 we discussed village rivalry and resentment when the District Council is dominated by members from one village. Each village has its interests, which could be expressed under the system of municipal councils more easily than under the current regime of a single council. While it is not likely that all disruptive rivalry would cease, I suggest that the Rapan polity would run more smoothly if something similar to the municipal council system of the pre-1887 period were reestablished.

and judicial organization were placed under the authority of the Administrator of the Austral Archipelago (Lacascade 1887b).

Except for the abolition of the monarchy and the increased authority of French officials, most of Lacascade's changes seem quite minor. The institution of French law had great potential for change, but this has not materialized since it is rarely applied. Lacascade's District Council was nothing drastically new, for the system of government by elected council had been in operation in Rapa for almost twenty years. On the other hand, the political organization instituted by Lacascade in 1887 is, with a few minor differences, the modern system described in Chapter 8. Thus, the major change in political organization occurred in the 1860s, when the government passed from the ramages and their chiefs to the villages and their elected councils. Lacascade added some finishing touches in 1887. Since then, Rapan political organization has remained much as he left it.

Two years later, in 1889, the new District Council redistributed the land. This sounded the death knell for the ancient ramages. Their territories were divided and awarded to individual owners, who are today remembered as the founders of the modern landowning ramages. However, while land distribution obviously had a drastic effect on the ramages themselves, it probably did not fundamentally change the ramage *system*. That is, the ramages that existed before land distribution in 1889 were not basically different in structure and function from the ramages of today. The ancient ramage was a politically important, discrete cognatic descent group; the modern ramage is a politically unimportant, nondiscrete cognatic descent group. We have argued that the change to nondiscreteness began in the 1830s and that the ramage had lost its political significance by the late 1860s. If this analysis is correct, then prior to their demise in 1889 the ramages would have been, like their modern counterparts, nondiscrete cognatic descent groups limited to the ownership and administration of property.

One important element of change in the ramage, however, remains to be considered. In the pre-European era the ramage closely controlled its territory, restricting its use to ramage members. Today anyone may establish improvements on unused land anywhere, with the result that new ramages, separate from those owning the land, have grown up with the sole function of owning improvements. The historical sources provide no information on when or how this change occurred, but I did elicit a local explanation. A Rapan who seems relatively well versed in history told me that when the land was redistributed in 1889 it was found that taro terraces which many persons had been cultivating for years were located on lands in which they no longer held rights of ownership. She said that to avoid problems of rent-paying or the inevitable confusion and disputes which would have accompanied a vast exchange of terraces, it was decided that all taro terraces would remain in the exclusive possession of their cultivators regardless of who owned the territory on which they were located. She said also that this decision was perpetuated when new terraces and other improvements were subsequently made. If her information is correct, the current rule that anyone may make and own improvements on unused land anywhere was established in 1889.

This historical analysis was prefaced by the assertion that events push a poorly adapted system over the brink of change and determine to some extent the course of change. We may now summarize the chain of critical events in nineteenth century Rapa. By 1830 a clear majority of the population had perished, rendering the social system poorly adapted and hence susceptible to change. For the aspects of society examined, the events which triggered the process of change were: (1) conversion to Christianity, and (2) the advent of trade and opportunities for wage labor. These promoted the development of Ha'urei as the island's religious and commercial center, which in turn produced a concentration of population in that village. We have interpreted this as a major cause of the change from ramage discreteness to nondiscreteness, a change which therefore probably began in the 1830s. Combined with other factors, ramage nondiscreteness eroded the chiefs' authority and this produced conditions favorable to the ramage's loss of all political functions. What precise events precipitated this change have not been discovered,[10] but the village had replaced

10 But see footnote 6, page 193.

the ramage as Rapa's political unit by 1868. With this development I submit that, in the areas of ramage structure and political organization, Rapan society completed the period of rapid change with the achievement of a new and satisfactory adaptation. Further modifications occurred in 1887–1889 with Lacascade's intervention and land redistribution. The separation of improvement ownership from landownership was a major development, although it had little effect on the purely structural aspects of the ramage or political organization. For these areas the events of 1887–1889 were relatively minor adjustments which did not drastically change the adapted social system that was established twenty years before and persists to the present.

CONTINUITY IN CHANGE

In addition to historical events, another and perhaps more important factor guiding the direction of social change is the nature of the changing society itself. Social scientists have come to realize that a social system plays an active rather than a passive role in its own history. After all, if change is adaptive, the process of adaptation must take as its raw material the social system before change sets in. Therefore, we may anticipate a relationship between the original system and that system at a later time. This point has been made in different ways. Developing his "Principle of Stabilization," Harding states that through adaptation a culture becomes specialized, and that such specialization is self-perpetuating. Hence the culture becomes conservative, resisting change which would alter its specialization. As a corollary to the principle of stabilization, "When acted upon by external forces a culture will, if necessary, undergo specific changes only to the extent of and with the effect of *preserving* unchanged its fundamental structure and character" (Sahlins and Service 1960:54, Harding's italics). Sorokin's principle of immanent change is another statement of the determinative force of a social system in its own development.

The totality of the external circumstances is relevant, but mainly in the way of retarding or accelerating the unfolding of the immanent destiny; weakening or reinforcing some of the traits of the system;

200

hindering or facilitating a realization of the immanent potentialities of the system; finally, in catastrophic changes, destroying the system; but these external circumstances cannot force the system to manifest what it potentially does not have; to become what it immanently cannot become; to do what it immanently is incapable of doing (Sorokin 1944: 602).

In studying social change, then, we should be alert for similarities as well as differences; we should look for *continuity* in change. Continuity may be demonstrated in two ways. One is to trace change historically, showing how each step developed out of its predecessor, as is attempted for Rapa above. The other way is to compare the system logically at two or more points in time, with the aim of isolating fundamental similarities. We turn now to a structural comparison of the ancient and modern Rapan ramages with this end in view.

Although the surface differences between the ancient and modern ramages are great, both rest on the same principles of organization. Most differences between them may be viewed as different manifestations of these principles, stemming from adaptation to different sets of environmental and especially political conditions. The structural principles are: (1) that rights in property (and therefore in the ramage — the property-owning group in both ancient and modern Rapa) pass by cognatic descent; and (2) that ramage members are differentiated by descent line seniority. Let us examine these in turn.

Although both are property-owning cognatic descent groups, the ancient and modern ramages differ considerably in that the former was discrete while the latter is nondiscrete. This difference stems from the fact that the ancient rule of descent was exclusive (one could activate membership in only one ramage at a time), while the modern rule is nonexclusive (one may be an active member of several ramages simultaneously). One could easily conclude that modern Rapa's nonexclusive cognatic rule of descent was borrowed from (or imposed by) the French. Thus, a remarkably precise rendering of the modern descent rule may be found in Article 745 of the *Code Civil* (54th edition), which reads in part: "Children or their descendants succeed to their father and mother, grandparents, or other ascendants without distinction of sex or primogeniture." The only difference from this European system of inheritance is the operational one that Rapans do not divide their property so frequently. Yet our analysis of the nineteenth century belies this explanation as historically unsound, for it is likely that the shift from ramage discreteness to nondiscreteness began in the 1830s, while active French intervention and the imposition of the *Code Civil* dates from 1887, a half-century later. I suggest that the modern descent rule developed out of the ancient rule, that both are based on the general and underlying principle that rights in property pass by cognatic descent. The considerable difference in form between the ancient and the modern ramage is the result of a relatively minor modification in the application of this principle, a modification which may be understood in terms of adaptation.

In conditions of heavy population pressure on land and frequent warfare between ramages, the ancient ramage required the undivided loyalty of its members for effective military action. The rule of exclusive cognatic descent was well adapted to these conditions, in that it generated a system of discrete ramages wherein the individual was limited to active membership in the ramage of his residence. Today Rapa is underpopulated and the ramage has lost its political and military functions; it therefore does not require the exclusive support of its members. What an individual should do as a member of one ramage seldom, if ever, conflicts with what he should do as a member of another. Here is a case where, as Sorokin predicted might happen, the external circumstances have facilitated "a realization of the immanent potentialities of the system." The previously exclusive descent rule has been expanded to become nonexclusive, enabling modern Rapans simultaneously to exercise active membership in all ramages in which they trace legitimate cognatic descent. As a result, of course, the modern ramage is nondiscrete. .

If the principle of cognatic descent has been manifested more fully in the modern ramage, the fate of the second principle — that ramage members are differentiated by descent line seniority — has been the reverse. In ancient times this principle was extensively realized in the elaborate system of stratification within the ramage and the related division of society into classes. The adaptive value of stratification was that it provided the basis for the ramage's network of authority, essential for effective action in large-scale coordinated enterprises such as warfare and the construction of the mountain forts. Manifestations of the principle of differentiation by descent-line seniority have been greatly inhibited by the events of the nineteenth century. As the ramage's political significance declined, and as it became a nondiscrete unit, its network of internal authority decayed and eventually vanished. Presumably, the system of stratification deteriorated contemporaneously. Today the principle of differentiation by descent-line seniority, now coupled with the distinction between generations, is visible only in the ideal order of succession to the office of ramage manager (see page 52).

But the point is that, however reduced, this principle still *is* visible. Although changing conditions have minimized one and maximized the other, the principles of differentiation by descent-line seniority and cognatic descent form the structural basis of the ramage, old and new. This implies that in the remaking of Rapan society, similarity is as important as difference, continuity as important as change.

DISASTER AND READAPTATION

Rapan history is relevant to an understanding of the long-range effects of disaster on human society. Specifically, Rapa is a case where an adapted social system was disrupted by disaster, and where ensuing social change has resulted in the formation of a new adapted system. Our findings confirm Chapman's general observation:

Many disaster studies note the fact that the impact of disaster upon a community . . . is not simply to disrupt this community's original state of equilibrium and to initiate processes which return it to a state of equilibrium, but is also sometimes to induce lasting social changes in the community. The consequence of a disaster may, therefore, be that from one system a new system is produced with its own quite different normal state (Chapman 1962b:322).

One point must be made clear: Rapan society was not struck by a single disaster and then given a period of grace for recovery and reorganization. Examining Table 1 (page 30) we note that epidemics and depopulation characterize most of the nineteenth century. The epidemic of 1863 was the last disaster which killed more than a majority of the population within a short time span, but the general trend of population decline was not reversed until around the turn of the present century. Yet, in the areas of ramage structure and political organization, the modern, adapted social system seems to have been forged by 1868. This means that social change in Rapa did not follow a disaster; it happpened during a period of successive disasters, with one of the most severe catastrophes (that of 1863) occurring just five years before the modern social system was established. Therefore, if disaster has any special effect on long-range social change it certainly should be evident in Rapa, where disaster struck throughout the entire period of readaptation.

What long-range effects might disaster have on a society? Change stemming from the disruption of an adapted social system is taken here to be a process of readaptation to a natural and human environment, the direction of readaptation being determined in part by the historical events of the period of change and in part by the nature of the original social system. The process of readaptation would occur whether the original state was disrupted by disaster or some other cause. However, disaster may have an effect on the direction and extent of readaptation. We might anticipate, for example, that change would be more extensive in a society undergoing a series of disasters than in a society recovering from one catastrophe. This is simply because in the former case the events of the period of change (such events being the successive disasters themselves) would be more disruptive. Again, disaster may affect the guiding role of the original social system in the process of readaptation. If the disaster destroys the ordering principles of the original system, that system could have little effect on the direction of change and we might therefore expect change to be extensive.[11] Or the impact of disaster may be selec-

[11] For example, epidemics may have had a more disintegrating effect on the social system of the Marquesas than elsewhere in Polynesia (Beaglehole 1957: 238; Suggs 1966:187–188).

tive, touching some parts of the social system more than others, and this would certainly affect the direction of change. Had Rapa's disaster been some blight which put an end to taro agriculture on the island, and had this not been accompanied by the loss of a majority of the population, Rapan history would have been quite different. In such a case, however, disaster may have no special consequences in the period of change itself. That is, although social change will differ according to which elements of the original system have been disrupted, the process, direction, and outcome of change may not vary significantly whether the disruption was produced by disaster or by something else.

The impact of disaster upon Rapa was severe by any measure. Although at times depopulation was gradual, disease did its most deadly work in several swift blows. Perhaps two-thirds of the population perished between 1826 and 1829, and a similar loss resulted from the epidemic of 1863. Moreover, we have argued that a series of disasters, such as struck Rapa, would be more devastating than a single calamity. There can be no question that disastrous epidemics disrupted the ancient social system, removed its adaptive value and hence rendered it highly susceptible to rapid change.[12] Yet, once the process of change had begun, disaster was not an important factor in the direction of change nor in the formation of a new, adapted social system.

Severe as they were, Rapa's disasters did not destroy the ordering principles of the ancient social system. We have seen, for example, that although altered conditions have led them to be manifested in different ways, the same structural principles underlie both the ancient and modern ramages. Nor were disasters the most important events guiding the social system through the period of change toward its new state of adaptation. Far more important were events such as the movements of population into a few villages — and this resulted from religious and commercial considerations, not disastrous epidemics. In fact, since the people scattered all over the island at the height of the epidemic of 1863 (see page 196 above), far from concentrating the population the

[12] The experience of Yap indicates that extreme depopulation need not always have this effect. See Schneider (1955:211–212, 217–218).

epidemics had the opposite immediate effect of dispersing it.[13]

On the basis of what happened in Rapa, then, we may conclude that disaster may be extremely effective in disrupting an adapted social system, thus leaving it highly susceptible to change. But disaster is not likely to play a unique role in the long-term process of change itself. Even when the society sustains successive disasters throughout the entire period of change, other factors guide the social system to a new state of adaptation.

From this perspective the most important lesson of Rapan history is an appreciation for the remarkable resilience of human society. During the decades following European contact, the population was nearly eradicated, Rapa became enmeshed in a network of inter-island trade, political authority passed to France, and religious authority to the Christian church. With so many potent forces raised against it, one might not be surprised had the traditional society disintegrated altogether. Yet this analysis suggests that social change in Rapa stems less from the imposition of institutions and laws from the outside than from adjustments made from within. The story of change in this island is not one of the French finding a prostrate community and remaking it after their own fashion, but of Rapan society retaining its viability in catastrophic circumstances and readapting to its new environment.

---

[13] It should be recalled that anomie resulting from the epidemics may have contributed to the erosion of authority of ramage chiefs. At most, however, this was but one of several causes.

The Descent System: Further Details

Cognatic descent systems such as the Rapan are not often found in anthropological literature. Especially because it generates overlapping descent groups, the Rapan system is highly relevant to a current theoretical controversy over the whole nature of descent. An expansion of the discussion in Chapter 3 and a few comments on some of the theoretical problems involved might be of interest to readers concerned with problems of descent and kinship (see also Hanson 1970).

SOME RAMAGE AFFILIATIONS

The best way I know to describe the system of overlapping ramages is to turn to actual cases, so we shall examine the ramage affiliations of two sibling groups related to each other as first cousins, and bearing the surnames Natiki and Nāri'i.[1] Figure 6

[1] Surnames pass from the father to his recognized children as in the Western system.

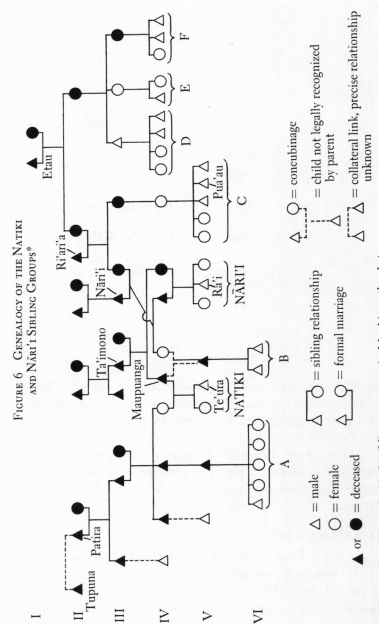

FIGURE 6 GENEALOGY OF THE NATIKI
AND NĀRI'I SIBLING GROUPS*

△ = male

○ = female

● or ▲ = deceased

[⌒ over △○] = sibling relationship

[⌒ under △○] = formal marriage

[⌐○ dashed] = concubinage

[△ dashed to ⌐] = child not legally recognized by parent

△ ⋯ △ = collateral link, precise relationship unknown

*The half-brother of the Natiki siblings was recognized by his mother but not by their common father.

208

presents the genealogy of these two sibling groups. The chart has been simplified in several respects. First, three or four collateral kinsmen on the upper generations who have no descendants and who are not important in matters pertaining to ramages have been left out. Second, for the sibling set which terminates each descent line, only those members presently living in Rapa are included. Finally, each of the terminal sibling groups is made up of adults, ranging in age from twenty to fifty; members of all these sibling groups have children, and some have grandchildren. Were these further descendants included, the genealogy would cover a span of seven generations rather than the six shown here. For example, there were originally thirteen Natiki full siblings. Of the eleven not included here, six are dead and five have emigrated to Tahiti. This sibling group has nine children and two grandchildren living in Rapa, and seventeen children and five grandchildren living in Tahiti. It should be remembered that such additional siblings, children, and grandchildren all belong to the ramages listed below, although for the sake of simplicity they are not considered.

The various ramages to which the Natiki and Nāri'i sibling groups belong are as follows:

1. *Tupuna.* This ramage was founded jointly by Patira, the mother's father's father of the Natiki sibling group, and a contemporary of his named Avae'oru. Tupuna, a collateral kinsman of Patira of unknown degree (connected with Patira by a dotted line on the genealogy) was awarded several tracts of land in 1889. Having no children, his property went to his collateral kinsmen, and two of the tracts were given jointly to his kinsmen Patira and Avae'oru. These tracts make up the estate of this ramage. Its present members are all legitimate descendants of Patira — the Natiki siblings, their mother, and sibling group A — plus all legitimate descendants of Avae'oru, who are not shown on the chart. The manager of the ramage is Ra'i, the male of the Nāri'i sibling group. My information is not totally clear, but I believe Ra'i is not a member of this ramage. He was probably chosen as manager because of his personal qualities, at a time when no member was considered to be qualified for the job.

2. *Patira 1*. This ramage was founded by Patira, mother's father's father of the Natiki siblings. Its estate is composed exclusively of land. It includes six tracts awarded to Patira in 1889, plus four tracts which Patira received individually from Tupuna. At present this ramage is composed of all legitimate living descendants of Patira; that is, the Natiki siblings, their mother, and sibling group A. In accordance with the rule that the manager be the senior male of the ramage, the manager here is Te'ura, the Natiki brother.

3. *Patira 2*. The founder of this ramage is the mother of the Natiki siblings. Its estate is composed of taro terraces and coffee groves created by their mother's father and mother's father's father. This ramage results from a division of all jointly owned taro terraces and coffee plots between their mother and mother's brother some twenty years ago. Patira 2 is made up exclusively of the Natiki siblings and their mother. (The other ramage resulting from this division, Patira 3, owns the groves and terraces given to the Natiki siblings' mother's brother, and is composed only of sibling group A.[2] This property division was the same sort mentioned in Chapter 3, where a ramage divides its improvements but continues to hold its land in common.) The manager of Patira 2 is Te'ura.

4. *Ngate Mato*. This is a very large and historically special ramage which owns only land. When the land was redistributed in 1889 some tracts were not included. Such tracts apparently remained in the hands of pre-1889 ramages and their descendants. These ramages have retained their ancient names and no one can identify their founders. Their large size today stems from the fact that current members affiliate by tracing descent from any member of a *group* of persons who lived in 1889. Ngate Mato is a case in point. The Natiki siblings affiliate to Ngate Mato through their mother's mother. Sibling group A belongs by merit of

[2] According to the Rapans, the name of all three of these ramages is Patira, the surname which has passed patrilineally from the original Patira, mother's father's father of the Natiki siblings. The numbers have been added for convenience in distinguishing them. The same procedure has been followed below to distinguish the several ramages named Natiki and Nāri'i.

descent from the same individual. I am not certain if the Nāri'i siblings and groups B, C, D, E, and F belong to this ramage. The manager is Te'ura.

5. *Okopou.* Here is another example of an extremely large and historically special ramage; this one probably includes the majority of Rapa's population. It owns only land. The Natiki siblings affiliate to Okopou through their mother's father's father, and sibling group A through the same person. The Nāri'i siblings also belong, probably affiliating through their father. For sibling group B, then, the link would be through their father's mother. I am not certain how sibling groups C, D, E, and F affiliate, but very likely some or all of them are members. The manager of Okopou is not shown on the genealogy.

6. *Natiki 1.* Ta'imono Natiki, father's father of the Natiki siblings and mother's father of the Nāri'i siblings, founded this ramage. Its estate is composed of a tract of territory awarded probably to Ta'imono in 1889, a coffee grove planted by a brother of Ta'imono (which, the brother being childless, passed to his closest kinsman, Ta'imono), and numerous taro terraces. Some of these terraces were made by Ta'imono and others by his father, but since Ta'imono was the only heir of his father who had descendants, they are all considered to have been included in his personal estate. This ramage is composed of the Natiki and Nāri'i sibling groups. Following the rule of succession by seniority, its manager is Te'ura.

7. *Natiki 2.* Here the founder was Maupuanga, father of the Natiki siblings. The estate of the ramage consists of two masonry houses, certain taro terraces and coffee groves created by Maupuanga himself, and other terraces and groves created by his father Ta'imono but awarded to Maupuanga in a property division between himself and his sister, Hurita. The ramage is composed solely of the Natiki sibling group; its manager is Te'ura.

8. *Nāri'i 1.* This ramage was founded by Nāri'i, father's father's father of the Nāri'i siblings. Its estate consists solely of territory. Present members are all descendants of the founder: the Nāri'i

siblings, their father's sister and her grandsons (sibling group B). The manager of this ramage is Ra'i.

9. *Nāri'i 2.* The estate of this ramage consists of coffee groves, taro terraces, and a masonry house. These formed the personal estates of the father and mother of the Nāri'i siblings which have merged by coming into the joint possession of their children. Members of Nāri'i 2 are the Nāri'i siblings, and the manager is Ra'i.

10. *Ri'ari'a.* Founded by Ri'ari'a, father's mother's father of the Nāri'i siblings, this ramage owns only the territory awarded its founder in 1889. Its membership consists of the Nāri'i siblings, sibling group B and their father's mother, and sibling group C and their mother. Consistent with the rule of succession by seniority, the manager is Ra'i.

11. *Tinohuri.* This ramage was founded by Etau Tinohuri, the only male on generation I of the genealogy. It owns the territory awarded to Etau in 1889. Except for Okopou and Ngate Mato, it is the largest of the ramages listed here. Its membership consists of the Nāri'i siblings, sibling group B and their father's mother, sibling group C and their mother, sibling group D and their father, sibling group E and their mother, and sibling group F. Incidentally, the children of Pua'au (second son in sibling group C) affiliate to the Tinohuri ramage in two different ways. One is through their father's mother, and the second is through their mother, for Pua'au is married to his mother's mother's mother's sister's daughter's daughter, the female of sibling group F. The manager of this ramage is again its senior male, the father of sibling group D.

Note that of the six grandparents of the two focal sibling groups, descent for purposes of ramage membership is traced from or through five of them. The sixth, father's mother of the Natikis and mother's mother of the Nāri'is, was an immigrant from Ra'ivavae, and therefore inherited no property in Rapa. However, these sibling groups claim they share property interests in Ra'ivavae, and very likely they trace their rights through this woman.

212

TABLE 5. RAMAGE AFFILIATIONS.

| | | | | | Sibling Group | | | |
Ramage	Natiki	Nāri'i	A	B	C	D	E	F
Patira 2	+	−	−	−	−	−	−	−
Natiki 2	+	−	−	−	−	−	−	−
Tupuna	+	−	+	−	−	−	−	−
Patira 1	+	−	+	−	−	−	−	−
Ngate Mato	+	?	+	?	?	?	?	?
Natiki 1	+	+	−	−	−	−	−	−
Okopou	+	+	+	+	?	?	?	?
Nāri'i 2	−	+	−	−	−	−	−	−
Nāri'i 1	−	+	−	+	−	−	−	−
Ri'ari'a	−	+	−	+	+	−	−	−
Tinohuri	−	+	−	+	+	+	+	+

Table 5 summarizes the affiliations of all sibling groups on the genealogy to the eleven ramages listed. While this chart gives the fullest information for ramage affiliations of the Natiki and Nāri'i sibling groups that my data allow, the list may not be exhaustive for either of them. The types of property considered here are only territory, houses, and presently cultivated coffee groves and taro terraces. It is possible that groves of orange or lumber trees or abandoned taro terraces in which one or the other of these sibling groups shares ownership stem from yet other ancestors. The ramage affiliations of the other six sibling groups mentioned here are of course far from complete. Since the purpose was to show the composition of as many of the ramages to which the Natikis and/or Nāri'is belong as possible, the other sibling groups have been examined only as they articulate with the two focal groups. Had we sufficient data and courage to attempt the tremendously complex job of filling in all the descent lines for these sibling groups and for the other groups with which they share membership in various ramages, eventually we would complete the tangled genealogical route that would show the composition of every ramage on the island.

THE PROBLEM OF OVERLAPPING

Under a cognatic descent rule it is possible for an individual to belong to more than one descent group because he may trace descent along several different lines. If individuals do in fact exercise simultaneous membership in several descent groups, those groups will not form discrete or mutually-exclusive segments of society, but will overlap in membership. This is the case in Rapa.

In some quarters the possibility that descent groups might overlap in membership poses a serious theoretical difficulty. Leach is unequivocal on this point: descent groups are discrete by definition; to include nondiscrete groups only results in confusion (Leach 1962:131). He registers hearty agreement in these matters with the earlier theorist Rivers, whose position Leach summarizes in the statement that the "notion of 'descent group' could only be useful if the groups in question were discrete and did not overlap; he [Rivers] therefore insisted that in practice a *descent group* should always be a *unilineal descent group*" (1962:130–131, Leach's italics). Perhaps others who prefer to restrict "descent" to "unilineal descent" (e.g., Goody 1959:66, 1961:7–8; Radcliffe-Brown 1929a:50–51, 1929b) are also motivated by the idea that descent groups must be discrete. In this connection Fortes may represent the exception which proves the rule, for he speaks of "bilateral descent groups" only if they are totally endogamous, and hence, discrete (1959:206).

As I understand it, "descent group" is a purely structural concept. It refers to a type of group defined by a particular means of recruiting members. The specific activities and responsibilities that fall under the jurisdiction of descent groups are *operational* considerations, and they vary tremendously from society to society. They have no place in the definition of a structural concept that aims at cross-cultural validity and utility.[3] Yet when the problem of overlapping leads us to limit descent groups to discrete groups by definition I think exactly this has occurred, for the problem of overlapping is rooted in operational considerations. This may be seen clearly in the curious but instructive fact that many of those theorists who seem most committed to the notion of discrete descent groups have for years been dealing with nondiscrete groups without sensing any particular difficulty: double unilineal

[3] My position on this point is quite similar to that more elaborately developed by Scheffler (1966).

systems. If each individual belongs to one patrilineage and one matrilineage, then descent groups of these two types overlap (or "cross-cut") one another in membership. No problems have been perceived in such systems because, in the most frequently discussed cases, while descent groups are nondiscrete *structurally* they are discrete *operationally*. That is, matrilineages and patrilineages engage in different spheres of activity, with the result that what the indivdual should do as a member of his patrilineage never conflicts with — indeed, is not even relevant to — what he should do as a member of his matrilineage. Fortes phrases his strictly defined idea of double descent systems: "The total universe of rights, duties, claims and capacities in relation to property, office, rank and ritual status are partitioned into equal and opposite categories for a person" (1963:60). Leach puts the same idea in the form of the hypothesis that "in all double unilineal systems the two sets of unilineal corporations, the patrilineal and the matrilineal, represent entirely different and sharply contrasted functional interests" (1962:134). (There seem to be exceptions to these statements, however, and our understanding of double descent might be deepened if more attention were paid to cases in which pátrilineages and matrilineages do not operate in totally distinct realms. In Pukapuka, for example, the two types of lineage overlap operationally to at least some degree in that they both own taro beds [E. and P. Beaglehole 1938:44].) .

Having argued that overlapping poses purely operational problems, we may explore just what these problems are. Schneider summarizes the position of those who demand that descent groups be discrete:

The whole person as an aggregate of different commitments must be able to provide unqualified solidarity with the unit to which he belongs. . . . But if a single person's solidarity is qualified by membership in two or more different units *of like order*, then his commitment to, his solidarity with, one of them is qualified by the claims of the other upon him (1965:46, Schneider's italics).

From this it is clear that at bottom the problem of overlapping is the possibility that the individual may be faced with conflicting obligations to the different descent groups to which he belongs.

The problem can be solved only by defining the individual's commitment to the descent group in such a way that he may belong to several without compromising his obligation to any.

It does appear that nondiscrete descent groups would pose an insoluble problem in the classic descent systems — such as many reported from Africa — which anthropologists most frequently discuss. Where descent groups are of great significance in a wide range of economic, political and religious affairs, and where much of the individual's activity is directly related to his descent group membership, to be equally committed to several groups of the same kind would inevitably place incompatible obligations upon him. But Firth (1963:25–26) has suggested that a system having nondiscrete descent groups could exist if these groups were restricted operationally to a specific resource or a specific activity or occasion. In this manner the problem of overlapping is solved — rather, avoided — in Rapa. A ramage undertakes no activity that is not directly related to its estate, and for the most part, these activities are very few. Because a Rapan is rarely called upon to act in the role of ramage member, and because his commitment to it is so narrowly defined, it is unlikely that his obligations as a member of one ramage would conflict with his obligations as a member of several others. In Rapa, then, the problem of overlapping is solved by reducing it to the vanishing point.

To be more specific, there are only two ways in which the individual's obligations to different descent groups may be thought to conflict. First, two groups to which he belongs might come into opposition, such as a feud or dispute. It might be thought that this could place him in a quandary as to which group to support. Second, the groups themselves may not be in opposition but the individual may be faced with incompatible duties to them. For example, he might be required to join with one group in one place and, at the same time, with another group in another place.

Although the narrow range of activities available to the ramage renders it unlikely, both types of conflicting obligations could occur in Rapa. Occasionally two ramages dispute the ownership of a piece of property, most common being arguments over the boundary separating adjacent coffee groves. It is possible that some persons may belong to both disputing ramages, but there seems to be no reason to anticipate that these circumstances would place the individual in an impossible situation — he could be ideally situated to arrange an amicable settlement. As for the second type of conflicting obligations, in Rapa this would again be limited to activities concerning coffee groves, for only here does the ramage act as a unit with any regularity. If two ramages to which he belongs appoint the same day for joint maintenance or harvesting of their coffee groves, the individual would encounter a conflict in that he could not join both parties. But Rapans solve this problem easily by recognizing the right of anyone involved in a joint activity to send a proxy in his stead (see also Silverman 1967). In this way an individual with conflicting obligations could be represented in two or more work groups simultaneously.

Bibliography

Aitken, Robert T.
1930   *Ethnology of Tubuai.* Honolulu: Bernice P. Bishop Museum Bulletin 70.
Barff, Charles
1858   Letter to Rev. A. Tidman, 2 December 1858. Archives of the London Missionary Society, South Sea Letters 1796–1906, Box 27, Folder 3, Jacket A.
Barff, John
1846   Visit to the Austral Islands. Archives of the London Missionary Society, South Sea Letters 1796–1906, Box 19, Folder 2, Jacket E.
Beaglehole, Ernest
1957   *Social Change in the South Pacific.* London: George Allen & Unwin.
————, and Pearl Beaglehole
1938   *Ethnology of Pukapuka.* Honolulu: Bernice P. Bishop Museum Bulletin 150.
Bell, F. L. S.
1931   "The Place of Food in the Social Life of Central Polynesia." *Oceania* 2:117–135.
Bidney, David (Ed.)
1963   *The Concept of Freedom in Anthropology.* The Hague: Mouton.
Buck, Peter H.
1934   *Mangaian Society.* Honolulu: Bernice P. Bishop Museum Bulletin 122.
Caillet, X.
1868   Caillet to La Roncière, 10 February 1868. Archives de la France d'Outre-Mer, Océanie A91.
1886   "Note sur Rapa." *Bulletin de la société bretonne de géographie,* 5ᵉ année, No. 26:207–219.
1886/87   "L'Île de Rapa." *Bulletin de la société de géographie commerciale de Paris* 9:280–287.
Caillot, A-C Eugène
1910   *Histoire de la Polynésie orientale.* Paris: Leroux.
1932   *Histoire de l'île Oparo ou Rapa.* Paris: Leroux.

219

Chapman, Dwight W.
1962a "A Brief Introduction to Contemporary Disaster Research." In George W. Baker and Dwight W. Chapman (Eds.), *Man and Society in Disaster*. New York: Basic Books.
1962b "Dimensions of Models in Disaster Behavior." In George W. Baker and Dwight W. Chapman (Eds.), *Man and Society in Disaster*. New York: Basic Books.
Charter, G., and E. Krause
1849 Visit to Rapa, dated Raiatea, 10 July 1849. Archives of the London Missionary Society, South Sea Letters 1796–1906, Box 22, Folder 1, Jacket C.
Chessé
1881 Chessé to minister, 10 March 1881. Archives de la France d'Outre-Mer, Océanie A122.
Darling, David
1836 Visit to Rapa, November 1836. Archives of the London Missionary Society, South Sea Letters 1796–1906, Box 11, Folder 1, Jacket B.
Davies, John
1827 "Extracts from the Journal of a Visit to the Islands of Rapa (or Oparo), Raivavai, and Tupuai. . . ." *Quarterly Chronicle of Transactions of the London Missionary Society* 3:323–332, 353–361 (July and October, 1827).
1835 Letter concerning Rapa, dated Papara, 8 October 1835. Archives of the London Missionary Society, South Sea Letters 1796–1906, Box 10, Folder 2, Jacket D.
1961 *The History of the Tahitian Mission, 1799–1830*. C. W. Newbury (Ed.). Cambridge: Cambridge University Press.
Deschanel, Paul
1888 *Les Intérêts français dans l'océan Pacifique*. Paris: Berger-Levrault.
Ellis, William
1829 *Polynesian Researches*. London: Fisher, Son, and Jackson, 2 vols.
Ferdon, Edwin N., Jr.
1965 "A Reconnaissance Survey of Three Fortified Hilltop Villages." In *Reports of the Norwegian Archaeological Expedition to Easter Island and the East Pacific*, Vol. 2: *Miscellaneous Papers*, Thor Heyerdahl and Edwin N. Ferdon, Jr. (Eds.). Monographs of the School of American Research and the Kon Tiki Museum, No. 24, pt. 2.
Firth, Raymond
1957 "A Note on Descent Groups in Polynesia." *Man* 57:4–8.
1963 "Bilateral Descent Groups: An Operational Viewpoint." In I. Schapera (Ed.), *Studies in Kinship and Marriage*. Royal Anthropological Institute: Occasional Paper No. 16.
Fortes, Meyer
1959 "Descent, Filiation and Affinity." *Man* 59:193–197, 206–212.
1963 "The 'Submerged Descent Line' in Ashanti." In I. Schapera (Ed.), *Studies in Kinship and Marriage*. Royal Anthropological Institute: Occasional Paper No. 16.
Goodenough, Ward H.
1955 "A Problem in Malayo-Polynesian Social Organization." *American Anthropologist* 57:71–83.
Goody, Jack
1959 "The Mother's Brother and the Sister's Son in West Africa." *Journal of the Royal Anthropological Institute* 89:61–88.

1961   "The Classification of Double Descent Systems." *Current Anthro-pology* 2:3–12.
Green, J. L.
1864a   "Austral Islands, Visit of the Rev. J. L. Green." *Missionary Magazine and Chronicle* (London Missionary Society) (September 1864), pp. 264–267.
1864b   Visit to the Austral Islands, dated Tahaa, 1 April 1864. Archives of the London Missionary Society, South Sea Letters 1796–1906, Box 30, Folder 1, Jacket A.
Hall, Captain Vine
1868   "On the Island of Rapa." New Zealand Institute, *Transactions* 1:75–83.
Hanson, F. Allan
1970   "Nonexclusive Cognatic Descent in Rapa." Forthcoming in Alan Howard (Ed.), *Polynesia: Readings on a Culture Area.* San Francisco: Chandler Publishing Company.
Hawthorn, H. B., and C. S. Belshaw
1957   "Cultural Evolution or Cultural Change? — the Case of Polynesia." *Journal of the Polynesian Society* 66:18–35.
Heath, T.
1840   Visit to Rapa, dated Tahiti, 8 December 1840. Archives of the London Missionary Society, South Sea Letters 1796–1906, Box 13, Folder 3, Jacket A.
Hoebel, E. Adamson
1960   "The Nature of Culture." In Harry L. Shapiro (Ed.), *Man, Culture, and Society.* New York: Oxford University Press.
Instructions
1882   Instructions pour le chef de poste de Rapa, 1 December 1882. Archives de la France d'Outre-Mer, Océanie A122.
Jaussen, Tepano
1949   *Grammaire et dictionnaire de la langue maori, dialecte tahitien.* Braine-le-Compte, Belgium: Zech et Fils.
Johansen, J. Prytz
1954   *The Maori and His Religion in Its Non-ritualistic Aspects.* Copenhagen: Ejnar Munksgaard.
Jore, Léonce
1959   *L'Océan Pacifique au temps de la restauration et de la monarchie de Juillet (1815–1848).* Paris: Besson et Chantemerle, 2 vols.
Lacascade
1887a   Lacascade to minister, 11 February 1887. Archives de la France d'Outre-Mer, Océanie A122.
1887b   Lacascade to minister, 12 July 1887. Archives de la France d'Outre-Mer, Océanie A122.
1887c   Lacascade to minister, 12 August 1887. Archives de la France d'Outre-Mer, Océanie A122.
La Roncière
1866   La Roncière to minister, 8 June 1866. Archives de la France d'Outre-Mer, Océanie K11.
Leach, E. R.
1962   "On Certain Unconsidered Aspects of Double Descent Systems." *Man* 62:130–134.
Lee, Dorothy
1959   *Freedom and Culture.* Englewood Cliffs, N.J.: Prentice-Hall.

Lucett, Edward
    1851   *Rovings in the Pacific from 1837 to 1849*. London: Longman, 2 vols.
McArthur, Norma
    1967   *Island Populations of the Pacific*. Canberra: Australian National University Press.
Malinowski, Bronislaw
    1922   *Argonauts of the Western Pacific*. London: Routledge.
    1959   *Crime and Custom in Savage Society*. Paterson, N.J.: Littlefield, Adams.
Marshall, Donald
    1961   *Ra'ivavae*. Garden City, N.Y.: Doubleday.
Méry
    1867   "Notes sur l'île Rapa." *Messager de Tahiti*, 16ᵉ année, 14 et 21 Septembre, 19 Octobre, 1867.
Moerenhout, J. A.
    1837   *Voyages aux îles du grand océan*. Paris: Adrien Maisonneuve, 2 vols.
Morris, George
    1862   Visit to Rapa, dated Raiatea, 29 March 1862. Archives of the London Missionary Society, South Sea Letters 1796–1906, Box 29, Folder 1, Jacket A.
Mulloy, William
    1965   "The Fortified Village of Morongo Uta." In *Reports of the Norwegian Archaeological Expedition to Easter Island and the East Pacific*, Vol. 2: *Miscellaneous Papers*, Thor Heyerdahl and Edwin N. Ferdon, Jr. (Eds.). Monographs of the School of American Research and the Kon Tiki Museum, No. 24, pt. 2.
Neal, Marie C.
    1965   *In Gardens of Hawaii*. Honolulu: Bernice P. Bishop Museum Special Publication 50.
Orsmond, J. M.
    1835   "Extracts of Journal." *The Evangelical Magazine and Missionary Chronicle* 13 (ns):518–520 (December 1835).
Ottino, Paul
    1965   *Ethno-histoire de Rangiroa* (publication provisoire). Papeete, Tahiti: O.R.S.T.O.M.
Panoff, Michel
    1964   "Les Structures agraires en Polynésie Française." École Pratique des Hautes Études, Vᵒ et VIᵒ Sections, Centre Documentaire pour l'Océanie, Rapports et Documents I.
Paulding, Hiram
    1831   *Journal of a Cruise of the U.S. Schooner Dolphin*. New York: Carvill.
Platt, George
    1848   With Mr. Darling on a visit to the Austral Islands, dated aboard the *John Williams*, 4 December 1848. Archives of the London Missionary Society, South Sea Letters 1796–1906, Box 21, Folder 2, Jacket E.
    1852   Visit to Rapa, dated Raiatea, 13 December 1852. Archives of the London Missionary Society, South Sea Letters 1796–1906, Box 24, Folder 8, Jacket D.
————, and E. Krause
    1845   On board the *John Williams* near Chain Island, dated 29 September 1845. Archives of the London Missionary Society, South Sea Letters 1796–1906, Box 18, Folder 4, Jacket C.

Pritchard, George
  1835 Visit to Moorea, Tubuai, Marquesas in the *Olive Branch*, 2 July–
        9 September 1835. Archives of the London Missionary Society, South
        Sea Journals, Box 8, 1834–1837.
  ———, and Alexander Simpson
  1830 "Extracts from the Journal of Messrs. Pritchard and Simpson, dur-
        ing Their Voyage to the Islands Tubuai, Raivavai, Rapa, Santa
        Christiana, Ouapuoa, Taaroa, and Taapoto." *Quarterly Chronicle
        of Transactions of the London Missionary Society* 4:161–170 (April
        1830).
Quentin, Alex.
  1867 "Rapport sur l'île Rapa." *Messager de Tahiti*, 16ᵉ année, 29 Juin
        1867.
Radcliffe-Brown, A. R.
  1929a "A Further Note on Ambrym." *Man* 29:50–53.
  1929b "Bilateral Descent." *Man* 29:199–200.
  1952 *Structure and Function in Primitive Society*. Glencoe, Ill.: Free
        Press.
Richard, Georges
  1886/87 "L'Île de Rapa." *Revue scientifique*, 3ᵉ série, tome XII, 2ᵉ
        semestre, pp. 23–24.
Ross, Angus
  1964 *New Zealand Aspirations in the Pacific in the Nineteenth Century.*
        Oxford: Clarendon Press.
Sahlins, Marshall D.
  1958 *Social Stratification in Polynesia*. Seattle: University of Washington
        Press.
  ———, and Elman R. Service (Eds.)
  1960 *Evolution and Culture*. Ann Arbor: University of Michigan Press.
Scheffler, Harold W.
  1966 "Ancestor Worship in Anthropology; or, Observations on Descent
        and Descent Groups." *Current Anthropology* 7:541–548.
Schmitt, Robert C.
  1965 "Garbled Population Estimates of Central Polynesia." *Journal of the
        Polynesian Society* 74:57–62.
Schneider, D. M.
  1955 "Abortion and Depopulation on a Pacific Island." In B. D. Paul
        (Ed.), *Health, Culture and Community*. New York: Russell Sage
        Foundation.
  1965 "Some Muddles in the Models." In *The Relevance of Models for
        Social Anthropology*, A.S.A. Monograph No. 1. New York: Praeger.
Scholefield, Guy H.
  1920 *The Pacific, Its Past and Future*. New York: Scribner's.
Silverman, Martin G.
  1967 "Participation by Proxy." *Journal of the Polynesian Society* 76:215–
        217.
Smith, Carlyle S.
  1965 "Test Excavations and Surveys of Miscellaneous Sites on the Island
        of Rapa Iti." In *Reports of the Norwegian Archaeological Expedition
        to Easter Island and the East Pacific*, Vol. 2: *Miscellaneous Papers*,
        Thor Heyerdahl and Edwin N. Ferdon, Jr. (Eds.). Monographs of
        the School of American Research and the Kon Tiki Museum, No. 24,
        pt. 2.

Sorokin, Pitirim A.
1941   *Social and Cultural Dynamics,* Vol. 4: *Basic Problems, Principles, and Methods.* New York: American Book Company.
Stokes, John F. G.
1930   "Ethnology of Rapa Island." Unpublished manuscript on file in the Bernice P. Bishop Museum, Honolulu, 5 vols.
1955   "Language in Rapa." *Journal of the Polynesian Society* 64:315–340.
Suggs, Robert C.
1966   *Marquesan Sexual Behavior.* New York: Harcourt, Brace & World.
Teissier, R.
1953   "Étude démographique sur les Établissements Français de l'Océanie." *Bulletin de la Société des Études Océaniennes,* No. 102:6–31.
t'Serstevens, A.
1950/51   *Tahiti et sa couronne.* Paris: A. Michel, 3 vols.
Vancouver, George
1801   *A Voyage of Discovery to the North Pacific Ocean.* John Vancouver (Ed.). London, 6 vols.

Index